Feis na nGleann

Feis na nGleann
A Century of Gaelic Culture in the Antrim Glens

Edited by

Eamon Phoenix,
Pádraic Ó Cléireacháin, Eileen McAuley
&
Nuala McSparran

Feis na nGleann
&
Stair Uladh

Ulster Historical Foundation is pleased to acknowledge support for this publication received from the Belfast Natural History and Philosophical Society, the Community Relations Council for Northern Ireland, Foras na Gaeilge and the Office of the Taoiseach, Dublin. All contributions are gratefully acknowledged.

Community Relations Council

This book has received financial support from the Northern Ireland Community Relations Council which aims to promote a pluralist society and encourage an acceptance and an understanding of cultural diversity.

First published 2005
by
Stair Uladh
an imprint of Ulster Historical Foundation
www.ancestryireland.com
www.booksireland.org.uk

Except as otherwise permitted under the Copyright, Designs and Patents Act 1988, this publication may only be reproduced, stored or transmitted in any form or by any means with the prior permission in writing of the publisher or, in the case of reprographic reproduction, in accordance with the terms of a licence issued by The Copyright Licensing Agency. Enquiries concerning reproduction outside those terms should be sent to the publisher.

© Feis na nGleann, 2005
ISBN 1 903688 49 3

Printed by Cromwell Press
Design and production by December Publications

Urraithe ag

Foras na Gaeilge

CONTENTS

	Réamhrá	xi
	Pádraic Ó Cléireacháin	
	Introduction	xii
	Eamon Phoenix	
1	**Feis na nGleann 1904–2004**	1
	Pádraic Ó Cléireacháin	
2	**Womenfolk of the Glens of Antrim and the Irish language**	15
	Diarmaid Ó Doibhlín	
3	**The Women Revivalists**	31
	Fred Heatley	
4	**Margaret Dobbs: Glenswoman, scholar and Irish language enthusiast (1871–1962)**	35
	Jack McCann	
5	**Extract from Miss Dobbs' Memoirs of Feis na nGleann**	41
	Margaret E. Dobbs	
6	**Ada McNeill (1860–1959), Protestant Gaelic Leaguer and Nationalist**	45
	Introduction *by Malachy McSparran*	
	Ada McNeill's recollections of Roger Casement (1929)	
7	**Roger Casement and North Antrim**	53
	Stephanie Millar	
8	**Francis Joseph Bigger: Historian, Gaelic Leaguer and Protestant Nationalist**	65
	Eamon Phoenix	
9	**Brothers in arts: Joseph and John Campbell and the first Glens Feis**	78
	Jack Magee	
10	**Eoin MacNeill (1867–1945): Glensman, language revivalist and state builder**	87
	Rev. Professor F.X. Martin, O.S.A.	

11	John Clarke: 'Benmore' (1868–1934) *Eamon Phoenix*	95
12	The founders of Feis na nGleann 1904 *Eileen McAuley*	98
13	Irish in the Glens – From decline to revival (1890–2004) *Eileen McAuley and Pádraic Ó Cléireacháin*	107
14	Gaedhilg Aondroma *Brian MacLochlainn*	124
15	Ealaíona agus Ceirdeanna (Arts and Crafts) Introduction *by Pádraic Ó Cléireacháin* 'From Moscow to the Moyle': Arts and crafts at the first Feis na nGleann *by Joseph McBrinn* Cushendall's toy-making industry *by Rosemary O'Rawe Brady* Patchwork quilting *by Rose Emerson* The story of flax from seed to linen *by Moira McNeill*	129
16	Feiseanna remembered: Reports and reminiscences	141
17	Field events at the Feis Introduction *by Pádraic Ó Cléireacháin* Carey Faughs GAC *by Pat McVeigh* Cushendun GAC *by Malachy McSparran* Cumann Oisin 1904–2004 *by Charlie McAllister*	158
18	Feis na nGleann: Glenarm's involvement *Felix McKillop*	169
19	Seamus Clarke: Local historian and chair of Feis na nGleann *Eamon Phoenix*	171
20	Centenary celebrations *Nuala McSparran*	173
	The poetry of Feis na nGleann	179
	Index	185

ACKNOWLEDGEMENTS

The Committee of Feis na nGleann wish to express their gratitude to Eamon Phoenix for his advice, help and above all the time he devoted to helping us with this publication.

A special word of thanks to all our contributors for taking the time and effort to submit articles and photographs.

The Committee of Feis na nGleann would also like to thank:

> Fergal Lynn, Cushendall, great-grandson of Joseph Duffy, for allowing us access to his grandfather's papers.
>
> Mrs Ann McMullan, for her patience and perseverance in helping to process the articles for this publication.
>
> Anne Marie McCloskey, Aileen Logan, Helen McAllister, Harry Boyle, Cait and Peig Dooey, and all members of the Committee of Feis na nGleann for their assistance with collating and sourcing photographic material, and especially Mary Blaney, Pádraic Ó Cléireacháin, Frank Rogers and Joseph McBrinn for the time and diligence given to proof reading the material.

We acknowledge our thanks to:

> The Glens of Antrim Historical Society,
>
> The Ulster Museum,
>
> Ulster Folk and Transport Museum,
>
> The National Museum of Ireland for permission to publish from their collections.
>
> The *Irish News* for providing material from their archives, and especially their paper-librarian, Kathleen Bell, for her kind assistance.

We would especially like to record our gratitude and thanks to all the other people who helped in anyway with sourcing information and providing photographs.

CONTRIBUTORS

Dr Eamon Phoenix
Principal lecturer in History at Stranmillis University College, Belfast. Author of a number of historical publications including *Northern Nationalism*.

Jack Magee
Historian and former lecturer in Marketing. He was formerly Marketing Manager with Bernard Hughes Ltd., Belfast, and is now based in Sydney. Author of *Barney: Bernard Hughes of Belfast (1808-1878)*.

Rev. Professor F. X. Martin O.S.A.
A native of Ballylongford Co. Kerry, and regarded as an authority on Eoin MacNeill. The late Professor Martin was professor of Medieval History at University College Dublin. This article is based on a lecture delivered by him at St Malachy's College, Belfast 18th November 1993. He died in 2000.

Brian MacLochlainn
Native of the Braid, retired academic, Celtic and Gaelic scholar.

Stephanie Millar
A teacher and graduate in History and Education of Stranmillis University College, Belfast.

Joseph McBrinn
A design lecturer at the University of Ulster, Belfast, living in Belfast.

Rosemary O'Rawe Brady
An accountant, born in America of Cushendall parents, and now living in Lurgan, Co. Armagh.

Moira McNeill
A native of Glendun Co. Antrim, *The Waking Quilt* was bequeathed to her by her grandmother Ellen O'Neill.

Augustine McCurdy
A native of Rathlin Island, he is the author of *Rathlin's Rugged Story* and *A History of the Irish Language on Rathlin*.

Paddy Burns
A member of Feis na nGleann committee, a retired businessman, a native of Cushendall.

Peadar O'Ruairc
A freelance writer and journalist based in Larne, he compiles the 'Duchas' column in the *Irish News*.

CONTRIBUTORS

Kevin Neeson
Resident of Ballymena and retired civil servant.

Patrick McVeigh
Treasurer of Feis na nGleann committee, retired businessman and native of Carey.

Charlie McAllister
A native of Glenariff, served as secretary to the Glenariff Hurling Club and is now a trustee of the Club. Charlie has had a life long interest in Gaelic games and has done much research on the history of his local club.

Felix McKillop
Head of Geography in St Comgall's College, Larne, author of *Glenarm: A Local History*, *Glencloy: A Local History*, *Larne and the Road to the Glens* and many other publications.

Pádraic Ó Cléiriacháin
A native of Co. Monaghan, a member of the committee of Feis na nGleann since 1952, presently holds the post of Vice-Chairperson; former Vice-Principal and Head of Chemistry of St MacNissi's College, Garron Tower.

Fred Heatley
Born in Belfast, a local historian and freelance journalist, he served for many years as a Governor of the Linen Hall Library, Belfast.

Most Rev. Donal McKeown
Auxiliary Bishop of Down and Connor, a native of Randalstown, who has strong ancestral ties with the Glens of Antrim, especially Glendun and Glenariff.

Diarmaid Ó Doibhlín
Senior lecturer in Irish in the Department of Irish Studies at the University of Ulster, Coleraine.

Rosemary, Lady Brookeborough
Wife of the late Viscount Brookeborough. Rose Maud Young was Lady Rosemary's great-aunt.

Malachy McSparran
Member of the Glens of Antrim Historical Society and well known local historian.

Eileen McAuley
Native of Glendun, retired bank manager and member of the committee of Feis na nGleann.

Mrs Nuala McSparran
Resident of Glendun and member of the committee of Feis na nGleann. Nuala has been in charge of the music section of the Feis for many years and is also the Publicity Officer.

Séamus Ó Cléirigh, Cathaoirleach

RÉAMHRÁ

Pádraic Ó Cléireacháin

Nuair a tionóladh Feis na nGleann don chéad uair i nGleann Áirimh in 1904, sé a bhí ann ná gné amháin den athbheochan Ghaelach a bhí faoi shiúl in Éirinn sa cheathrú deireannach den naoú aois déag. Bunaíodh Cumann Lúthchleas Gael in 1884 chun cluichí dúchasacha na hÉireann a eagrú agus a chaomhnú. In 1893 cuireadh tús le Conradh na Gaeilge le príomh-chuspóir an Ghaeilge a choiméad mar teanga bheo.

I gcúrsaí polaitíochta bhí iarracht á dhéanamh chun Riail Dúchasach páirteach a bhaint amach, agus bhí Conradh na Talún ag iarraidh deireadh a chur le córas na dtiarnaí talún.

B'é príomh-aidhm na Feise gnéithe uile de cultúr na hÉireann a chur chun cinn – teanga, stair, ceol, amhránaíocht, rincí agus cluichí. Chomh maith, tugadh cothú do na tionscail dúchasacha agus maireann an roinn tábhachtach seo go dtí an lá inniú. I rith na blianta thug coistí éagsúla i ndiaidh a chéile go dícheallach faoin obair ag dréim le cuspóirí na mbunaitheoirí a bhaint amach.

Tháinig athruithe leis na blianta. Tá staid cumasach buan ar na cluichí dúchasacha anois, agus tá an ceol traidisiúnta ag dul i dtreise gach bhliain ó bunaíodh *Comhaltas Ceoltóirí Éireann* in 1951. Tá réimsí na Gaeltachta ar anchaoi ach tá uimhir na nGaelscoileanna ag dul i méadaíocht ar fúd na tíre; is cúis mhór dóchais an fhorbairt seo. Úsáideann daltaí ó na scoileanna seo an Ghaeilge mar gnáth-theanga le blianta tar éis aistriú go meánscoileanna dóibh. D'féadfaí an toradh seo a chomhlánú dá mbainfaí níos mó úsáid as an Fháinne. Casann na mílte daoine le chéile gach lá gan smaoineadh go dtiocfadh leo a gcuid chomhrá a bheith go hiomlán i nGaeilge. Chuirfeadh an fáinne beag óir nó airgid in iúl dá chéile gur mhian leo an Ghaeilge a labhairt.

Sé an príomhchontúirt inniú ná easnamh suime díreach mar a bhí céad bliain ó shin. Gach bliain cuireann Feis na nGleann i gcuimhne dúinn go bhfuil a lán oibre le déanamh go fóill, go háirithe i gcaomhnú na teangan. Tá súil ag Coiste na Feise go dtiocfaidh go leor daoine chun tosaigh sna blianta atá romhainn agus de dhualgas orthu leanstan leis an obair go dtí go mbainfear amach na haidhmeanna uile.

INTRODUCTION

Eamon Phoenix

The Glens of Antrim formed one of the last Gaeltacht areas in Ulster up to the early 1900s. Until the opening of the Antrim Coast Road in the 1850s, Irish was universally spoken in the Glens and on Rathlin. As late as 1897, the Belfast Gaelic League, composed mainly of middle-class Protestants such as F.J. Bigger and Dr John St Clair Boyd, made a field visit to Glenariff to meet and speak with the remaining native Irish speakers. This was the background to the establishment of Feis na nGleann – the 'Feis of the Nine Glens' – in June 1904, which this book seeks to commemorate.

In 1900, Joseph Duffy, a local teacher in Cushendall, estimated that whereas in 1875, 20 per cent of the population of the Glens could speak Gaelic, the figure had fallen to a mere 5 per cent. The 1904 Feis – the first Gaelic festival in eastern Ulster – harnessed the talents of the people of the Glens and was supported by leading 'Big House' families in the district. The founders of the festival included such local aristocratic women as Miss Rose Young of Galgorm Castle, a member of a leading Ballymena Unionist and landed family, Miss Ada McNeill of Cushendun, a first cousin of the Unionist MP, Ronald McNeill, and Miss Barbara McDonnell of Glendun, a prominent member of the Church of Ireland in the locality. Ronald McNeill (later Lord Cushendun), a prominent supporter of Sir Edward Carson in the later struggle against Home Rule, donated a prize to the Feis and recalls in his memoirs that his grandfather, Edmund Alexander McNeill (who was born in 1785) 'talked the native Irish as they all did in those days at Cushendun'. Sir Roger Casment, then a British diplomat, also became interested in the Feis and the language revival and this marked his conversion to Irish nationalism.

The cross-community involvement in the first Glens Feis, an affirmation of Gaelic culture in north Antrim, resonated throughout Ireland at the time. The event was widely reported in the Unionist press as a worthy cultural event that transcended class, creed and politics in the north of Ireland. Much was made of the fact that the last Gaelic poet of the Glens was John McCambridge, a Protestant and the author of the beautiful lament, Áird a' Chuain. McCambridge was an uncle of Sir Daniel Dixon, Unionist MP for North Belfast in the early 1900s and a former Lord Mayor of Belfast.

Yet in the centuries before the partition of Ireland, Ulster Protestant interest in the Irish language was much greater than might be imagined today. Many of the original Plantation settlers were native Scots Gaelic speakers, capable of conversing with the native Irish of Antrim or Donegal. The late Canon Coslett Quin, a Church of Ireland rector and Gaelic scholar, could write in 1973 that: 'Protestants share this Gaelic heritage with the Psalm-singing sabbatarian Gaels of the Western Isles and the Irish Catholics of Saxon, Welsh and Norman ancestry'.

INTRODUCTION

In the seventeenth century, the English-born William Bedell (1571–1642), Bishop of Kilmore and Ardagh, devoted himself to the study of Irish and was responsible for the translation of the Old Testament into Gaelic. The Presbyterian Church, too, showed an early interest in the language, partly for reasons of proselytisation, and in 1710 the Belfast Synod sent six ministers and three probationers to preach to the Catholic masses.

By the early nineteenth century Irish was in general decline along the east coast of Ireland. As late as 1820, however, it is estimated that 56,000 people in Co. Antrim (21 per cent of the population) could speak Irish. In Co. Tyrone the figure was 141,000 (53 per cent). The spread of English through the National Schools after 1831 and the impact of the Great Famine in the 1840s had a devastating effect on Irish in the north, as in the rest of Ireland.

Yet this inexorable decline was partly counterbalanced in Ulster by an upsurge of interest in reviving the language. In the liberal atmosphere of Belfast in the 1790s, the *Northern Star* – the organ of the United Irishmen – published the first ever Irish language magazine, *Bolg an tSolair*, a miscellany of Irish grammar, poetry and prayers in 1792.

In the 1830s a new organisation, the Ulster Gaelic Society, was formed in Belfast by a group of learned Protestants including the third Marquess of Downshire, Robert Shipboy McAdam and Dr Reuben Bryce. McAdam, part owner of the Soho Foundry in Belfast's Townsend Street, made a huge contribution to the work of collecting Irish manuscripts and recording songs and folktales in the oral tradition. He brought Gaelic scribes to Belfast and compiled a grammar in Irish for use in the language classes conducted at his old school, the Royal Belfast Academical Institution.

The general acceptance of Irish in the northern capital was highlighted during Queen Victoria's visit to Ireland in 1849. Mottoes in Irish adorned the route of the royal procession through the town and Victoria noted in her diary for 11 August 1849: 'I have all along forgotten to say that the favourite motto written up on most of the arches etc and in every place was "Cead Mile Failte", which means "a hundred thousand welcomes" in Irish … They often called out, "Cead Mile Failte!" and it appears in every sort of shape.'

There are countless examples of northern Protestants actively involved in the language revival in the late nineteenth century. These included Bishop William Reeves of Down and Connor, the antiquarian and a former headmaster of Ballymena Diocesan School, Sir Samuel Ferguson, the poet and lawyer, and James McKnight, the journalist and land reformer. A native of Rathfriland, Co. Down, McKnight was the son of a Presbyterian native Irish speaker. A lover of the language, he was a firm Unionist in politics.

The Gaelic League, founded in 1893 by Douglas Hyde and Eoin MacNeill, attracted significant Ulster Protestant support in its early years. The Belfast branch, founded in 1895, grew out of the Belfast Naturalists' Field Club. Its first president was Dr St Clair Boyd, senior surgeon in the Samaritan Hospital and a firm Unionist who lamented the decline of 'such a beautiful and noble language'. A vice-president of the League was Rev. R.R. Kane, the leading Unionist and Orangeman.

Outside Belfast, and the nationalist parts of Ulster, the League took root in the

Non-Subscribing Presbyterian soil of Moneyrea, Co. Down, where Rev. Richard Lyttle organised Irish language classes in the early 1900s. As a direct result, 1 per cent of the inhabitants of this rural district recorded a knowledge of Irish in the 1911 Census.

The politicisation of the Gaelic League after 1910, with the rise of separatist nationalism and the inclusion of a clause in its constitution supporting Irish independence at its 1915 Ard-Fheis, certainly marked a turning point in northern Protestant identification with the language. However, interest did continue and in the 1940s a Gaelic Fellowship was founded in Belfast at the YMCA by John (Seán) Pasker, a Presbyterian civil servant. Pasker's objective was to help towards healing ancient wounds through mutual understanding.

Since the 1980s, the establishment of the Ultach Trust and, more recently, Foras na Gaeilge has enabled a fresh effort to present the Irish language as the historical and cultural inheritance of all those rooted on this island, of whichever tradition. This was the vision of those generous-minded men and women, Catholic, Protestant and Dissenter, Unionist and Nationalist, who met in the vale of Glenariff a century ago to celebrate the unique language, culture and traditions of the Glens of Antrim. This book is a tribute to them.

In Chapter 1, Pádraic Ó Cléireacháin traces the origins of Feis na nGleann against the background of the Gaelic Revival during that 'crease in time' between the death of Parnell in 1891 and the 1916 Rising. The central roles in the foundation of the Feis of Rose Maud Young (Róis Ní Ógáin), Ada McNeill and Margaret Dobbs is the focus of Dr Diarmaid Ó Doibhlín in Chapter 2. As the author shows, these privileged women were assisted in their mission to promote the language by the Belfast-based writer, Mrs Margaret Hutton, member of the Senate of Queen's University and a friend of Patrick Pearse. This theme is explored further by Fred Heatley in Chapter 3, where he throws light on such additional literary figures as the 'Glens of Antrim poetess', Moira O'Neill of Rockport, Anna Johnston (better known as the poetess 'Ethna Carbery'), and Alice Milligan, who worked for the Gaelic League in the Glens.

In Chapter 4 the late Jack McCann provides a graphic pen picture of Margaret Dobbs, who 'found in the quiet of the Glens what had been drowned out by the bustle of her native Dublin – spoken Irish'. Her unique memoir of the Feis is reproduced in Chapter 5.

Local historian Malachy McSparran profiles Ada McNeill in Chapter 6. An ardent Irish separatist, in contrast to the gentle and mildly Unionist Rose Young, 'Miss Ada' was in love with Casement. Her poignant memoir of her tragic friend, written in the 1920s, is published here for the first time.

No history of the Glens Feis would be complete without reference to Roger Casement, whose gravitation to Irish nationalism coincided with his involvement in the 1904 pageant in Glenariff. Casement's deep North Antrim roots, his education in Ballymena and tragic fate in 1916 are chronicled in Chapter 7 by Stephanie Millar, a teacher and historian.

Among the colourful figures in the creation of Feis na nGleann was the Belfast lawyer and antiquarian, Francis Joseph Bigger. The career of this Gaelic revivalist and Protestant nationalist – described as 'Belfast's cultural Don Quixote' – is examined by Eamon Phoenix in Chapter 8.

In Chapter 9, the author and historian Jack Magee details the contribution to the inaugural Feis of two of Bigger's 'Ard Righ circle', the talented Campbell brothers, John and Joseph. Joseph Campbell, the author of myriad poems including 'The Blue Hills of Antrim' and 'My Lagan Love', was in Glenariff that June day along with his artist brother John (Seaghan Mac Cathmaoil), who designed the first Feis programme. The author links the Belfast brothers to a galaxy of talent including Herbert Hughes, the composer, R.L. O'Mealy, the Belfast-based uileann piper, and the celebrated Irish poet, Pádraic Colum.

Present also at the 1904 Feis was Eoin MacNeill (1867–1945), historian, founder of the Gaelic League and a native of Glenarm. MacNeill's fascinating political and intellectual career is outlined in Chapter 10 by the late Professor F.X. Martin, historian and Augustinian friar, who knew MacNeill.

In Chapter 11, Eamon Phoenix describes the career of John Clarke ('Benmore'), the Glenarm-based cultural figure, while in Chapter 12 Eileen McAuley provides crisp biographies of the key figures in the early Feiseanna including Joseph Duffy, the Mayo-born schoolteacher and Irish speaker, Mrs Annie McGavock of Glenarm, a sister of Eoin MacNeill, and Mrs Frances Riddell of Ballycastle, who helped set up the Irish Peasant Home Industries shop in that town.

A major focus of Feis na nGleann over the past century has been the preservation and revival of the Irish language. In Chapter 13, Eileen McAuley, Padraic Ó Cléireacháin and Eamon Phoenix explore the fortunes of the language in the Glens through a series of unique and previously unpublished historical documents, school reports and memoirs. In Chapter 14, Brian Mac Lochlainn, a Gaelic scholar, uses the Antrim Gaelic dialect to recall some native speakers in the area including John McCambridge, who wrote Áird a' Chuain, Seán Mac Maoláin, the Glenariff-born writer, and the last Glens speaker of Irish, 'Big Jim' McAuley, who died in 1983.

In Chapter 15, a series of writers stress the importance of Irish arts and crafts in the Feis and Gaelic revival. As Joseph McBrinn points out, men such as F.J. Bigger and Sir Horace Plunkett, the pioneer of Irish agricultural co-operation, saw the revival of rural crafts as vital not only for the continuation of native traditions but also for the fostering of a sense of national and regional identity. As a result of the first Feis, Mrs Riddell opened a toy-making enterprise in Ballycastle while in Cushendall, Miss Barbara McDonnell started a toy factory in the coach house of her estate.

Chapter 16 draws together a series of reports and personal reminiscences of Feiseanna over the decades. Field events and the role of early hurling clubs are discussed in Chapter 17, while Chapter 18 considers Glenarm's involvement in the Feis. The life and times of Seamus Clarke, local historian and the current Chair of Feis na nGleann, are covered in Chapter 19. In Chapter 20, Nuala McSparran reports on the centenary celebrations held in 2004.

The volume concludes with a selection of verse relating to Feis na nGleann by such poets as Joseph Campbell, Siobhan Ní Luain of Glenravel, Roger Casement and Joseph Duffy. It closes appropriately with the beautiful Gaelic lament from the Antrim coast, Áird a' Chuain.

Feis dancers *(Courtesy Ulster Museum/MAGNI)*

1

FEIS NA nGLEANN 1904–2004
Pádraic Ó Cléireacháin

Sa cheathrú deireanach den naoú aois déag, cuireadh tús le hathbheochan i gcúrsaí Gaelacha in Éirinn. In 1884, ag cruinniú i nDurlas Éile, bunaíodh Cumann Lúthchleas Gael le príomh-chuspóir cluichí dúchasacha na hÉireann, iománaíocht agus peil Ghaelach, a eagrú agus a chaomhnú. I gcúrsaí polaitíochta bhí iarracht á dhéanamh chun Riail Dúchasach páirteach a bhaint amach, agus bhí Conradh na Talún ag iarraidh deireadh a chur leis an gcóras éagórach ina raibh mórchuid de thalamh na tíre i seilbh na dtiarnaí talún agus a d'fhág cuid mhaith daoine de thógáil na hÉireann i riocht táirísleachta.

The later years of the nineteenth century saw the beginnings of a Gaelic revival in Ireland. In 1884 the Gaelic Athletic Association was founded at a meeting in Thurles to organise and preserve the native games of hurling and Gaelic football. On the political front there was a campaign for a limited form of Home Rule, and the Land League was trying to end the iniquitous system of landlordism, which had reduced many Irish people to an attitude of servility.

In 1892 Dr Douglas Hyde, in a speech to the Irish National Literary Society in Dublin, pointed out that while many Irishmen professed to despise England and wanted recognition as a distinct nationality, they rejected the Irish language which would have made that distinction. He said: 'In order to de-Anglicise ourselves we must arrest the decay of the language'. A meeting was held in Dublin on 31 July 1893 to put Dr Hyde's ideas into effect. The result was the formation of the Gaelic League, with the main aim of preserving Irish as a spoken language.

The first secretary was Eoin MacNeill, a native of Glenarm in Co. Antrim, who was born on 15 May 1867. His father, Archibald MacNeill, and his mother, Rosetta MacAuley, both came from old and respected Glens families. Eoin was educated in St Malachy's College and the Royal University of Ireland. He then went to Dublin to work in the Civil Service, and obtained his BA in 1888. Immediately afterwards MacNeill started to study Irish seriously, and he spent some time in Inis Meán on the advice of Fr Eoghan O'Growney. He was aware that Irish was still spoken in the Glens of Antrim because, when he was growing up in Glenarm, an old family nurse, Peggy Carnegie from Glenariff, had been a native Irish speaker.

MacNeill applied himself diligently to the establishment of Gaelic League branches throughout Ireland. The main aim was always to preserve the spoken language. He wrote: 'No language can be kept alive by mere book-teaching.

Holden's Hall, venue for arts and craft exhibition 1904 *(Courtesy Ulster Museum/MAGNI)*

Additional means must be employed. Indifference is the chief danger to the language and must be replaced with enthusiasm.'

One of the first branches of the Gaelic League was founded in Belfast, and with it are linked the names of Ethna Carbery and Alice Milligan. At the turn of the century branches were formed in the Glens and concerts, *céilithe*, language classes and visits to historic places attracted considerable interest. GAA clubs were formed and the native and ancient game of shinny became known as hurling under rules that were being standardised on an all-Ireland basis. Many well-known and indeed famous names are connected with those early days of the revival in the Glens. Visitors who took part included Francis Joseph Bigger, Bulmer Hobson, Sam Waddell (who sometimes used the pseudonym Rutherford Mayne), Carl Hardebeck, John and Joseph Campbell and Cathal O'Byrne. Among the Glens people who became involved were Margaret Dobbs, Ada McNeill, Rose Young, Barbara McDonnell, Roger Casement, John Clarke, Stephen Clarke, Joseph Duffy and Hugh Flatley.

At a meeting in Cushendall on 28 February 1904, it was decided to hold a Feis. A committee was elected with Barbara McDonnell of Monavart as President, Ada McNeill as Secretary and F.J. Bigger as Treasurer. Barbara McDonnell was a direct descendant of Dr James McDonnell, who was the main organiser of the Belfast Harp Festival in 1792. F.J. Bigger was active in the Gaelic League in Belfast and was President of Belfast Coiste Ceantair. The other committee members were: Daniel McAllister, Joseph Duffy, Margaret Dobbs, Hugh Flatley (Cushendall), Mrs Frances Riddell, Dominic Maguire, Roger Casement (listed as 'Consul Casement'), Stephen McKeown, Neil McAuley (Carey/Ballycastle), Denis Black, Miss McGonigle, William McLaughlin (Glendun), John McCambridge (Laney), John McNamee (Glenann), Rose Young (Galgorm), Thomas Moorhead, John McKillen (Glenariff), John Higgins (Glenravel), Bernard O'Donnell, Miss Johnston, P. Hamill (Carnlough/Glencloy) John Clarke, Mrs Annie McGavock (a sister of Eoin MacNeill), and James McRann (Glenarm).

The Feis took place in Glenariff on Thursday, 30 June 1904. It was preceded by a large procession from Cushendall starting shortly after 9 a.m. and led by pipers from Armagh. The procession included some competitors, a hurling team and many spectators. Banners were carried representing the nine glens and some North Antrim clans. In an old photograph of the procession passing the Red Arch it is possible to identify F.J. Bigger, Margaret Dobbs and Ada McNeill. Roger Casement had organised a group of native Irish speakers from Rathlin Island who arrived by boat with their own piper.

Competitions covered vocal and instrumental music, dancing, history and language, and the Feis was almost unique in having a Local Industries section, which was held in Holden's Hall beside Waterfoot. (This survives to the present day as the Arts and Crafts section.) The *Irish News* of Friday, 1 July, published the results from the industrial section but the reporter complained that he had been unable to get results from other sections in time. The prizes were presented by the pioneer of Irish agricultural co-operation, Sir Horace Plunkett, at a concert on Thursday evening in Holden's Hall. He praised the high standard and diversity of the exhibits and the work of the Gaelic League. Eoin MacNeill also spoke, emphasising the importance of preserving the language. At that time there were native speakers in Glenariff, Glendun and Rathlin Island. A hurling match for the Shield of the Heroes took place on the beach, with Carey Faughs defeating Cushendun Emmets, who had earlier beaten Glenarm Shane O'Neill's. This shield, a magnificent piece of work fashioned in copper, was specially commissioned by F.J. Bigger and is still in the possession of Carey Faughs GAA Club. It is of interest that Roger Casement – on leave from his diplomatic duties – was one of the umpires at this match.

The Feis was held in Cushendall in 1906 and 1912, in Carnlough in 1907, in Ballycastle in 1909 and in Garron Tower in 1911. In all the other years it was held in Glenariff. The 1912 Feis featured a pageant devised by the Bangor-based poetess and Protestant nationalist, Alice Milligan, and entitled *The Masque of the Nine Glens*. It involved pipe music and dancing and featured nine maidens, representing the nine glens, paying homage to the High King and Queen of Ireland.

For both Feiseanna in Cushendall, Legge Green was used as well as that part of the present golf course alongside Shore Street. Roger Casement is recorded as helping to prepare the ground in the week before the 1906 Feis by cutting weeds. At that Feis several prizes in the literary section were won by a teenager called Brian O'Byrne from South Armagh, who was later to achieve fame as a novelist under the name 'Donn Byrne'. Seamus Ó Searcaigh from the Donegal Gaeltacht judged the spoken Irish competitions and complimented the schools, especially Martinstown and Kilmore, on their very high standard. The standard in adult evening classes, especially in Glenravel, was also highly praised. At that time there were over 200 Irish speakers on Rathlin out of a population of 325, and there was an Irish College on Rathlin during the summer months, sponsored by F.J. Bigger.

The 1913 Feis in Glenariff was restricted, due to the destruction of Holden's Hall. The literary and history competitions, however, took place in the tea-house at the top of the glen. The Feis was suspended after the outbreak of the First World War. Roger Casement, a member of the original committee, was executed in 1916 for his part in the background to the Easter Rising. The struggle for independence and the Civil War that followed during the years 1922–23 left many people disillusioned. The work of rekindling the national spirit was not easy, but throughout the country earnest men and women worked quietly and assiduously towards that end.

Some of the original Feis committee remained and succeeded in re-establishing the Feis in 1928. They included Margaret Dobbs, Ada McNeill, John Clarke and a local schoolteacher, Hugh Flatley. They were joined by others including Andy Dooey, Pádraic and Sibéal Mac Cormaic and Mrs Sydney Parry (née Gertrude Bannister), a cousin of Roger Casement and the last person to visit him before his execution. They also included Anna McAllister, who was elected secretary; she was to carry out her arduous duties in a wonderfully efficient manner for 27 years.

The hurling match in 1928 was North v. South Antrim, and this contest was a feature of the Feis until the late 1950s, when the North Antrim Board allowed the final of the North Antrim championship to be played at the Feis. A cup was purchased for this competition, which attracts good crowds each year. Since then, also, the finals of the North Antrim junior and under-16 championships have been played at the Feis and, in more recent times, junior and senior camogie competitions have been added, making it necessary to have some games on the Saturday as well as the Sunday.

Two of the entrants in the history section in 1928 were Frank McAuley of Layd, who was later to become treasurer of the Feis for many years, and Peter Madden, later to become a priest in the diocese; it was he who presented the Madden Cup for history to the Feis. John H. McAuley of Ballycastle, composer of the famous song 'The Ould Lammas Fair', presented one of the prizes in the industrial section.

Street dancing at Cushendun *(Courtesy Ulster Museum/MAGNI)*

The Feis remained in Cushendall in 1929 and 1930. One of the adjudicators in the Arts and Crafts section in those years was the already famous artist, Humbert Craig, and a first prizewinner whom Craig encouraged to take up painting seriously was a young Charles McAuley, who went on to develop his own unique style and achieve a reputation to equal that of Craig. (Incidentally, Humbert Craig lies buried in the Church of Ireland graveyard in Cushendall and Charles McAuley in the Catholic graveyard a little further on.)

The Feis continued successfully during the 1930s, moving to different venues. In 1931 all competitions were held in Ballymena except hurling and athletics, which were held in Cushendall. In 1932 the Feis moved to Glenarm, and in 1933–4 to Cushendun; it was here that the competition for the Bishop Mageean Cup for the Irish language was first held. The 1934 *clár* (programme) noted the death of John Clarke of Glenarm ('Benmore'), one of the founders of the Feis and a noted writer and Gaelgeoir. The venue was Carnlough in 1935–6, Cushendall in 1937–8, and Ballycastle in 1939–40.

Seamus Clarke, the present chairperson, has been a committee member continuously since 1937, giving him a remarkable 67 years' service to date. Mr Clarke is a cousin of 'Benmore' and has long played a pivotal role in GAA and Gaelic League circles in North Antrim, as well as writing an acclaimed history of Feis na nGleann.

During the Second World War (1939–45), with its attendant restrictions and

Boy dancer
(Courtesy Ulster Museum/MAGNI)

petrol rationing, it was decided to cancel the annual Feis. It resumed after the 'emergency'. Literary and history competitions were held in St Louis Convent, Ballymena, because bus and rail connections were available. All other competitions were held in Glenariff. In 1946 the Rev. John MacKechnie, a Church of Scotland minister from Glasgow, gave an inspired address. He noted that unlike the Scottish Mod (festival), the adjudicators spoke Irish among themselves during the intervals. He also praised the association of the language with the wider culture of music, athletics and games. He said that the Romans had destroyed local cultures by imperial power, and urged those present not to let modern-day imperial power destroy the native Gaelic culture of the Glens.

The Feis moved to Ballycastle in 1950–1. All the competitions were held there, and drama in Irish was introduced for the first time. The 1951 oration was given by Tomás Mac Curtain, son of the murdered Lord Mayor of Cork. It returned to Glenariff in 1952–3, to Cushendun in 1954–5 and back to Glenariff in the years 1956–60 inclusive. In 1951 the committee decided to organise a summer school in Cushendall for children too young or with an insufficient knowledge of Irish to go to the Gaeltacht. The school was approved by Comhaltas Uladh, and, with Matt McAteer, as headmaster it proved very successful, but it was discontinued after four years owing to the difficulty of finding accommodation in competition with visitors from Scotland. However, Comhaltas Uladh continued the school in Omeath for some years and it was later moved to Garron Tower, where it is still held each year during the first half of July.

The late Fr Brian Brady was a powerful presence on the Feis Committee from 1954 until 1966, when he was transferred to St Joseph's Training College in Belfast. Fr Brady, later to receive a doctorate from Columbia University, ran the drama competitions virtually on his own and worked tirelessly each year in preparing the field for Feis Day, helping to erect dancing platforms and looking after the orator.

1961 saw the death of Pádraic MacCormaic, who had been on the Committee since 1928. In the early years of the century, Pat had been a member of the Supreme Council of the IRB, representing Scotland. He was very proud of the fact that he was given the task of proposing Pádraig Pearse as a member of the Supreme Council. His wife, Sibéal, had taken Irish classes in Glendun for many years.

Around 1957 Miss Dobbs requested that committee meetings be held in her home at Portnagolan as she felt too frail to leave the house, having been hospitalised for a short time the previous year. For the next four years almost all committee meetings were held there and each meeting began with Amhrán na bhFiann played on a gramophone. This grand old lady died early in 1962; the whole Feis committee and many of the general public attended her funeral in Cushendall. She was the last of the original 1904 committee.

From 1960 the literary and history competitions were held in St Louis Convent Grammar School, Ballymena; the headmistress at that time was Sr Dervile, a daughter of the well-known Irish scholar, Enrí Ó Muirgheasa (Henry Morris), whose published work included five collections of Ulster Gaelic poems. The Feis moved to Ballycastle in 1961, where the oration was given by Rev. Albert McElroy, leader of the Ulster Liberal Party, who reminded the listeners of the 1798 tradition still alive among some groups of Presbyterians. Apart from those already mentioned, active members of the committee at that time included Eddie Brogan (Cushendun – chairperson), Patrick J. Clerkin (Cushendall – secretary), Frank McAuley (Cushendall – treasurer) Fr Tom Bartley (Garron Tower), who was the main organiser of the literary and history competitions, John McAleese (Loughgiel), Hugh McCamphill and Pearse Dooey (Dunloy), Harry Scally (Cushendun), Pádraig Ó Cléirigh (Ballycastle – later Chairperson),

Joe McMullan (Glenariff) and Agnes McMullan (Cushendun).

In May 1971 buses taking children to the literary and history competitions in Ballymena came under attack in Harryville. In the interests of safety it was decided to suspend competitions in this section indefinitely, and scholarships were allotted to schools that had traditionally sent entries. How the money was divided was a matter for the schools themselves. This procedure continued until the single-day competitions were renewed at the Feis in Carey in 1992. They have continued to be held in Carey each year since then under the very capable direction of Mrs Aileen McCarry.

The dancing competitions were always held on platforms in the field on Feis Sunday except in the event of inclement weather, when they were moved to a local hall. In the late 1950s and the 1960s it took three platforms to accommodate all the competitions. From the early 1970s onwards, however, dancing competitions were held indoors over two days at the insistence of the dancing teachers. It was also becoming more difficult to obtain insurance for outdoor events.

Dancing competitions took place under the rules of the Irish Dancing Commission. Before the 1973 Feis, some dancing teachers had broken away from the Commission and formed their own organisation, Comhdháil le Rincí Gaelacha. Several of these turned up at the parochial hall in Glenariff on Feis Day with a large number of children in dancing costume and in fact occupied the hall, preventing competitions from taking place. The committee member in charge of the dancing, John O'Connor, made a number of efforts to effect a compromise but eventually had to call off the competitions. Dancing was suspended for a year and then reinstated under the rules of the Comhdháil, which now controlled nearly all the dancing schools in the Feis area. The competitions were run for 21 years under James McAuley, who was appointed dancing secretary in 1977, and in the early 1990s separate competitions were organised for Comhdháil and Commission schools, since the latter were gaining in strength again. For the past six years, dancing has been under Irish Dancing Commission rules only.

John Turnly of Drumnasole was an active member of the committee during the 1970s, bringing to the proceedings an intense enthusiasm that was an inspiration to everyone. He was murdered by loyalists in Carnlough on 4 June 1980, and his death was a tragic loss to all the causes he had espoused, as well as a great personal loss to his wife and sons. Those of us who knew him were impressed by the genuineness of his beliefs and his determination not to be diverted from whatever course of action he had decided to take in a particular situation. He was a modern-day Roger Casement, and indeed he was proud to display in his home a signed photograph of Casement, which is now in the possession of the Feis Chairperson, Seamus Clarke. Several years after his death, when the Irish Independence Party, which he had helped found, was being wound up, funds were made available to the Feis committee to purchase a trophy

Fiddler at Feis in Cushendun *(Courtesy Ulster Museum/MAGNI)*

in his memory. The result is a magnificent three-foot-high carving in bog oak, commissioned from Rathlin artist Paddy Burns, depicting Deirdre and the Sons of Uisneach. It has been named the 'John Turnly Memorial Trophy' and is competed for annually by schools in a history project competition.

With the development of club grounds during this period, more venues became available. The Feis moved to Cushendall in 1987–9, to Dunloy in 1990–1, to Carey in 1992–3, back to Glenariff in 1994–6, to Carey in 1997–9, to Dunloy in 2000 and to Loughgiel in 2001–3. In 2000 the North Antrim Board arranged an under-12 ground skills competition with a number of teams from Munster participating along with teams from all the North Antrim clubs. Matches took place during the week at various venues including Glenariff, Cushendall and Cushendun. The semi-finals and final were played in Dunloy on Feis Day. The tournament, organised by a hard-working committee under Seamus Elliott and Chris Campbell, was favoured with fine weather and was an unqualified success, resulting in a surge of interest in under-age hurling throughout North Antrim.

The late 1980s and early 1990s brought great sorrow with the untimely deaths of three very active members of the Feis committee. Mrs Annie Harvey died on 25 October 1986, at a relatively young age. Annie, who was a niece of the late Pádraic MacCormaic, played a very important role, along with Miss Mairéad McMullan, in revitalising the Arts and Crafts section during the 1970s and 1980s when the Feis was held in Glenariff. The amazing displays in this section have been a feature of the Feis in recent years. John McKay died on 27 February 1992, after a short illness. For a number of years he had given freely of his time in the lead-up to the Feis, helping to erect platforms, attending to the P.A. system, erecting the Feis banner and performing dozens of unexpected tasks as they arose, to make sure everything ran smoothly on the day. On one memorable occasion after a Feis concert in Cushendall, when an artiste from Donegal town, who did not have transport, had to get home for the following morning, John drove him all the way, leaving Cushendall at 1 a.m. and returning after daylight the next morning. For this he refused to accept any recompense, not even the cost of his petrol. Two years later, on 17 February 1984, Alastair McAllister died unexpectedly, following what should have been a relatively minor operation. Alastair had been a most efficient treasurer for a number of years. Not only did he keep a close eye on the finances, but he himself arranged all the personnel for the collection of money at the various gates and venues. As well, especially when the Feis was in Glenariff, he spent many hours in helping prepare the field, erecting platforms, liaising with the local GAA club and performing the many thankless and unseen tasks associated with a big occasion. His quiet efficiency was greatly missed.

The Feis was planned for Loughgiel for the first time in 2001, but an outbreak of foot-and-mouth disease in the Glens led to travel restrictions. The dancing, music, and arts and crafts competitions, which were to have been held in the Community Centre, had to be cancelled and only the hurling and camogie competitions took place. The literary and history competitions had been held in Carey in May. The Feis did take place in Loughgiel in 2002 and was planned again for 2003 but the sudden death of Loughgiel's parish priest, Fr Willie McKeever, the day before the Feis was due to open, caused the cancellation of all the weekend events. The hurling and camogie competitions were completed later in the year.

The Feis returned to Glenariff for its centenary in 2004. Celebrations commenced with a dinner in Ballycastle in March at which the guests included

Some members of the committee at Feis na nGleann held in Glenarm in 1932: John 'Benmore' Clarke, Rev. Liam Kirkwood, Miss Madge Logue, Rev. Edward Diamond, Hugh Flately, Annie McAllister (Waterfoot), Rev. George Clenaghan, Maggie O'Boyle (Glenarm) Archie McKinley (Carnlough)

Sean Kelly, President of the GAA, Miriam O'Callaghan, President of the Camogie Association of Ireland, and noted historian, Dr Eamon Phoenix. Literary and history competitions were held in Carey on 8 May. Music and dancing competitions took place in Kilmore House in Glenariff on the weekend 12/13 June, and the field events in Glenariff on 19/20 June. The various displays included historical memorabilia, handcrafts and dancing, and the celebrations concluded with a concert in November, featuring the National Folk Theatre of Ireland group from Tralee, Co. Kerry (Siamsa Tíre).

The present committee consists of Seamus Clarke (Ballycastle – chairperson), Patrick J. Clerkin (Cushendall – vice-chairperson), Marie McAllister (Garron Point – general secretary and dancing secretary), Pat McVeigh (Carey – treasurer and field events secretary), Nuala McSparran (Glendun – P.R.O. and music secretary), Mairéad McMullan (Glenariff – arts and crafts secretary), Aileen McCarry (Carey – literary secretary), Eileen McAuley (Glendun), Kathleen Burns, Cathal McNaughton, Paddy Burns (Cushendall), Patricia Dennis, Mary Kane, Chris Campbell (Carey), James McCarry (Carey), Fiona Mackle, John Connolly, Vincent Harvey (Glenariff), Anne-Marie McCloskey, Aileen Logan (Portglenone), and Bobby McIlhatton (Loughgiel).

The past 100 years have seen many changes, some good and some not so

Procession at first Feis, 1904, from Cushendall to Glenariff *(Courtesy Ulster Museum/MAGNI)*

good. Gaelic games are on a very sound footing and traditional music, song and dance received a great boost with the formation of *Comhaltas Ceoltóirí Éireann* in 1951. There are at present eight branches of *Comhaltas* in Co. Antrim, including the Ballycastle and Glens of Antrim branches. On the negative side the Gaeltacht areas have shrunk under increasing exposure to English language media and sometimes the indifference of the Government in Dublin. The growth of Gaelscoileanna throughout Ireland is perhaps the most promising development since the foundation of the Gaelic League. Their success is demonstrated by the fact that many of their pupils continue to use Irish in everyday conversation long after transferring to secondary school. This success could be complemented by better use of the Fáinne. Hundreds, perhaps thousands, of people meet regularly without realising that they could easily carry on their conversations in Irish. The little gold or silver badge would identify them as being able and willing to do so. It has the potential to transform the restoration of Irish as a spoken language.

The men and women who organised the first Feis na nGleann in 1904 had a great belief in the value of preserving Gaelic culture in all its forms, and were prepared to work hard to achieve that aim. Successive committees down through the years have ensured that this work continues. In this short account it has been possible to mention only a few names from the past, but the contribution of all those who have given of their time on the committee or as helpers over the years is greatly appreciated.

The greatest danger today is indifference, as it was a century ago. The annual Glens Feis serves to remind us that in some areas, especially in the preservation of Irish as a spoken language, there is still a long way to go. The present committee are confident that enough men and women of all ages will come forward, as they have done over the past 100 years, to carry on the work with enthusiasm and commitment into another century until all the aims have been achieved.

Sé an príomhchontúirt inniú ná easnamh suime díreach mar a bhí céad bliain ó shin. Gach bhliain cuireann Feis na nGleann i gcuimhne dúinn go bhfuil a lán oibre le déanamh go fóill, go háirithe i gcaomhnú na teangan. Tá súil ag Coiste na Feise go dtiocfaidh go leor daoine, idir fhir is mhná, sean agus óg, chun tosaigh sna blianta atá romhainn agus de dhualgas orthu leanstan leis an obair le díograis agus le dúthracht go dtí go mbainfear amach na haidhmeanna uíle.

Cassie *(Courtesy Ulster Museum/MAGNI)*

2
WOMENFOLK OF THE GLENS OF ANTRIM AND THE IRISH LANGUAGE

Diarmaid Ó Doibhlín

'Ireland is a closed book to those who do not know her language. No one can know Ireland properly until one knows the language. Her treasures are as hidden as a book unopened. Open the book and learn to love your language.' So spoke Margaret Dobbs (1871–1962) in 1945 when the committee of Feis na nGleann in the Glens of Antrim made a special presentation to her to mark her contribution to the promotion of Feis na nGleann and its activities. The Feis had, and indeed still has, a wide range of cultural activities under its banner and to its credit, and here was Miss Dobbs, of solid Unionist stock and a close friend of Roger Casement, putting her finger on the kernel of the whole matter.

Margaret Emmeline Dobbs was born in Dublin but spent most of her long life in the Glens of Antrim. Remarkably, she was one of a group of women from the Protestant and Unionist tradition at that time in the Glens of Antrim who devoted their energies and considerable talents to the language and cultural values of the plain people of Ireland. In a certain sense they gathered round Miss Dobbs; her home in Portnagolan, Cushendall, became for them a focal point where they came frequently to renew their energies and their close friendships.

There was Rose Maud Young of the Youngs of Galgorm House in Ballymena, known as Róis Ní Ógáin, who came to live in the Glens in her final years. She learned her Irish at Gaelic League classes at home in Belfast and in London. There was Ada McNeill, of the McNeills of the Glens, whose *Cú na gCleas*, published in 1914, contained the very first literary effort of Seamus Ó Grianna; there was Margaret Hutton, translator of the *Táin* and close friend and supporter of Patrick Pearse in his efforts to establish his Irish language schools in Dublin; there was Gertrude Parry and her sisters Una and Eilis Bannister, who were cousins of Roger Casement; and there was Barbara McDonnell of Glenariff, whose ancestor, Dr Séamus Mac Dónaill, had done so much in the late eighteenth and in the nineteenth century in Belfast to promote the Irish language and to foster the welfare of the poor in that city. Indeed, in many ways it is with Dr James McDonnell, or Dr Séamus Mac Dónaill, of Glenariff that we should begin our story.

The Irish Revival of 1893 – the founding of the Gaelic League – had been preceded by almost a century by a very similar revival in eighteenth-century Belfast, and most significantly in the very heart of Presbyterian Belfast. In 1795

Patrick Lynch of Loughinisland, Co. Down, a member of the Lynch family who ran a classical school in Co. Down where Catholics and Protestants were educated together, published *Bolg an tSólair* – a literary magazine and the first of its kind to be devoted to the Irish language. It contained poems and stories, and translations by Charlotte Brooke, who had died two years earlier.

Lynch was a scribe and a poor scholar in the Irish mode. The *Northern Star* newspaper, which carried an announcement about the publication, had this to say:

> an attempt to revive the grammatical and critical knowledge of the Irish language in this town [Belfast] is generously made by Mr Lynch: he teaches publicly in the Academy and privately in several families. It [the language] is particularly interesting to all who wish for the improvement and union of this neglected and divided kingdom. By our understanding and speaking it we could more easily and effectively communicate our sentiments and instructions to all our countrymen, and thus mutually improve and conciliate each other's affections.[1]

Dr Séamus Mac Dónaill of the Glens was at the very heart of that revival. He was to a very large extent the driving force behind the Harp Festival of 1792. It was, after all, in the bosom of nationalist Presbyterian Belfast, as Máire McNeill has written, that the renaissance of Irish music took place. The 1798 Rising drastically undermined the effectiveness of Lynch and McDonnell, but McDonnell was back in 1833 and elected chairperson of Cuideachta Ghaeilge Uladh with the young Robert MacAdam as secretary.

Cuideachta Ghaeilge Uladh, or the Ulster Gaelic Society, was in many ways a unique society in nineteenth century Ireland. The Gaelic Society of Dublin (founded in 1806), the Iberno Celtic Society (1818), the Irish Archaeological Society (1840) and the Celtic Society (1845), to mention only a few, placed their emphasis and interest almost exclusively on the past, and were greatly influenced by European romanticism. They concentrated to a large extent on antiquarianism and quietly ignored the living language of the great numbers of the poor Irish who were everywhere around them throughout the Irish countryside. MacAdam, McDonnell and the members of the Ulster Gaelic Society, on the other hand, placed their emphasis on the Irish of the poor and the marginalised, the living language that carried their intellectual and emotional life. Thus MacAdam was up in the Glens sitting with the old speakers, recording their stories and songs and speaking their language.

Tomás Ó Fiannachtaigh was in Ballinascreen trying to set up a school where he could teach the language – the written language, that is – to the hundreds who were native speakers but had never had the opportunity to write or read their own language. This crucial difference – this emphasis on the living language – was an idea that the Gaelic League borrowed effectively at the turn of the last century, and that sent the Pearses and Ó Gramhnaigh and MacNeill to Inis Meán and to the west coast of Ireland to get a grasp of the living, spoken Irish of the ordinary people. It was perhaps the most central idea that the League had, and because it helped to break down the barriers between peoples and between classes it brought the educated middle classes from the towns into contact with the ordinary Irish of the countryside and gave the Irish country person, the bearer of the tradition, a status and a place in society that he or she had not possessed in over three centuries.

MacAdam was a wealthy businessman. He was a Presbyterian, yet he sat in the cabins of the poor Irish Catholics, noting down what they had to say, preserving the traditions that they had received orally and that they were only too willing to transmit. Gaelic manuscript no. xxxi in the Belfast Public Library contains some examples of the recordings MacAdam made in the Glens of Antrim.

    (p. 52) Dia Sathairn mo lean ar éirigh don ghréin. On the landing of the French. Taken down from Lane when he was blind drunk.

55   'Is air maduin andé a chualamas sgéul' 2v, Cushendall dialect. J. McCambridge.

56   Bhí oiread Osgair ann a dá bhonn i.r Description of a giantess. From John O'Neill of the Glens.

57   Cuirim mo bheannacht chon an tigh tá a naice na gcrann 4v. An Draighneán Donn from Cushendall. P.H. Garrett.

In 1833, three years after the founding of the Ulster Gaelic Society, a Ladies Gaelic Society was founded in Belfast with similar aims. It is there, I believe, that the origin and antecedents of the above-mentioned Protestant women of the Glens lie.

There is just one other point, I think, to be made here about the Ulster Ladies Gaelic Society. In 1841 it published a little book called *An Irish Primer Compiled and Published under the Patronage of the Ladies Gaelic Society.* It added to that the publication of a short catechism and some religious materials, and the ladies speak in that section of the importance in the work for the language of avoiding anything and everything that might lead to *mioscais agus mírún* (malice and ill-will). One could spend a lot of time tracing the fortunes of the Ulster Gaelic Society, following its publications and activities, but that is a topic for another occasion.

I might, however, digress briefly from my central topic: in the 1840s the Irish language world in Ulster was riven by a most unseemly, bitter and acrimonious row between Protestants and Catholics over the teaching of the Bible through the medium of the Irish language. This row is well documented, as it was fought out in the leading papers of the day. In many ways it is quite meaningless to us today. Distinguished clerics from the Presbyterian and Catholic sides launched into each other without restraint and with language that at times knew no bounds. They ended up – indeed they began – by calling each other liars, brigands, fools and rogues. It all did irreparable damage to the language cause in the north, and it is no harm at Éigse na nGlinntí, some 160 years later, to ask forgiveness for all the harsh things that were said, for all the cruel innuendo, and to assert again, as the Ladies Gaelic Society with great wisdom had asserted when it published its little primer, that malice, or ill-feeling and hatred have no place whatsoever in our work for the language.

Irish had to a great extent been on the run in the nineteenth century. The decline of the language had been under way since the collapse of the Gaelic system in the seventeenth century. The Irish language and the cultural tradition the language carried had few protectors and few promoters in the new dispensation after the seventeenth century. Throughout the eighteeenth century, in spite of penal laws, in spite of the constant process of marginalisation inflicted on the native Catholic Irish (and, it should be added, to a great extent on the Presbyterian community here in Ulster), the language retained its vigour and the cultural and literary tradition was still vibrant.

Eibhlín Dhubh Ní Chonaill in Macroom, Co. Cork, lamented her husband Art Ó Laoghaire, who was murdered treacherously near Carraig an Ime in West Cork on 4 May 1773. The lament is a most original and unique piece of literature. Eibhlín recalls their good days together:

> Is domsa narbh aithreach:
> Chuiris parlús á ghealadh dhom
> Rúmanna á mbreacadh dhom
> Bácús a dheargadh dhom
> Brící ar bhearraibh dhom
> Mairt á leagadh dhom;
> Codladh i gclúmh lachan dom
> Go dtíódh an t-eadartha
> Nó thairis dá dtaitneadh liom.
>
> I left my Father's house
> And ran away with you
> And that was no bad choice
> You gave me everything
> There were parlours whitened for me
> Bedrooms painted for me
> Ovens reddened for me
> Loaves baked for me
> Joints spitted for me
> Beds made for me
> To take my ease on flock
> Until the milking time
> And later if I pleased.

Eibhlín Dhubh is working in a tradition that is as old as the hag of Béarra, and she is confident and in control. Art Ó Laoghaire, she reminds us, was related to anyone who was anyone within the Gaelic tradition, including the Earls of Antrim in the Glens.

Eoghan Ó Neill, of Bannville in Co. Down, was drowned in the River Bann in September 1747. He was a distinguished member of the old Irish family Ó Neill of Clandaboy, with roots stretching back to Tulach Óg in Tyrone and further back to Aileach in Donegal and the beginnings of recorded history in Ireland. His untimely death was a tragedy for his family and the entire local community. Séamus Mac Póilín, Vicar General of the Diocese of Dromore, preached the funeral sermon over Eoghan Ó Néill, and Patrick Lynch, whom I mentioned earlier, made a copy in a manuscript and recorded it for posterity. The sermon is a plea for mercy on the soul of Eoghan Ó Néill. The sermon and the lament both show that Irish was still the language of the heart even among the aristocracy, or what was left of the Gaelic aristocracy.

Nevertheless, the language had been cut adrift. The most graphic description of the state to which it had been reduced is to be found in Aindrias Ó Doinnshléibhe's catechism in the Irish language, published in Paris in 1742. Ó Doinnshléibhe was prefect of studies at the Irish College in Paris. In the catechism he puts his finger on the weakness of the position of the Irish language within Irish society:

> It is no wonder then ... that a language of neither Court nor city nor bar nor business, ever since the beginning of King James the First's reign, should have suffered vast alterations and corruptions, and be now on the brink of utter decay, as it really is to the great dishonour and shame of the natives ... Irishmen without Irish is a great bull.

Irish, even in the eighteenth century, was cut off from the major areas of life and experience. It was not in the universities or schools; it was not in the courts; it was scarcely in the churches and throughout the nineteenth century even the Catholic Church neglected the language. It was the property of the poor masses and became identified with poverty and backwardness. Those who were seeking to get on in the world had to opt for the world of English. In 1950 Professor Ó Cuív published a paper on the state of the language throughout the nineteenth century and the early years of the twentieth century, and had this to say: 'a century ago we would have found Irish in every county in Ireland and Gaeltachtaí either *fíor* or *breac* in probably twenty-two or twenty-three counties'.[2]

Irish was still strong in the Glens of Antrim in 1893, particularly in Glenarm, Carey and Glenariff. It was in the late 1930s that Professor Holmer of Uppsala University came over to study the Irish language both in the Glens and on Rathlin Island. Indeed, all over Ulster there were in the 1920s, 1930s and 1940s Gaeltachtaí or communities of native Irish speakers displaying varying degrees of vigour. In Muintir Luinigh in Co. Tyrone there was a strong Gaeltacht – the last Irish speaker died there in the 1960s. The last speaker of South Derry Irish died in 1943. And there were native speakers in South Armagh and Down until the late 1940s.

The basic Gaelic League objective was to halt the decline of Irish and to spread its use back into the cities. To a certain degree – indeed, palpably – it failed. But most importantly, like the Belfast Revivalists of the 1830s, the League placed its whole emphasis on the spoken language of the Gaeltacht. It lifted up

Rosemary, Lady Brookeborough great-niece of Rose Young

those poor forgotten people who were speakers of Irish and who had been marginalised in Irish society; it gave them prestige, restored their self-esteem and assured them of a role and importance in post-Famine Ireland. And so, in my view, this gave the Gaelic League a crucial role in developing Irish society. The middle classes in the towns and the countryside, the upper classes, Catholic, Protestant and Dissenter came together in the early years of the twentieth century to learn and to cultivate the language and cultural traditions of the ordinary people of Ireland. This was the crucial aspect of the League's success. So it was that Margaret Dobbs, Rose Maud Young, Ada McNeill, Margaret Hutton and Gertrude Parry had become involved in the effort to rescue a language and a culture. Their role is unique and, I believe, particularly significant to the times in which we live.

Miss Dobbs, Miss Young, Ada McNeill and Margaret Hutton came from solid Unionist backgrounds. They were relatively well off. Miss Dobbs could afford in the early years of the century to give £600 to the Casement defence fund – a considerable sum in those days. Born in Dublin, she first came into contact with Irish/Scottish Gaelic through a servant who was employed in her home. Her father, Conway Edward Dobbs, was High Sheriff of Carrrickfergus and Co. Louth, and Justice of the Peace in Co. Antrim. When he died in 1898 she came north to the Glens, where she spent the rest of her life. She was a founding member of Feis na nGleann in 1904 and maintained her interest in the Feis and its activities until her death in 1962. She had a solid command of Irish and had articles published in leading learned journals of the day. She lectured in early Irish in the Irish College in Cloch Cheannfhaolaidh. Her brother, James Dobbs, had been one of the Unionists involved in the Larne gun-running, yet Margaret Dobbs was perhaps Roger Casement's closest friend. Whatever about the politics, Margaret Dobbs continued her work for the language and its culture right up to the time of her death, and was a driving force in Feis na nGleann. Her funeral was to be a private family affair but the ordinary people of the Glens turned out in their hundreds, and the private funeral became a most public one.

Margaret Hutton was the wife of a Belfast industrialist, a member of the Gaelic League and a scholar. Her home on the Malone Road was a centre of cultural and artistic activity in Belfast. She was frequently in the Glens with Miss Dobbs. She was a close friend of Pearse and a benefactor on many occasions to his educational and cultural projects. A letter from Pearse to her in 1910 runs: 'A Chara Dhíl, a thousand thanks for your generous promise of £50 towards the development of Scoil Eanna. I am proud of this proof of your confidence and approbation.' Pearse, on a visit to Belfast in 1904, had stayed with Margaret Hutton: 'It is very kind of you to offer me hospitality during my stay in Belfast … mise le meas mór, do chara Pádraig Mac Piarais'.

In the summer of 1909 Mrs Hutton was in touch with Pearse; she wanted to go to the Ros Muc Gaeltacht and wished to stay at the Pearse cottage. He wrote back to her giving detailed directions of how she might reach Maam Cross, and says, 'I am writing to Broxley Park, as Miss Young told me you would be there next week …' The Miss Young referred to may well have been Miss Rose Maud Young of Galgorm House, Ballymena, the seventh of twelve children born to John Young, chief sheriff and deputy lieutenant in Antrim, and Grace Charlotte Savage. She was reared in Galgorm and tutored privately. The Youngs were staunchly Unionist and Miss Young, when she died in 1947, was almost certainly still a Unionist. The Youngs had been prosperous merchants in Ballymena and had acquired Galgorm with its 2,000 acres in 1850.

They were on good terms with most of the landed gentry in Antrim, and there was much toing and froing between Galgorm and the other county houses, especially among the young people, for parties and outings. In addition, the Youngs were prolific diary writers. I have benefited greatly from reading the diaries of Rose Young – Róis Ní Ógáin – that were kindly placed at my disposal by Rosemary, Lady Brookeborough, whose great-aunt Rose Young was.

Rose Young's great claim to fame was her splendid anthology of Irish verse (*Duanaire Gaedhilge*), which was published in three volumes – Volume 1 in 1921, Volume 2 in 1924 and Volume 3 in 1930. These dates are important as

> ASHBROOKE,
> BROOKEBOROUGH,
> CO. FERMANAGH, N.IRELAND.
>
> Aunt Rose 17. 7. 004.
>
> My memories, as a child, of my great Aunt Rose Young, were of a frail elderly lady. A much loved member of a large family – we visited her quite often at Cushendall, and in turn, she regularly came to Galgorm, staying overnight on many occasions, as is commemorated by her signatures in the Galgorm Visitor's book. I had little knowledge of her cultural interests, and involvement, in the language, and literature, of the Glens. With such a variety of older relatives, all involved with varieties of interests and professions, children, as we were, only absorbed a smattering of knowledge of their activities.
>
> With best wishes
> Rosemary Brookeborough

Extract from letter by Lady Brookeborough recalling her memories of her great-aunt Rose

they reveal that her interest in Irish survived the political upheavals of 1916–23. These three volumes reveal a sense of taste and fine literary judgement as well as a competence to deal with solid academic matters in which she had little formal training.

Breathnach and Ní Mhurchú suggest that Rose Young got her interest in Irish from Bishop Reeves, and this may well be true.[3] There are three references in the diaries to Bishop Reeves, but only one of these – that of 14/16 November 1889 – has any connection with Irish. She had stayed with the bishop at Conway House, Dunmurry 'to see some Irish manuscripts he had bought'. I suspect that she and other members of her family circle even at this early stage may have had some knowledge of spoken Irish.

She was interested in the manuscript tradition from an early stage. On a visit to Oxford in 1891 she went twice to the Bodleian; on the first occasion (1 April) she saw the 'mss of the Annals of Tigearnach' and on her second visit (9 April) she saw and examined 'the Life of Colmcille by O Donnell'. On 7 June she lunched with Professor Rhys at Oxford.

On a visit to London in March 1903 she stayed with her sister Ethel at 7 Stanley Gardens and began attending Micheál Breathnach's Irish classes and also classes conducted by Miss Drury. Back in Galgorm in 1904 she noted that 'Miss Ada McNeill came to read Irish with me'. In the same year she noted that she was having Irish classes from Mr Rooney, and that she and her sister Mary and brother Willie went down to Glenariff to the first Glens Feis. In 1905 she was at the Oireachtas in Dublin and lunched with Hyde and Úna Ní Ógáin; she attended the competitions and Irish language plays. Later in the year she was in Belfast with Mrs Hutton and they both went to the an Irish language play in St Mary's Hall; in July she was up in the Glens 'to see W. McShane, Rose McGrogan, and Biddy McVeigh to talk Irish', and eight days later she was back with McShane 'to record his Creggan Song', presumably Art Mac Cumhaigh's *Úirchill an Chreagáin*, which had made its way up to the Glens from South Armagh.

All the time that she was immersing herself in the living tradition of Irish, family life went on as usual. In 1908 she joined Coláiste Chomhghaill in Belfast and went religiously to the Saturday classes and to the written and oral examination. Seán Ó Catháin had set up Coláiste Chomhghaill at the bottom the Falls Road, and his reputation as a teacher was second to none. It was probably Ó Catháin who introduced her to the richness of the Munster folksong tradition in Irish, which is reflected in the *Duanaire*.

Normal life at Galgorm, as I have said, went on, and this entry in the diaries for 7 December 1910 is revealing: 'Ballymena Unionist meeting. Colonel Rowan came for the night to go to it. Captain O'Neill and Lady O'Neill came to early dinner. I went with the whole party to the meeting.' Ten days later, on 17 December, there is this entry: 'I went to Belfast to the Irish College'. On 22 June 1911 she records a huge party at Galgorm to celebrate Coronation Day, and at the end of that month she records the Glens Feis at Garron Tower. All the while she is moving between two worlds.

As noted above, Miss Young's crowning achievement is her *Duanaire Gaedhilge* in three volumes. There she selected and presented some of the most moving and most beautiful songs in the Irish language tradition. An tAthair Lorcán Ó Muireadhaigh, writing in *An tUltach*, said, 'ón uair gur foilsíodh an chéad imleabhar den duanaire seo is minic a moladh an obair go léir agus ní haon ionadh é' ('Since the first edition of this anthology was published the work has often been praised, and no wonder'),[4] and Aodh de Blacam in the *Sunday Independent* wrote, 'This is what we have long been wanting, a really tasteful anthology of Irish verse. A book in which every piece is pure gold.'

The selections Miss Young made for the *Duanaire* reveal a sense of taste and literary judgement that is in many ways unparalleled:

> A Mhuire dhílis, cad a dhéanfad má imíonn tú uaim
> Níl eolas chun do thí agam, do thine ná do chluid,
> Tá mo mháithrín faoi leatrom is m'athair san uaigh
> Tá mo mhuintir ar fad i bhfeirg liom is mo ghrá i bhfad uaim.

This song, like so many in the collection, has in it all the bare passion of brokenhearted love, a work of great literature. 'It is a most beautiful love song,' Miss Young writes in her notes, 'full of poignant pathos.' She was getting in touch with the ordinary people, searching out their emotional and imaginative life, their ideas and their feelings and presenting them accurately and in a scholarly fashion. In the same volume she presented 'Thugamar Féin an Samhradh Linn' and added the following note: 'I have added the second verse which was taken down by me many years ago from old Mrs Hamilton in Cushendun, Co. Antrim'. Also included is 'Caoineadh na d'Trí Mhuire' ('The Lament of the Three Marys'), a religious poem.

> A Pheadair, a aspail, an bhfaca tú mo ghrá gheal
> Ochón is ochón ó
> Chonaic mé ar ball é á chéasadh ag na saighdiúir
> Ochón is ochón ó.

Miss Young writes: 'A keen with this name used to be chanted at funerals and wakes in Glendun Co. Antrim. Three women took part in it, and keened as they marched in procession to the grave. Mrs Nellie O'Neill who died in Glendun some years ago has acted in this way as one of the three Marys.'

She was out there in the Gaeltacht, going up the glen to meet with native speakers, to gather their lore, and her book has the breath of the living Gaeltacht about it. For Rose Young the Gaeltacht stretched from Carraig na bhFear in Cork to Cushendun in Antrim, through Rafferty's poems and Miss Brooke's collection and the Hardiman collection and the Petrie collection and the Walsh collection, right through to Nancy Tracey of Binn an Phréacháin in Tyrone. She opened up these treasures to the enthusiastic and wide body of readers who were rediscovering Irish and the Gaelic world, and she did it with discernment and judgement.

Douglas Hyde wrote in the introduction to her *Duanaire*: 'Tá obair shármhaith déanta ag Róis Ní Ógáin. Do chuir sí dánchruinniú le chéile nach furas a shárú as bhinneas agus as mhaitheas' ('Róis Ní Ógáin has performed a valuable task. She has made available a collection of poems that are incomparable for their excellence and melodiousness.') Róis Ní Ógáin had in her much of the spirit of Hyde and the early Gaelic League. Writing to Hyde, Pearse had said, 'When the Gaelic League was founded those who had adhered to it should have left the city behind and headed for the rural areas. They should have gone among the people who spoke and lived there with them.' Rose Young did precisely that. Hyde moved among the ordinary folk of Roscommon, and as the son of an Anglican minister it was a big step for him. Rose Young moved among the ordinary folk of Cushendun, and it was an even bigger step for her – from the big house in Galgorm to the country cottage or cabin in Cushendun, all the while reaching out beyond her religious and political affiliations to touch and experience the lives of the ordinary Irish and to share in their emotional life and ideas.

It has been said and written that her interest in Irish led to her expulsion from the family circle and that she was ostracised. This is simply untrue. Lady Brookeborough assures me that she can recall her Aunt Rose quite clearly as a frail old lady, and that they as children were brought to visit her in Cushendun and Ballycastle on a regular basis. When she died in the Glens she was taken home to be buried with her own people in Ahoghill. My feeling is that some Gaels might be more comfortable with a Miss Young that had been ostracised from her family because of her love of and devotion to the Irish language. The truth is that Miss Young, like many of us, found it impossible to define Ireland in political or religious terms, but that down there with the ordinary people was a rich cultural world based on a wide human experience, whose secrets and values Rose Young sought to explore and, most importantly, reveal to a wider audience, and within which she could find space.

On 1 June 1909 Miss Young has this entry in her diary: ' I went to Donegal with Ada, I met Ada at Ballymena station at nine thirty, Miss Gough joined us at Coleraine. We arrived in Caiseal na gCorr at three o clock and walked to Meenaboy.' She stayed eighteen days as a student at Colaiste Uladh, the Ulster College there. Ada was Ada McNeill. She was not related to Eoin MacNeill of Glenarm, the founder member of the Gaelic League. She was a cousin of Lord Cushendun, lived in Cushendun and was one of the McNeills who were the agents for the Whites of Ballymena. It seems that it was through Francis Joseph Bigger – who, it must be said, played a crucial role in attracting fellow Protestants to the native Irish culture – that she got interested in Irish. She was an early member of the Gaelic League and was on the organising committee of Feis na nGleann. She was involved in the Irish College on Rathlin Island and, most importantly, she was on the organising committee of Colaiste Uladh, and acted as the secretary in the early years.

Colaiste Uladh had been set up in Gort an Choirce in the parish of Cloughaneely in Donegal in 1906. It brought together all creeds, classes and political affiliations. Miss Dobbs was treasurer. Patrick Pearse came there to lecture, as did Eoin MacNeill and Professor Rhys from Oxford. Joseph Mary

Róis Ní Ógáin

Plunkett and Roger Casement came there to study the language. Séamus Ó Searcaigh was teaching there, as was Eamonn Ó Tuathail, and Una Farrelly was president. There were solid courses of study in modern Irish, medieval Irish and Irish history, with a strong emphasis on creative writing and of course the living language. There were walks out in the mountains, trips to the islands of Tory and Arainn Mhór, and parties and aeraíochtaí on sunny days up in the Bealtaine. The day ended with the céilí in the College when all the students would gather with the local people.

Joseph Mary Plunkett catches the whole atmosphere in a love poem he wrote centred around his reminiscences of Colaiste Uladh and the pleasures of life there.

> Cloughaneely Irish College,
> Has a wealth of wit and knowledge,
> Not to speak of health and beauty
> Grace and graciousness go lore
> But among its charms entrancing

Men and maidens, songs and dancing,
There is nothing so delightful
As yourself mo mhíle stór

Loud the sound that hails awaking
Banbha's son, for the dawn is breaking
And the waves of Cloughaneely
Help to swell the ocean roar
But the breeze that sweeps above them
Fills their song and makes us love them.
For it's laden with music
Of your heart mo mhíle stór

When the moon is shining palely
On the evening of the céilí
And purple stars are peeping
Through the open College door
There is music in the night
Of the dance and voices laughing
But 'tis nothing like the music
Of your heart mo mhíle stór.

Miss McNeill, Miss Young and Miss Dobbs were at those céilís. They may have been standing by too when the president of the college gave Pádraig Mac Piarais a stern reprimand for turning up late for a lecture.

There were writers there too. In many ways Colaiste Uladh provided a breeding ground for such writers as Séamus Ó Grianna, who was a student there, and 'Fionn Mac Cumhaill', who was really Maghnus Mac Cumhaill. He was a great athlete and his fellow students at the Irish college nicknamed him Fionn Mac Cumhaill; the name stuck and all his books, full of beautiful Donegal Irish, were published under that name. It was Ada McNeill that first spotted the talent in Séamus Ó Grianna and wrote down from him his first literary effort in *Cú na gCleas*, which was published in 1914.

We could perhaps dismiss all this as upper-class, well-off women – dilettantes – toying with and pottering about in this strange archaic language; women who had little else to do and were just following a whim or a fantasy. This, I believe, would be a gross misreading of the situation and a grave injustice to their memory. There had always been within the Protestant and Unionist tradition a strand that devoted itself to Irish and saw the cultivation of the living language as important. It stretches back through MacAdam and Mac Dónaill and Bryson in nineteenth-century Belfast, to Richardson, Bedell and Pól Ó hUiginn. For the native Irish tradition was in reality a set of values, a vision or view of the human condition, an outlook, a storehouse of human experience.

We recognise today the valuable contribution to the development of Irish of Rose Young, Margaret Hutton, Ada McNeill and Margaret Dobbs. They knew, as we should all know today, that the language and the culture enshrined in the language are a vast human resource there for all, Catholic, Protestant and

Dissenter; that it has a beauty and a reality and a great human tug at the heart that are as powerful today as when Miss Young began to make her trips to Belfast to learn Irish from Seán Ó Catháin.

In the early years – before politics took over – the language movement was a force for drawing people together. It broke down the barriers between the well-off, the middle classes and the poor mere Irish; it gave the opportunity to people, regardless of sex, background, religious persuasion or political affiliation to come together for a common purpose – the cultivation and sharing of a rich and varied human tradition that had evolved and was continuing to evolve, and to which Miss Young, Miss McNeill, Miss Dobbs and the others contributed so positively.

In *Duanaire Gaedhilge* Volume 1 (1921), Miss Young gives the text of 'An raibh tú ag an gCarraig':

> An raibh tú ag an gCarraig no an bhfaca tú ann mo ghrá
> Nó an bhfaca tú gile na finne nó scéimh na mná
> Nó an bhfaca tú an t-úll ba chumhra is ba mhilse bláth
> Nó an bhfaca tú mo Vailintín nó an bhfuil sí dá cloí mar táim

She based the text on Walsh's *Irish Popular Songs* and O'Daly's *Poets and Poetry of Munster*; and she adds the following note:

> Walsh thought the song was a southern one, but could not fix its locality. Dr .Joyce heard it sung hundreds of times in Munster, which seems to confirm Walsh's opinion. O'Daly says it is the chef-d-oeuvre of Dominic Ó Mongáin, a County Tyrone poet, and was written in the 18th century in honour of Eliza Blacker of Carrick, Co. Armagh, afterwards Lady Dunkin of Upper Clogher Court, Bushmills, Co. Antrim, now called Dundarave.

Miss Young seems to me to be bringing all of Ireland together here: poor poet and landed gentry, north and south, as if the language and the cultural tradition might provide the basis for cohesion in Ireland so that we might bring different classes and creeds together and might, in Hyde's telling phrase, make the present a rational continuation of the past.

Miss Young, Miss Dobbs and Miss Ada McNeill remained faithful to the Gaelic League spirit to the very end. On 6 May 1935 Miss Young records the celebration of the King's Silver Jubilee with bonfires on the Antrim coast; the very next day she was at a meeting of the Feis na nGleann Committee. At the age of 73 she made the journey to Dublin and found a vantage point at the Pillar to watch her old friend Douglas Hyde pass on his inauguration parade as President of Ireland. In November of the previous year she had been taking a Mrs McCormick and a Mr Brogan through the new Irish linguaphone course. The following year she was at her brother George's funeral: 'an enormous procession of 'B' Specials and Orangemen marched after the hearse to Ahoghill and gave George a military funeral'. Ireland was going its different ways, and political opportunists would exploit and highlight the differences, but Miss Young within the Irish language and Irish cultural movement found the space and the understanding to make creative and positive contributions, and prepared in a fashion the way for others of her background and disposition to find their place within the Irish language and cultural tradition.

1 Frank O'Connor, *Kings, Lords and Commons* (Dublin, 1962), p. 110.
2 B. Ó Cuív, *Irish Dialects and Irish-Speaking Districts* (Dublin, 1971), p. 26.
3 D. Breathnach and M. Ní Mhurchú (eds), *Beathaisnéis a hAon* (Dublin, 1986), pp. 30–1.
4 D. Breathnach and M. Ní Mhurchú (eds), *Beathaisnéis a Dó* (Dublin, 1990), p. 116.

Women at work in the Glens, planting potatoes *(Courtesy Ulster Museum/MAGNI)*

3

THE WOMEN REVIVALISTS
Fred Heatley

Many of us who know the haunting beauty of the Antrim Glens seldom pause to think of just how hard, in the past, life was for the people who lived there. For the men there was the scraping of a living from a soil deep in rock or marshed in water, as fishermen or sea-going, mainly in coastal vessels. For the women there was the assistance, where necessary, around the farm, the upkeep of small, cramped houses and the rearing of the children. For all there were the often long distances to be walked to shops, schools, places of worship. And there was the heartbreak of enforced emigration. Not an easy existence.

As elsewhere where similar conditions existed, it was mostly the women who kept the homes together; yet, in general, they are written – deliberately or otherwise – out of the historical record. It is mainly of men that historians and writers tell, with only the odd woman emerging from the gloom. But north-east Antrim, despite its alleged dour Scottishness, has had several women speaking out for the area, and at no place were they more prevalent than at Feis na nGleann.

The first president of the Feis was Miss Barbara McDonnell of Monavart, Cushendall, and Miss Anna McAllister was to become secretary – a position held for 27 years. Other women throughout the long years have been committee members. But the women who spoke most for the Glens spread their activities somewhat further afield.

Nesta Higginson, who wrote under the pseudonym 'Moira O'Neill', was to earn a reputation as 'The Poet of the Glens of Antrim' due to her use of verse to depict the area in which she lived for so many years. She resided in Rockport, described as a 'big, white, roomy house … beside the sea at Cushendun', but was not to spend all her days there as she married Walter Skrine, with whom she went to farm in North-West Canada; on their return to Ireland they settled in the Skrine family home at Ferns, Co. Wexford. Moira O'Neill's poetry is redolent of the Glens and displays an awareness of the life then lived there, with its verse-tales of emigration and tragedy. Her own homesickness is shown in 'Back to Ireland' with its opening lines:

> Oh tell me, will I ever win to Ireland again,
> Astore! From the far North-West?
> Have we given all the rainbows, an' green woods an' rain,
> For the suns an' the snows o' the West?

The sadness and hopelessness of life is captured in 'Sea Wrack'

> There' a fire low upon the rocks to burn the wrack to kelp.
> There' a boat gone down upon the Moyle, an' sorra one to help!
> Him beneath the salt sea, me upon the shore,
> By sunlight or moonlight we'll lift the wrack no more.

Songs of the Glens of Antrim and her *Collected Poems* were published in several editions in Britain and America.

Another 'big house' woman who left her memory in the Glens was Margaret Emmeline Dobbs of Portnagolan, Cushendall. Her family had long links to Irish parliamentarianism, and her father, Conway Edward Dobbs, was J.P. for the County of Antrim and High Sheriff for Carrickfergus and for Co. Louth. Margaret was reared in Dublin, with holidays spent at Glenariff Lodge, at the head of the Glen of that name.

Upon her father's death in 1898 the Dobbs family moved to Glenariff as a permanent residence. Margaret's schoolgirl love of the Irish language deepened on finding it still the spoken tongue among many of the Glensfolk, and she was to spend the remainder of her life (she died in 1962, aged 90) in its study and encouraging its growth. Though a brother was one of the Unionist gun-runners to Larne in 1912, Margaret's own political views, if any, are unknown. She was romantically linked with Roger Casement (whose sexuality was until fairly recently disputed): Mick Leitch of Callisnagh in the heart of Glenariff informed this writer of Margaret and Casement being many times seen walking hand in hand. In a newspaper interview many years later, she was extremely circumspect, stating of Casement that: 'Not only was he my friend but he was a friend of all the Irish people. But I have not the same admiration for his judgements.' Whatever her politics, she remained to the last a staunch supporter of Feis na nGleann.

Ada McNeill, another founder of the Feis and a member of its committee, was of the Glendun McNeills and was unabashed about her strong Republicanism. Rose Maud Young (Róis Ní Ógáin) was, however, a Unionist, born in 1865 and reared at Galgorm House near Ballymena; she lived her final years with Margaret Dobbs in the Glens. Her three-volume anthology of Irish verse, published between 1921 and 1930, assured her a place in Irish language literary studies. Her involvement with the language is believed to have occurred through friendship with Bishop William Reeves (1815–92), Bishop of Down, Connor and Dromore from 1886. Rose Young/Róis Ní Ógáin died in 1947 and is buried in the Presbyterian churchyard in Ahoghill. Some believed that she was a Unionist all of her life while others thought that she had to leave Galgorm House because of her pro-Irish views.

Other women prominent in the Irish language world who became identified with – though not necessarily living in – the Glens included Una and Eilis Bannister and their sister Gertrude Parry, and, perhaps most unexpectedly of all,

THE WOMEN REVIVALISTS

Margaret Hutton. All were from Protestant and Unionist backgrounds, the Parry/Bannister sisters being cousins of Roger Casement and Margaret Hutton the wife of a wealthy Belfast man resident on the upper-class Malone Road. She was a friend of Patrick Pearse, who led the Irish Rebellion of 1916, though whether she supported that enterprise is doubtful. As it was, Pearse stayed in the Hutton home at Deramore Park, Belfast, and Margaret donated a hefty (for the period) £50 to Scoil Eanna, Pearse's Irish-Ireland enterprise in Co. Dublin. Hutton was a member of the Gaelic League and translated the Irish saga, *Táin Bó Cualinge*, into English.

There were, of course, many more women supporting Feis na nGleann, such as Ethna Carbery. Born in Ballymena in 1866, Carbery's true name was Anna Johnston, later Anna MacManus through her marriage to author, Seamus MacManus. A poet and songwriter, her best-known song was 'Roddy MacCorley'. She died in 1911. The long-lived Alice Milligan from Omagh was another poet who, with Anna Johnston, published and edited a couple of Republican literary papers, *The Northern Patriot* and *Shan Van Vocht*. Their efforts marked them out as early feminists, as they traded with the male-dominated thinking of their period.

Sadly left out of the Feis story are those women without whose help the event itself might have proved a disappointment: the women who prepared the tables, who scrimped so that their children could have appropriate dress for dance or sport, and who displayed a willingness to do the needful. Their names or deeds may never resound with those of the prominent women mentioned above, but their help was and is essential to maintain the success of a unique occasion. This brings to mind the little 'An Tuirne Beag' premises in Ballycastle, which owed its origin to Stephen Clarke, who was involved with Feis na nGleann since its inauguration, and his wife. When he died his wife maintained the business for a number of years, selling items from the Ballycastle Toy Factory. This was a relic of a local industry set up as an aim of those behind the Feis, and it was her remaining stock that formed the nucleus of Ballycastle's little museum. History in itself.

Margaret Dobbs and Rose Young with group of Irish dancers at the Feis, Ballymena, in 1931

4

MARGARET DOBBS
GLENSWOMAN, SCHOLAR AND IRISH LANGUAGE ENTHUSIAST (1871–1962)

Jack McCann

'Dear Maggy, Many thanks for your letter. No I'm afraid the Abbey people would not do it just now, when they are trying to produce paying plays ...' The budding playwright to whom this letter was addressed in 1910 was Miss Margaret Emmeline Dobbs of Cushendall. Unlike the writer of the letter, John Masefield, who was to become England's longest serving Poet Laureate, Margaret Dobbs was to have little impact outside her chosen ground, the Glens of Antrim. Her fate was to outlive her generation and, like her plays, to end up almost forgotten. In the end, did any of her dreams come true or had she grown too old to dream?

She was born on 19 November 1871. Her father, Conway Edward Dobbs, was a J.P. for Co. Antrim, High Sheriff for Carrickfergus (an assize town) in 1875, and High Sheriff for Co. Louth in 1882. The Carrickfergus appointment was due to a long family association with the town. In 1690 an ancestor as Mayor had welcomed William, Prince of Orange, to the town on his way to victory at the Boyne. The Louth post could be traced to his marriage with Sarah Mulholland, one of six daughters of St Clair Kelburn Mulholland, himself a High Sheriff for Louth. The Mulhollands of Co. Down are the family from which Lord Dunleath is sprung.

Margaret's grandfather, also Conway Edward, had married his own cousin, Maria Sophia, only daughter of Francis Dobbs, Member of Grattan's Parliament. Before looking further at Margaret's life, a peep at Francis might prove of interest. He was called to the Bar in 1775 and in the following year wrote a play, *The Patriot King and the Irish Chief*, which was never performed. A leading member of the Irish Volunteers, he was their Northern representative at the Dungannon Convention of 1782, a close friend of Lord Charlemont and a fanatical opponent of legislative union with England. He published a volume of poetry of high quality in 1788, but his pungent political pamphlets attracted a wider readership.

Francis Dobbs is best remembered for a speech delivered against the Union on 7 June 1800, not so much for its political content as for the argument that the Union was forbidden by scripture. In support he quoted from Daniel and *The Book of Revelations*, and while on his feet took the opportunity to foretell the second coming of the Messiah! It had all the ingredients of, and was, a best-seller

– 30,000 copies. In spite of Francis Dobbs and Daniel, the Act of Union, for better or worse, was passed in 1800 and Francis faded into obscurity to die eleven years later in dreadful financial distress.

Was Margaret influenced by this flamboyant eccentric? I think so. He was the only other green branch in the family tree, a staunch Protestant who kept faith with his country and his church. Margaret was known to refer to him as 'Francis the incorruptible', for unlike many of his creed and class he could not be bought in the chicanery leading up to the Act of Union. And of course he had written a play.

Margaret's family lived in Dublin, then the undisputed capital of an undivided Ireland, but she was soon to learn that it was an English city. In 1886 she expressed a desire to learn the Irish language. Her parents did not object. Indeed, in later life she was to comment that her feelings for things Irish might have stemmed from the Mulholland in her. I think, however, that the twelve-year-old was encouraged by her governess, a Scot with a Gaelic background. In those far-off days a governess had almost unlimited control in matters educational. Anyhow, Margaret and governess searched Dublin in vain for an Irish teacher.

Remarkably, a young man from Glenarm, Eoin MacNeill, in 1887 placed an advertisement in a Dublin paper for a tutor in the Irish language and got one reply – from a man who knew only the pronunciation of Irish place names. MacNeill went west to Inis Meán in the Aran Islands, but age and background debarred Margaret from taking such a step, so her young dream went unfulfilled.

Her parents had fallen in romantic love with Glenariff, and they built Glenariff Lodge at the head of the glen where the family spent their summer holidays. When Conway Dobbs died in 1898 Sarah and the children moved permanently to Glenariff. Margaret was 27. The family name had long been linked with the glen. Almost a century before Sarah moved there the Rev. Richard Stewart Dobbs lived at the foot of the glen in Bay Lodge, where he wrote his *Statistical account of parishes of Ardclinis and Layd*. And an even earlier Richard Dobbs had taken a close look at Glenariff in 1683 when surveying the County of Antrim for William Molyneux's Irish atlas. No strangers they.

Margaret found in the quiet of the Glens what had been drowned out in the bustle of Dublin – spoken Irish. More importantly, she found others of her faith who shared her love of the language and scholars like Hugh Flatley, the Mayo schoolmaster, who were prepared to teach it. And things were happening. Miss Higginson from down Cushendun way had instant success with her *Songs of the Glens of Antrim*, published in 1900; our seeker after an Irish tutor, Eoin MacNeill, became vice-president of the Gaelic League; and Constance Crommelin from up Layd shore married an English poet named John Masefield. Oh, indeed things were happening. If Dublin remembered 1904 as the year in which the Abbey Theatre was founded, the Glens remembered it as the year of the Big Feis. There is a contemporary photograph of the great Feis procession and up front Miss Margaret Emmeline Dobbs, for whom life was only beginning. A member of the Feis committee from the start and later a tireless literary secretary, her Dobbs scholarship to a Gaeltacht college was the most coveted award in the literary section for many years.

Folk memories of the Big Feis abound in the Glens. John Hewitt in his poem 'Fame' tells how Roger Casement brought the Raghery (Rathlin) men over for the day. Casement acted as umpire at the hurley match on Red Bay strand for the 'Shield of the Heroes'. But for me it is the folk-memory of Roger Casement shirt-sleeved, sickling the rushes to clear the Feis field, for it links Casement with Margaret; the British Consul and the daughter of the big house promoting the cause of Gaelic Ireland. It is said that Casement could not master the Irish language. He was less determined in this one respect than Margaret, who went off to the Irish College at Cloughaneely in the Donegal Gaeltacht. Often she would recall the hardships encountered by teachers and students in those primitive days. She became treasurer of the summer school and brought back to the Glens of Antrim the message from the Gaeltacht: know your own language.

There is an unfortunate inclination to link the language with Catholics only, but when Margaret Dobbs was spreading the gospel in the Glens she gathered around her a group of ladies from well-known Protestant families – names like Young, Hutton, McNaughten, Richardson – who shared her zeal for the spread of the language.

One of them, Rose Young, is worth more than a passing reference such as this. Possibly ostracised by her family because of her pro-Irish views, she came to live with Margaret Dobbs at Portnagolan House, Cushendall, and died there in 1947. She compiled an anthology of Irish verse with the help of Douglas Hyde, first president of the Gaelic League and first President of Ireland. Rose Young is buried in the Presbyterian churchyard at Ahoghill, Co. Antrim. Mrs Hutton devoted ten years to her translation of the Irish epic, *The Cattle Raid of Cooley*: Protestant pride in our past.

I turned up the Feis programme of 1930 to find Margaret Dobbs and Ada McNeill on the committee and Rose Young, with one J. Humbert Craig, judging the Arts and Crafts exhibition. In passing it is worth noting that the winner of the senior section for Celtic design was a young man named Charles McAuley, while in classes for knowledge of Irish history Glendun folk swept the boards.

In 1946 the Feis committee decided to honour Margaret Dobbs for her devotion to the Feis and language by presenting her with an illuminated address. It can be seen today at Portnagolan House, with its stained glass windows commemorative of a great Irishwoman. Returning thanks for the praise lavished upon her on that presentation day, she recalled that it was exactly 60 years before that she and her governess searched in vain for an Irish teacher in Dublin, and how she achieved her ambition only when she became a member of Feis na nGleann. She went on to say:

Ireland is a closed book to those who do not know her language. No one can know Ireland properly until one knows the language. Her treasures are as hidden as a book unopened. Open the book and learn to love your language.

Let's turn to her plays. Playwriting occupied a decade or more of her life prior to 1921. In all she wrote seven plays, three of which were publicly performed, though only one was produced outside the Glens – *The Doctor and Mrs McAuley*, which won the Warden trophy for one-act plays at Belfast festival in 1913. Her plays were published by Dundalgan Press in 1920. In the Glens they were performed in what she described as a hayloft turned into a hall at the rear of the Glens of Antrim Hotel in Cushendall. One player appeared in all three plays: Dan McMullan, the tailor, of whom Lynn Doyle wrote in the December 1931 issue of *The Glensman*: There was a great comic actor lost to the world in Dan 'to all the world that is but Cushendall'. Nicholas Crommelin, brother of the above-mentioned Constance, appeared in two plays. It is interesting to note the Crommelin connection with both the Dobbs and Mulholland families. In 1776 Maria Dobbs married Samuel de Lacherois Crommelin, and in 1851 Annie Mulholland wed Nicholas de Lacherois Crommelin.

By far the most interesting play was never performed (shades of 'Francis the incorruptible'). It was entitled *A Man and a Brother*. Described as of three acts, it ran to only 36 pages and must have been the fastest three-act play in theatrical history. Miss Dobbs gave as her reason for its non-performance 'fear of political misunderstanding'. When she sent the draft to Masefield, he described it as the best constructed of her plays but added a prophetic note (the letter was dated 3 January 1921): 'I hope that we may see it acted, but I think the Irish world will change so soon and so much that it will be old fashioned before we come over. However you would not mind that I'm sure.'

Masefield knew her mind better than most, for the change that was to come was what she and others had dreamed of for years – Casement's dream, Hyde's dream and the dream of that fierce Republican, Ada McNeill, of whom Pádraic Mac Cormaic was to say, 'Miss Ada's all right – all right all the way'. But Margaret was not so politically outspoken as Miss Ada, and she was probably satisfied to see the play in print. Though she worked hard for ten years at her craft, she failed as a playwright. Her friend and mentor, Masefield, foresaw this, and in his letters he was kindly critical. In the letter that opens this chapter he discounted Abbey interest in the kindliest possible way, made a brief reference to the Belfast Literary Theatre's possible interest, but said firmly and frankly: 'It would pay you to stage it yourself at the garage, rehearse your own company, and play it yourself; amply pay you'. I think that says it all.

Harking back to Masefield's letter and the Abbey producing paying plays, it is ironic to think that from the pen of a playwright in Carnlough, a few miles down the shore, would come plays that would keep the Abbey open – George Shiels! Remember Yeats's riposte when Ernie Blythe said it was time to give Shiels a rest: 'A rest? And close the place!' For Margaret such a dream never came true.

But her plays were only a part of a very interesting life. In a letter to a friend of mine years later, setting out her interests, she made no mention whatever of her plays; after 1920, she never wrote another line for the theatre. In the end Masefield quietly got his way. She gave her main interest as research work in historical and archaeological matters. She had articles published in the *Ulster Journal of Archaeology*, in a German magazine for Celtic studies, in the French *Revue Celtique* and in the Irish magazine *Eriu*. It is impossible to deal with all she wrote: I will content myself, and hope you will be content, with three references to articles in the *Ulster Journal*. One, in 1939, was a lengthy look at the Ui Dercu Cein – a section of the Cruitne, the Picts of Dalriada – and traced their development from about 500 A.D. to around 1030 A.D. Rather too heavy for me, but then it was written for those who read and understood; it has 38 references from such tomes as *The Book of Leinster*, *The Annals of Ulster* and *The Book of Rights*. In 1950 she was writing about the name 'Dalriada', linking it with a race of horse breakers and riders claiming descent from Conall Cearnach of *Táin* fame, of whom it was said, so she noted, 'He was the third who rode a single horse first in Eire'. And if that is not an Irishism what is?

An article in Vol. 19 in 1956 looks at Lough Neagh and the traditions concerning it, and shows careful research of genealogical tracts in Laud 610 (Bodleian Library). To make easier reading of a transcription quoted, she gives the English translation of a number of Gaelic names of people and places. Oh, she would have been pleased with *The Glynns*!

There was a hint of romance between herself and Casement; that he was certainly more than an acquaintance was evidenced in an interview she gave some years before her death, in which she said, 'Roger was my friend. He used to stay here week-ends after his return almost broken in health from Putamayo.' (It was Casement's exposure of the conditions under which natives worked that earned him his knighthood.) The interviewer, mindful of renewed interest in the notorious Casement diaries, asked Miss Dobbs for her views on the scandal. Her reply is interesting: 'I have always had the highest admiration for Roger. He was a gentleman, humanitarian, poet and patriot. Not only was he my friend but he was a friend of all the Irish people. But I have not the same admiration for his judgements.'

Sadly, the journalist did not press her to explain and we therefore have to make conjecture. Her admiration for his virtues certainly ruled out any acceptance by her of the behaviour attributed to him by the alleged diaries. Was she then referring to his political judgement? Possibly. She considered herself a friend of all the Irish people, but was it an Ireland within the British Empire? Remember, 'Home Rule' was the cry in Casement's day. Talk of a Republic was still behind hand. In Ulster people were arming to defy, if necessary, the will of Parliament, while in the South they were arming to support the rule of Parliament. Where stood the Dobbses of Cushendall? I can tell you. Motor car number 3 on that night in Larne brought from the *SS Clydevalley* four bundles of German Mausers to the home of Mr Dobbs of Cushendall. I took that to be

Henry Hugh Dobbs, Margaret's brother. But other German guns changed all that and, instead of fighting on Bannside, the U.V.F. were soon fighting in France.

And of course there were Dobbses in the line: Margaret's brother Nithsdale, a colonel; her nephew the brigadier, her cousins, Chaplain Rev. Conway Ed. and Lieutenant Conway Ed. For the Dobbses there was a war on. Hard to believe that the handsome knight who sat at a table in Portnagolan would be plotting with the Germans to bring guns to Ireland, not in support of Parliament but to destroy its power over Ireland. What side was Margaret on?

Margaret Dobbs died at Portnagolan in 1962, aged 90 years.

This article was first published in 'The Glynns', Journal of the Glens of Antrim Historical Society, Vol. 2, 1983.

5
EXTRACT FROM MISS DOBBS' MEMOIRS OF FEIS NA nGLEANN
Margaret E. Dobbs

It was F.J. Bigger and his young friends who started Feis na nGleann when spending a holiday in Cushendun. They included Sam Waddell ('Rutherford Mayne'), Fred Hughes, Denis McCullough, Joseph Campbell and his sister. They consulted with Roger Casement, Miss Ada McNeill and others and, as a result, a committee was formed and Feis na nGleann was started in 1904. Denis Maguire of Belfast was helping, also Miss Barbara McDonnell was asked to be president as representing the McDonnells of Antrim.

The first Feis na nGleann took place in Glenariff. There was a large wooden hall near Waterfoot which served to hold the industrial and art exhibits and the evening concert and speeches. There were local pipers in Co. Antrim at that time; two of them played. I don't remember what language competitions took place. The next Feis was held in the same place; I think the oration was given by Mr Gill of the Congested Districts Board.

The next year the Feis was moved to Cushendall where there were halls and schools convenient for the language examinations. I wrote a play dealing with Glens history which was acted by the Ulster Theatre Group despite great difficulties, such as a makeshift stage in a garage, with candles the only light. I have no records after this until 1910, when Fr Domhnall Ó Tuathall came to Glenariff. He set out to save the Glens Irish and spread it. He was a great and earnest worker and soon had the children and young people at work. Classes were formed and the children went to the few old native speakers left for lessons. An open-air Feis was held in Glenariff in 1910. On the platform that day were Fr McGowan, Fr Ó Tuathall, Hugh Flatley, Ada McNeill, Rose Young, myself and others present included Carl Hardebeck, Louis Walsh, Andrew Dooey and P.T. Finlay (Cú Uladh). Roger Casement was not present that day.

Very soon special competitions were organised for native speakers, a thing now past. Travelling teachers were at work in Ballymena, Glenariff and Glenravel. It was in Glenravel that Sibéal Ó Luain learnt her Irish, which after her marriage to Pádraic Mac Cormaic, she taught so well in Glendun. In 1911 the Feis met again in Glenariff. Owing to an increase in the number of language competitions we had to appeal for help in the judging to Alice Milligan, Rose Young, Mrs McGavock and Seamus Ó Searcaigh. There was not so much to do in music and dancing sections as there is now.

In 1912 the Feis was held in Cushendall. The language examinations took

Margaret Dobbs

place the day before and Glenravel entrants were most prominent in the list of prize winners. A pageant was staged in the open air on Legge Green, beginning with a procession and including 'Homage of the Nine Glens to the Ard-Ri', a dance and Druidical ceremonies. I have no notes on the 1913 Feis and the World War of 1914 and the civil unrest 1916–1922 put an end to activities till 1923.

By that time, of the original committee only Pádraic MacCormaic, Ada McNeill and myself were left. A new committee was collected including Fr McCracken, Fr Lenaghan, Fr Fogarty, Séan Ó Clérigh, Áine McAllister, Arthur McAlister, Peter Marley, Eileen Kearney, Sibéal Mac Cormaic, Mrs Gertrude Parry, Ada McNeill, Andrew Dooey, Joseph Gregg and others.

The Feis of 1928 was held in Cushendall and since then has been held without interruption. One day has proved insufficient for the work. The 1929 Feis was again held in Cushendall and largely attended, both by competitors and visitors. Lughaidh Walsh opened the day with a speech in Irish and English. It took two days to get through all the work.

In 1931 a change was made by holding the Feis in Ballymena – with great success. Lord Ashbourne spoke in Irish and work lasted three days. Competitors came from outside Co. Antrim and there was a great increase in music and dancing. Though Ballymena Feis was so successful, many people felt it should not go outside the Glens. The next year, 1932, it was held in Glenarm and was opened by Una Ní Fhaircheallaigh. In 1933 I think the Feis was in Cushendall and also in 1934. In 1935 and 1936 it was in Carnlough. There were competitions for scholarships presented by the Feis Committee and the Bishop of Down and Connor presented a cup for the language competitions. Dr

Madden presented a cup for history. In 1941 the music and language examinations were held in Kintullagh Convent schools while the sports and dancing took place on a later date in Glenariff. This arrangement worked well for several years. In 1942 and 1943 the sports day in Glenariff was favoured with fine weather but in 1944 a very wet day spoilt the Feis.

After this date it was decided to keep the Feis in Glenariff for ten years running and Fr O'Neill and Archibald McMullen undertook the local management. By 1945 the number of competitors had greatly increased from 200 in 1943 to 800 entries. It took two days for the language examinations alone. In 1945 American and Belgian soldiers were present while camping in this county. In 1946 we were lucky in having very fine weather The oration was given by a well-known Scottish scholar, the Rev. John McKechnie; Larne led in the competitions thanks to Fr Byrne PP, President of the Feis.

In 1947 the language took two days' work in examination. Rev. E. Devlin, President of Comhaltas Uladh, was the orator. Bad weather spoiled things in 1948 and it was thought wise to move to Cushendun for shelter, dividing the examinations between Cushendun and Cushendall. In 1950 the Feis went to Ballycastle. Since then it has been held twice in Glenariff and now, for the second consecutive year, it is being held in Cushendun.

I have said nothing of the arts and crafts side, which has been organised every year. It was run many times by Mrs Mooney and Miss Logue, both now retired from their labours. It is impossible to name all who have worked freely and voluntarily in the cause but it is to Pádraic Mac Cormaic most credit must go for founding and reviving the work. He and Mrs Mac Cormaic did great things for the Gaelic cause in the Glens. The work Fr O'Toole did in Glenariff can be felt in the work done by his pupil, Aine McAllister, secretary of the Feis for many years. Now retired, she is missed at every moment; I am glad to say she is still with the committee.

Memoirs written to mark the Golden Jubilee of the Feis in 1954.

The soothing sound of the fiddle

6
ADA McNEILL (1860–1959)
PROTESTANT GAELIC LEAGUER AND NATIONALIST

Introduction
Malachy McSparran

Ada McNeill, better known in the Glens as Miss Ada, was born in England in 1860. She was the only child of Daniel McNeill and his wife Nanette Astley. Daniel McNeill had served for a time in the Indian Army and retired with the rank of captain. He then spent a few years working in the Bankrupcty Court, but due to the serious illness of his wife he returned to Cushendun, where he spent the rest of his life. His wife never regained full health and remained an invalid until her death in 1883. Ada was brought up in Cushendun.

Although Ada was a first cousin of Ronald McNeill, later Lord Cushendun, she did not share his political beliefs. Lord Cushendun was a staunch Unionist, a friend of Carson and Craig, and at one time was reckoned to be a possible first Prime Minister of Northern Ireland. Ada was an early member of the Gaelic League and, along with Margaret Dobbs and Rose Young, was enthusiastic in the local promotion of the Gaelic Revival. She was a member of the First Feis Committee in 1904, and a founder member of the Ulster College of Irish, in Cloghaneely in Donegal.

Ada McNeill was a friend of Roger Casement and he stayed many times in the McNeill home in Cushendun, when he was on holiday from his work overseas. She seems to have had a romantic attachment to him – whether it was reciprocated on his part is unknown. Ada certainly visited him while he was in prison in Brixton in 1916.

Even after Casement's death and the division of Ireland in 1921, Miss Ada continued with her promotion of the Irish language. She regularly visited the school in Cushendun where she read Irish legends and folklore to the pupils.

Miss Ada died in 1959 at her residence, Glendun Lodge, Cushendun. She is buried in the small graveyard attached to the Church of Ireland in Cushendun.

Ada McNeill's recollections of Roger Casement (1929)

You ask me a hard thing, that is to write my recollections of Roger. They belong not to the outside of life, to details of actual happenings but to the influence that such a friendship has had on my life, my character – shall I say – if I have any, which I sometimes doubt – that is the reason that it is a hard thing. I think when we first met I was 24 and he 21 or so? That I remember very distinctly. I think

An extract taken from notes written by Ada McNeill about Roger Casement

for a good many years of his life, his headquarters was at Churchfield – the other side of the mountain from us – our cousin Charlotte Miller had married Mr Casement of Churchfield, Uncle Roger. I was very fond of this cousin and he was hospitality itself. They kept an open house. Her relations were always welcome. There was a great friendship between Charlotte Casement and my father. They were first cousins. When anything took me over to Ballycastle – a twelve mile drive in those days before motors – I nearly always called with her, for lunch or tea and often stayed the night.

It was an early call I made going from Ballycastle, and I could not stay for lunch. Cousin Cha said, 'Roger is here now. I'd like you to meet him.' He was disturbed at his work and came from the dining room, his hand full of MS – tall and slight and handsome. So unlike any of the Casement family that it was quite a shock. He looked very untidy and dishevelled like someone who'd been writing since 7 a.m. and had no time for his breakfast. I think he was home from Africa. He walked about the room talking delightfully – about what I forget. I seemed to have talked a lot too – and forgot it was time to go – I seemed to be meeting a friend of a long time ago, not a stranger.

There was a great friendship – shall I call it – at this time between me and the youngest son at Churchfield, afterwards Admiral Casement. He rode over a few days later bringing Roger.

We were a horrid cynical transplanted family. In the West Highland homes of the past, we should have been among our own set and neighbours. There was really great enmity between ourselves and the Casements. In spite of the hospitality and good heartedness of the Churchfield people, it was never really abridged. My father's remark was, 'What a charming lad, absolutely unlike a Casement – I don't believe he is one.' After this, whenever Roger was at Churchfield, he came over to see us. I don't remember we ever did any exciting things. I don't connect his visits with exciting picnics or yachting or boating – it was now and again, a few days at the time and we were both great walkers and strode over the hills and up the glen – and both discovered we could talk without stopping about Ireland. This was a great joy to me, because there was no-one to talk to on that subject except the country people who had sworn to make me a red hot Republican and Fenian like themselves. I was in a Unionist milieu and Roger was too – on the Ballycastle side of the mountain. It was not surprising we made friends. Roger had the history of Ireland at his finger ends and influenced me till it became a passion to see Ireland free. We often argued and fought out our battles of long ago. I criticised the Irish side – but he always made excuses for them. At Churchfield were delightful books which never would have been found in our house. I remember rainy grey days in the dark old library there – which were anything but grey for us – with the open doors of the big bookcases. Roger refuting my gutsy excited arguments with quotations upon which he could always lay his fingers. I learned a lot like this – and to read for myself. Then there were more walks over the moors at home over Torr Road; my conversion was complete and life seemed to hold only Ireland and all the more so that I couldn't talk about it to the People. Among them a lot of my life was passed which was my father's wish and he said to make up my mind on everything and read for myself. One summer Roger came over for a few days, when we had a full house and gathered people around him under the big sycamore that was our roof tree. I can see him now – with a party converted on arguing and proselytizing.

With my father late into the night he talked of Africa and interested him intensely, then my father said after bidding him goodbye – as the king of Italy said of Mussolini, 'that youth will go far, we have not heard the last of him'.

Then there seems to come a long gap. Busy interests for us both and I expect little remembrance of each other.

1903 – could it have been after my father's death that I met him again? By

Ada McNeill

this time Roger was a celebrated man. His wonderful report on the Congo had brought him fame.

I remember once how his earnestness influenced me on another subject besides Ireland. I had lost my faith and only scoffed at religion and having a biting tongue and certain power of influencing others, this gave my father great pain and vexation, my greatest and best friend. I remember a long walk up the glen with Roger and as we turned home he talked eloquently and earnestly against scoffing at religion. I listened, actually paid attention and listened. His enthusiasm was as great as my own about things and he was far more earnest and simple. There was something always very young and boyish and yet so very true and earnest about his character that he made you pause and think. I remember at a picnic at Murlough – his actually sitting on the rocks and talking so earnestly about Faith and Religion that we all listened and bicycling home that night we agreed that no-one could have done it but Roger. In 1903 there was no abatement in my passion for Ireland and I was then in the Gaelic League and meeting a good many of the Gaelic League people. My first essay in writing a letter in the Gaelic was from the Aran Isles to Roger, I think in Dublin. Somewhere about this time I remember a delightful visit of Roger's to Cushendun House where he met a very artistic cousin of mine. I seem to recollect attempts at conversion all round – the cousin to the Irish cause and Roger to paintings. The artist in him came out in poetry and music. The attempts were not successful but we all three had a time to remember.

The first Glens Feis was – I think – 1905. Roger's name was on the Committee as representing Glenshesk. We worked hard for it together – sitting up writing till one or two a.m. and when all done – sitting by a dying fire to say how the Feis and the movement it stood for, had grown beyond all bounds and how when the day came a chaos we couldn't prevent would take the place of the organisation we intended – and hadn't the time to manage. Roger was a person of many sided character. One was always finding some new side; the side of hard steady work I had not seen before. You could have absolute reliance on what he said he would do – being done – this I fear is rare among us Celts. I so far had met only the pleasant agreeable person who helped a house party at home or in Ballycastle to go off well, as far as public work went! He was hard down on the others who promised and did nothing – hated idleness and never failed to carry out, at all cost, whatever he had promised to do. You could depend on him utterly.

Our dreams were coming true. A spirit was wakening in Ireland. Even in the sleepy old Glens, people turned out to meetings – came to committees – got enthusiastic about reviving old customs – about remembering the grand old past which is our inheritance. We were no longer Ireland of the Gall – the stranger. We tried to revive dancing – Roger took his place in the four hand reels. Strode about the roads hatless, encouraging, working up the heedless. I was not long ago talking to Stephen Clarke and he drew a picture of Roger – so full of energy and prompt work. There was a Feis in Cushendall and all our negotiations had failed to get the field we wanted for a hurling match. Another field full of weeds and dockens and thistles had to suffice the much persecuted Gael. Immediately Roger went for the scythe in hand and while we were talking and cursing, began to work hard cutting down the weeds and preparing the ground.

Like myself he was a person of moods – sometimes full of cheer – of hope – a glorious future for Ireland and so on – other times telling of civilisations that had passed away into oblivion …

I was delighted at last to be fighting in the last ditch with my Gaelic ancestors – to me it was the last ditch – I didn't hope for victory till much later.

Roger's influence was splendid with all the people younger than himself. A sort of inspiration to work and unselfishness and manliness for the young men and boys – in the girls he seemed to inspire a sort of hero worship – making them more thoughtful and earnest.

The nice old times when we could walk through the hills and talk and talk were over. Only seldom had one time to talk about Ireland in those Feis days. One evening in my garden, I remember in the old Coast Guard station – for though still in C'dun we were no longer in my old home. We went out late after a hard day – to plant carnation cuttings in my sadly neglected garden. We began to talk of Ireland.

'What are you doing, Alana?' said Roger.

'Oh! Heavens,' I said, 'I have planted them upside down too!'

Then we laughed and agreed it was best when talking about Ireland not to be doing anything else at the same time.

I was always for battle and bloodshed and vengeance without end and joy and delight in cruel vengeance – and how Roger hated all such thoughts and cruelty and war. Bulmer Hobson and he and I often talked together at this time and both were for the victory of good over evil but I always to do evil if necessary – do it thoroughly and hope that good would come out of it, but to win without suffering and lots of it for the enemy, wasn't in my prayers.

Roger often said I was a savage – worse a primitive savage – he had seen lots of suffering doubtless in Africa. Of Africa he never spoke to me. I didn't want to hear about what my Glens people called 'them Blacks' and I think we grudged Roger to Africa and thought he should have been in Ireland all the time.

We were nearly some of us arrested over anti-recruiting literature of which my house was full … Roger's fear always for others always thoughtful and considerate. Never a pin of care for himself.

Ambitious? I wonder?

He left the Glens and work of the Gaelic League for larger fields of usefulness and I didn't see him again till his return from the Putamayo.

That was at Cloghaneely Co. Donegal where I was working for the Summer School of Gaelic in Ulster. I had a dreadful little cabin of four rooms, where I entertained a great many friends – many too many for the space – Roger came often then and never can I forget how full that place became of newspapers which he imported. I'd never seen so many – they were heaped up in piles everywhere. Sometimes I helped to cut out bits and post them off – but with greater joy burn them. We sat once or twice by a large turf fire in my cabin – talking far into the night – as in the old days – in peace with no-one to disturb

– things were moving in Ireland – we seemed to tread the lightning talking of it all and piling up a glorious future for the old race and land that had come through so much – Roger was much altered – strained and ill but with just the old enthusiasms for all things Irish – we argued and disagreed often. I was on the wing for India and he tried hard to dissuade me from going but I would not listen but I learned then how much better his idea and judgment was – of the real values of life – I could never get my values – as artists say either in painting or in life.

It struck me more than ever – then – his horror of cruelty and oppression of the weak. In horror of all suffering and anger against those who cause it. I had a useless idiot of a maid from the Glens and was well reproved for being an absolute slave driver – and maker of slaves – I was a hard hearted disillusioned person – and would have liked, at that time to have driven a lot of people I had to work with not into slavery but to the shambles. This style of mind met with no response or sympathy from Roger. I thought he imagined people were as good hearted as he was himself and that he was often and often taken in – so we argued and disagreed.

The day I left I took with me a wild little hare of a Donegal lass as maid to see life and learn about the world in the Antrim Glens. On the way to the station the whole sole came off her shoe. We shall none of us forget Sir Roger helping her and disturbing the whole peace of the station in the fat bags to find a hammer and nails to mend her shoe.

Always good and kind to people that others never noticed or worried about. When I came back from India we met several times as he was in Ireland.

Up to the neck in the fight. In 1913 I imagine it was he came to Cushendun to speak at Shane O'Neill Carn. He then said war was coming in four or five years. We little thought how near the blaze it was. It might have been June 1914. For I remember picking my favourite rose for him in the garden when he said goodbye.

I saw him again in Brixton Prison in 1916. Today I took out of my dressing case his goodbye letter to me from Pentonville. It has lain for twelve years carefully hidden there.

Roger Casement

7

ROGER CASEMENT AND NORTH ANTRIM
Stephanie Millar

Casement's origins

The surname 'Casement' is of Manx origin and it was Sir Roger Casement's great-great-grandfather who brought it to Northern Ireland. Hugh Casement emigrated from Ramsey in the Isle of Man in the early eighteenth century and married the daughter of the Rector of Ballinderry. This local marriage introduced the Casement surname to Ulster. Sir Roger Casement's great-grandfather, also named Roger, came from Ballymena. He was from Henryville, now known as Harryville, and lived in a large house beside the Braid River. In 1790 this Roger Casement bought the lease for Churchfield House, Ballycastle. The lease cost £4,600 and the property was to become the Casement family seat, down to the present day.

Sir Roger Casement's paternal grandparents were Hugh Casement and Agnes Turnball, who gave birth to Roger's father, Roger Casement, on 23 May 1819. Roger's father was born into a Protestant house with a tradition of service to the Union. His maternal grandparents were James Jephson and Anne Ball. The Jephsons came from Mallow Castle, Co. Cork; Anne gave birth to Roger's mother, Annie Jephson, on 14 July 1834. Annie Jephson was born into the Catholic branch of one of the most illustrious Protestant houses in Irish history.

Roger Casement, the father, met Annie Jephson in Paris and the pair were married on 24 April 1855 at St Anne's in Belfast. Roger was 35; Annie was only 20. Agnes Jane was born a year later in Ulster. Charles Adam William Ball – Charlie – was born on 5 October 1861. The next son was Thomas Hugh Jephson, who was born 'at sea' and registered in Boulogne on 3 January 1863. Finally, Roger David was born on 1 September 1864 at Doyle's Cottage, Lawson Terrace, Sandycove, near Dublin. The Casement family tended to rely on handouts from relatives as Roger's father had got them into a parlous financial state.

When he was nine, Roger's mother died in Sussex. Cirrhosis was the primary cause of death, and her passing was the precursor of family and domestic breakdown. On the family's return to Ireland after their mother's death, Roger went to live with his father's brother, Uncle John, at Magherintemple (formerly Churchfield House). Roger's father chose to live 27 miles away at the Adair Arms Hotel, Ballymena. He had become increasingly divorced from reality and his physical health was not good, while his mental health was deteriorating. Casement's biographers, Sawyer and Dudgeon, recall Roger's father having conducted seances at the Adair Arms Hotel. It was here that he died on Saturday, 26 May 1877, and it was a sad and lonely death. An inquest followed that evening and it was presumed that tuberculosis was the primary cause; yet another Casement had succumbed to the 'white death'.

At twelve years of age, Roger became an orphan. At this stage in his life he was a tall, dark, slender lad who looked serious and spiritually troubled. After his mother's death he had turned more and more grave and inward. On his father's death he found himself, along with his siblings, wards of Chancery, dependent on the sympathy of Uncle John and of other relations. In 1877 John Casement became adviser and substitute father to the poor orphaned boy named Roger David Casement.

Childhood and education
Although Roger was sent to live with his Uncle John at Magherintemple when he was nine, little is known about his time there before he went to boarding school in Ballymena. Mackey's book on Casement informs us that his Uncle John had a well-stocked library at Magherintemple, and during his early time there he spent a lot of time reading books on Ireland and Irish history.[1]

Casement was educated at Ballymena Diocesan School, the forerunner of today's Ballymena Academy, under the academic management of the Rev. Robert King. His school career there can only be confirmed for the three academic years from September 1877 to summer 1880. Dr King was a good classical scholar and from him Roger acquired an adequate knowledge of the classics. The school was essentially for day pupils but Casement boarded, along with half a dozen others. The only school chum he had was the headmaster's seventh son, Travers King. Roger tended to join the headmaster and Mrs King every weekend for Sunday lunch.

At school Casement was very bright and adventurous, thoroughly enjoying every moment of his life. His surviving exercise books, which are kept in the National Library of Ireland, tell of his prizes for classical studies. He also developed a taste for poetry, particularly that of Keats, Shelley and Tennyson. He tended to spend many a quiet moment honing his own poetic efforts and, according to evidence in his notebooks, writing poetry was a habit he started in Ballymena.

He also acquired a good grounding in French, Greek and Latin, and he was reasonably fluent in Portuguese. History was his great love but he deeply resented the fact that the curriculum paid little attention to Irish history. Casement was to state categorically that he was not given any Irish language or history teaching. Both Dr King and another master, Dr William Reeves, were graduates of Trinity College Dublin and could speak Irish. Casement knew this and, as he was so devoted to Ireland, this privileged knowledge about his masters irritated him greatly. It was one of the major reasons why he turned down a request from the same school in 1912 for financial assistance.

Before leaving the school Casement, at the age of 15, had become something of a cricketer. He played for three separate local teams in the months of June and July 1880, including one for a school in the nearby Moravian village of Gracehill. He occasionally lent a hand to the men of the Young family from Galgorm who were associated with Ballymena Cricket Club. It was with the Young family that he spent much of his free time in the town, and he holidayed with them in Galgorm.

Due to lack of money and not academic talent, Casement left his formal education in Ballymena at the age of 15. He had been left penniless by his father's extravagance, and Dudgeon reflects on this departure by putting the blame on Magherintemple. He believes that if his ancestral home had been more generous, Casement might have proceeded to Trinity College Dublin.

By the age of 16 Casement had nearly reached his full adult height of six feet and two inches, and had the frame and movement of an athlete. His favourite pastime was swimming off the rocks in the bays of Co. Antrim or taking long walks in the mountain glens. Straight after his school departure, his Uncle John and a friend of his Bannister cousins, Alfred Jones, got Roger his first job as a clerk in the Elder Dempster Shipping Company in Liverpool. Office work upset Casement and so he became a purser on board the SS *Bonny*. It was his short time with Elder Dempster that initiated his consuming love of Africa. After five years of African life Casement returned home in October 1889, at the age of 25. On 23 October he spent a night in Portglenone and then set out for Ballycastle. We cannot be sure how long he stayed, but he did return to work, this time in the Congo.

In 1895 Casement visited Uncle John at Magherintemple, as he was at a bit of a loose end. According to Reid, 'he bathed, swam, walked, scribbled and began to think seriously of putting together a volume of verse'.[2] Uncle John had got an extension built on to the family home in 1894. The architect, John Lanyon, had designed it, but in 1895 Casement found the new part of the house draughty and cold, largely due to the exposed location.

Casement spent much of 1898 on sick leave, making long visits to his uncle at Magherintemple. On 17 May 1898 Casement wrote to a friend regarding a big Casement gathering that took place at his uncle's, which he attended. By 19 September of that year he was back in Ballycastle and he luxuriated in swimming in the bay. Due to sick leave, Casement was again in Ballycastle between August and November 1900. Much of this leave was spent at Magherintemple, where he always had free bed and board and the opportunity to walk, swim, read and tinker with poems.

At Christmas 1903 Casement arrived for a four-day stay at Magherintemple. His diary for Christmas Eve 1903 makes bleak reading:

> … on to Ballycastle, train late, 20 minutes stoppage at Armoy. No one to meet me. Cold and black. I will not go up there again. Aunt C. [Charlotte] up, all well … Spent day in house, cold worse – much worse, very miserable place during day. Others to church, I to bed early …[3]

On Christmas Day and for the next two days he worked on the revisions to his Congo Report, but he felt bored and stifled at his uncle's house. He continually repeated the word 'miserable' in his diary entries for this festive period.

This was to be the last time that Casement stayed at Magherintemple, although he was back in Ballycastle several times. This is significant as he was beginning to discover, through the Gaelic League, 'Irish Ireland' rather than 'English Ireland', and he knew he would have found little sympathy for this new passion among the entrenched Ulster Casements.

Casement's involvement in Feis na nGleann
In 1893 the Gaelic League was established with the aim of restoring the Irish language and winning back the allegiance of the Irish people to their own music, customs and games. The idea of a Gaelic League was Eoin MacNeill's; it was established in Dublin on 31 July 1893 with Douglas Hyde as its first president and MacNeill as vice-president.

Casement returned to Ireland in early 1904 due to impaired health, and took a great interest in the advancement of the Gaelic League and all it stood for. As soon as he joined the League he realised that the spoken Irish language was dying fast. From then on his main policy was to preserve Irish as a living tongue, and he made up his mind to try to learn the language. Ada McNeill was one of the womenfolk of the Glens who devoted their energies and considerable talents to the language and the cultural values of the plain people. 'Miss Ada' was a Protestant Nationalist who lived in Cushendun; she became involved with the organising of the first Glens Feis. Casement and Ada became good friends through their allegiance to the Irish language. He admitted to her that he found it hard to learn the language, and she advised him to take a correspondence course.

The best example of the gathering strands of the Irish movement in Ulster can be seen in the first Glens Feis. Discussions were held on the feasibility of holding a Gaelic 'Feis of the Glens' on the Antrim coast. The planning took place in Cushendall, where it was decided that the aim of the Feis was to proclaim the common Irish heritage of the coastal towns and the nine Glens between Ballycastle and Carnlough. At a meeting in the schoolhouse in Cushendall on 28 February 1904, at which Casement's friend, the Belfast solicitor F.J. Bigger was chairman, it was resolved to hold a Feis that summer. At that meeting Casement made a dramatic arrival, as retold by the following letter that Mrs Annie McGavock, from Glenarm, sent to her brother, Eoin MacNeill, in Dublin, dated 8 March 1904:

> Mr Clarke [John Clarke, one of the Feis committee] told me that at a meeting on Sunday week in Cushendall he said a few words about the movement and when he finished, a tall soldierly looking man came over to him and said: 'I agree heartily with all you have said; these have been my own thoughts for years.' Mr Clarke thought no more of the incident but on Friday last he got a letter from the

Boats provided by the Casement family to transport Rathlin Islanders to Red Bay to attend first Feis in 1904 *(Courtesy Ulster Museum/MAGNI)*

gentleman telling him he is greatly interested in the Feis, hopes he will be here at the time, but as he is going to South Africa soon, he fears he may have to leave before 30 June. He subscribes £5. Mr C. says he can hardly believe that a Casement of Ballycastle could hold such views.[4]

This remarkable letter seems to mark Casement's first public embrace of Irish nationalism.

The Feis was to occupy several days in late June. There were to be shows and competitions in traditional arts, crafts, games, spinning, weaving of tweed and flannel, the culture of eggs and fowls, of vegetables and flowers, storytelling in Irish, dancing, piping, solo and choral singing and a hurling match. The date was fixed for 30 June 1904 and Miss Barbara McDonnell was elected first president. Meetings were held all over the Glens and no stone was left unturned to make the festival a success. Subscriptions and prizes poured in dramatically, while F.J. Bigger spared no expense to make the scene a brilliant one. Secretary for the event was Miss Ada McNeill; Miss Rose Young, a close friend of Casement's from Galgorm Castle, was a member on the committee for Glencorp.

The first Feis was duly held in Glenariff and the weather was sunny and fine. Around 2,000 people attended the pageant, and Jeff Dudgeon describes the opening event as 'magnificently well organised and visually memorable'.[5] Casement had been especially anxious that the Rathlin Islanders, a Gaelic enclave six miles off Ballycastle, be involved in the Feis. Before the event he begged the loan of a small steamer from a local squire, Hugh MacEldowney, to ferry these native speakers over to the Feis. However MacEldowney refused on the grounds that he did not want Papists in his craft. The result was that Casement chartered a steamer at his own expense and brought over a party of 200 'Rachary men' for the ceremony. The steamer put into harbour at Red Bay, where the islanders disembarked; with Casement at their head they marched to the pipe music of Neil McCurdy to the Feis field.

Eoin MacNeill, himself a Glensman, spoke on the language and there were competitions covering the entire field of native industries, vocal and instrumental music, dancing, history and language. Casement was especially pleased when the Rathlin men he had transported to the Feis took first prizes in the war pipes and solo dancing. Casement's sister, Nina, (this was her pet name) and his brother, Tom, were both present at this Feis; Nina supported him by presenting a prize. Casement also took on the honour of presenting three prizes. Two of these went to the best-dressed boy and girl wearing the best Irish material outfits that had been made in the Glens. His other prize was awarded for the most decorative work in Irish wood. The writer and Nationalist M.P. Stephen Gwynn adjudicated the literacy and Gaelic competitions.

For that day in June 1904 sectarian differences were invisible as the upper and intellectual classes of the North combined with the coastal Catholics of Antrim in what Dudgeon has termed 'a celebration of Irish life, locality and culture'.[6] The men and women of the Glens were filled with pride that the Feis had affirmed their age-old Gaelic heritage and traditions. They were determined that the Feis would not end with one demonstration of their national outlook.

The Feis continued to be held annually in the month of June, and the venue for the 1906 Feis was Cushendall. The North Antrim Unionists had been quite tolerant of the activities of the Gaelic Leaguers for the past two years. However, in 1906 a local landlord, Francis Turnley, threatened to victimise one of his tenants who had offered to lend a field to the Feis committee for the sports. The nervous tenant withdrew his offer and the committee was left fieldless. At the first Glens Feis Turnley had provided a £1 prize; he had clearly undergone a major change of heart by June 1906. Immediately Casement went into a rage, cursing all loyalists: 'Loyalists are the devil and it is enough to make anyone who is decent and kind-hearted declare himself a Fenian just to differentiate himself from them'.[7]

The only other field available to the committee was overgrown with weeds and thistles. This did not in any way daunt Casement, who armed himself with a scythe and set out to work clearing the field; he managed to put it in order for the events. The 1906 Feis turned out to be a resounding success.

The 1906 dancing and singing competitions had been arranged to commence at 11.30 a.m., and the dancing competition took place on a specially erected platform in the Feis field. The contesting sides in the hurling match were Carey and Glenarm; the event proved to be very interesting and was greatly enjoyed by the large crowd. After an exciting struggle Carey won by 17 points to 10. The

ROGER CASEMENT AND NORTH ANTRIM

Casement's defence team

examinations in the school competitions took place prior to the Feis, but the results were given on the day. The Ballymena competitors did very creditably despite the language obstacle compared with districts where Irish had a stronger hold. The propitious weather added much to the success in 1906. Everything passed off without a hitch under the careful arranging of Miss Margaret Dobbs and Mr Hugh Flatley, a local schoolteacher.

The Glens Feis had certainly become firmly established by 1906. It continued annually, attracting competitors and spectators as it moved around different venues. While attending the 1911 Feis – his first real Irish gesture in about a year – Casement was kept family-bound in Ballycastle, much to his annoyance. His cousin, the Admiral Casement, had died suddenly in the night of heart failure and he felt obliged to stay for the funeral. In the autumn of 1927 Feis na nGleann acquired an interesting new member who carried on the Casement tradition: his favourite cousin, Gertrude Bannister, followed in his famous footsteps.

Casement, Home Rule and North Antrim
In May 1913 Sir Roger Casement retired from the Foreign Office and went home to Ireland. For a while after his return he avoided north Antrim because of the embarrassing fact that Ada McNeill had fallen passionately in love with him. At this time neither Sinn Fein nor the Irish language cause was having much success, and Casement warmed to the demand for Home Rule. He turned his attention to Sir Edward Carson's movement against Home Rule. The prospect of some Antrim Protestants standing up to fight Carsonism and proclaim their faith in a United Ireland was too good for Casement to resist. He wrote to the Presbyterian minister in Ballymoney, Rev. J.B. Armour, a leading Protestant

Home Ruler, suggesting a Home Rule meeting to attack the policy of Carson, to be held in the North Antrim town. Casement's biographer, Reid, notes that Casement hated everything Carson stood for, but the man himself still subtly fascinated him.

Captain Jack White, a Cushendall landowner and son of Sir George White from Broughshane, had a similar idea to that of Casement. White is traditionally regarded as the instigator of the 1913 Ballymoney meeting. White's aim for the meeting was to show the 'lovelessness' of Carson and the bigotry and stagnation of the Unionist party. However, prior to the meeting Casement wrote to Alice Green informing her that he hoped with the assistance of every drop of Fenian blood 'in my soul' to 'light a fire' that would 'set the Antrim hills ablaze' and would 'unite Presbyterian and Catholic farmers and townsmen at Ballymoney in a clear message to Ireland'.[8] However, Armour made it clear to Casement that an Irish-Ireland meeting was nor permissible, while a liberal Home Rule gathering was feasible.

Casement visited Ballymoney to meet with local Liberals at Trinity Manse. Armour had previously advised Casement that the speakers and those attending the meeting should be Protestant in order to underline the message that not all Protestants in Ulster were Carsonites. At the meeting between Casement and the local Liberals, Armour suggested Sir Roger as chairman but Casement refused. White, who had not been present at the discussions, objected to all the decisions taken, and a stormy row ensued between Casement and White in Belfast following Casement's visit to Ballymoney. Armour soothed the situation by guaranteeing that White would be at the forefront of the speakers. He also took it upon himself to find a local chairman; John McElderry, an old Ballymoney Liberal, took up the position. From this point on Armour and his committee of local Liberals and solicitors took on most of the organisation of the meeting. The scheduled date was the evening of Friday, 24 October 1913; the venue was Ballymoney Town Hall. In early September Casement had secured Alice Green, the Nationalist historian, as one of the speakers.

In all his political manoeuvring Casement was passing himself as a Protestant, as he always had done in Ulster even though he had been baptised a Roman Catholic on 5 August 1868 and he believed he 'was brought up really nothing'.[9] He did not raise any objection to being classed as a Protestant, despite his Nationalist leanings, and exploited the position to promote himself publicly.

The Protestant Home Rule meeting took place in Ballymoney Town Hall as scheduled. The hall was decorated with Union Jacks and other flags, and over the platform was a large banner inscribed with: 'No Provisional or Provincial Government for us.'[10] The estimated attendance varied between 400 and 600. Most of those present were local businessmen and farmers; Roman Catholics were excluded. After the opening remarks by the chair, John McElderry, two resolutions were proposed by John McMaster and seconded by Robert Carson. The first protested against the claim that Sir Edward Carson represented the

Protestant community of north-east Ulster, and pledged lawful opposition to his Provisional Government. The second consisted of a rejection of the sectarianism that separated Irishmen and invited the Government to help bring all Irishmen together. This second resolution was Sir Roger's handiwork.

Casement was the third speaker to take to the platform that evening; Mrs Green had preceded him. He began his speech by stating: 'I have lived amongst Ulster people many years of my life and in quiet and daily contact with them I learned to know them well'.[11] In similar vein to the previous speakers he continued in the spirit of reconciliation and stressed the need to look to Ireland's past. He argued that it was not politics that was important but the welfare of the common country of Ireland. On one point he was absolute, and that was that the exclusion of Ulster would not be a solution to the Home Rule crisis. He also used the occasion to air his views on Irish nationalism, and he concluded his speech dramatically: 'We want Ulster for Ireland and Ireland for Ulster'.[12]

The influence that the Gaelic League had had on them was evident from the tone of Green's and Casement's speeches. Significantly, the meeting ended with the singing of the British National Anthem.

The *Ballymoney Free Press* quoted Casement's speech, which pleased Armour greatly. The London *Times* dismissed the event as representing only 'a small and isolated 'pocket' of dissident Protestants'.[13] The *Belfast Evening Telegraph* published the most scathing report of the meeting, terming it 'The Ballymoney Farce'. Unsurprisingly, the Nationalist paper, the *Irish News*, presented the most positive report, endorsing the Protestant Home Rulers. Immediately after the meeting Mrs Green and Casement went to Ballycastle for a 'rest', and they visited Rathlin Island to make a bit of propaganda. On 25 October 1913 Casement described the meeting to his cousin Gertrude as 'a grand success'. Even the fact that the besotted Ada McNeill came to the meeting failed to spoil it for him. The meeting had boosted Casement's morale sky high, and he hoped to organise a similar one in Coleraine; however, this venture was thwarted by the power of the local Unionists who dominated the Town Council.

The Ballymoney meeting had seen Casement's first public speech, and after this he became a major figure on the Irish stage. Within a month he had written to Mrs Green explaining that he had 'in mind a great scheme of volunteering for all Ireland'.[14] As early as December 1913 he had become a member of the Provisional Committee of the National Volunteers, and became involved in a tour of Ireland to recruit Volunteers.

Casement's Nationalist persona
By 1914 Casement was a dedicated Irish Nationalist, and he began to take a more active part in the movement for Irish independence. He sought help for the Irish cause first in America and then, after the First World War broke out, in Germany, where he remained until 1916. In Berlin he aimed to negotiate for a supply of armaments and military assistance. Finally, in March 1916 the

Germans agreed to send 20,000 rifles to Ireland to help with the IRB-inspired Easter Rising. The consignment was scheduled to arrive in Tralee Bay immediately before the Rising was due to begin on Easter Sunday. Owing to a misunderstanding the German arms arrived early and were intercepted by British warships, which forced the steamer *Aud* to sail to Queenstown. Here the ship was scuttled and the precious cargo of guns went to the bottom of the sea.

Equally disastrous was Casement's landing in Ireland on 21 April 1916. He was put ashore at Banna Strand, Co. Kerry, and was almost immediately taken into custody. He attempted to warn the Volunteers to call off the Rising, but he failed. The Government authorities wrongly believed Casement to be the chief figure in the plot. He was imprisoned in a rat-infested dungeon in the Tower of London. He was tried in July 1916 and convicted of high treason, sabotage and espionage against the English Crown.

Casement was sent to Pentonville Prison to await execution; while there he made two unsuccessful suicide attempts. From prison he wrote a letter to his cousin, Gertrude Bannister, asking her to make sure his last wish was granted. This was that he be buried at Murlough Bay, Co. Antrim, after his execution. This had been a favourite haunt of Casement's where he spent much leisure time swimming, reading and writing.

Roger Casement's Fate
Casement was hanged at Pentonville Prison on 3 August 1916. The executioner, Albert Ellis, recalled: 'He appeared to me the bravest man it fell to my unhappy lot to execute'.[15] Great crowds gathered to hear of his execution on that fateful day. His last wish was not granted; he was buried at Pentonville after the execution. His remains were repatriated from England in 1965 and reburied in Ireland. Crowds filled the streets of Dublin to watch the reburial at Glasnevin in March 1965; a headstone was erected at the burial site in his memory.

In the 1990s doubts were cast as to whether the skeleton buried at Glasnevin actually was Casement's. It was suggested that when the prison grave was reopened it proved impossible to distinguish his bones from those of other prisoners. Some day, DNA testing on Casement's current relatives may give closure on these doubts. However, Sir Roger's last wish was never to be granted.

It is important to note that no relatives travelled from Magherintemple or Co. Antrim for Casement's reinterment in Dublin. This reiterates the loneliness that had surrounded him for most of his life.

Roger Casement's Legacy
To some extent Casement was the author of his own destruction. His optimism about the possibility of capitalising on Irish discontent by raising an Irish Brigade in Germany from prisoners of war had inflated expectations. The miserable failure of his initiative clearly dented his credibility. Casement is a transitional figure, the last great Protestant martyr of the Republican struggle against the

English. He was a man who played a key role in Irish independence but whose memory was for a long time an uneasy one for Nationalist writers. The lingering controversy over the so-called 'Black Diaries' and his alleged homosexuality greatly affected Irish public opinion though today, in a more liberal age, there is a greater disposition to consider Casement an Irish patriot and a great humanitarian. On 12 March 2002 the results of the first ever fully independent forensic examination of the Black Diaries were announced at a press conference in London. The verdict was: 'Each of the five documents collectively known as the Black Diaries is exclusively the work of Roger Casement's hand'.[16] This provides us with some closure on the controversy of the Black Diaries.

The young boy who had been orphaned at only twelve years old had come a long way in Irish history by 1916. On 21 June 1953 the Gaelic Athletic Association named its new sports ground in Belfast after Roger Casement. This ensures that the surname has a daily resonance in Nationalist circles. In addition a small memorial is situated at Murlough Bay, though it was recently vandalised. The local committee has decided to start work on the creation of a new and fitting monument as a replacement. This will probably be a bronze statue of Casement. The committee's hope is that the statue will reflect not only his work in the struggle for Irish freedom but also his humanitarian work world-wide, in the Congo and in the Amazon Basin. This monument seems fitting, given that Sawyer concludes: 'Even in Ireland, few today are well-informed about Casement's brave, practical work on behalf of those who are least able to protect themselves'.[17]

1 H.O. Mackey, *Roger Casement: The Truth about the Forged Diaries* (Dublin, 1966).
2 B.L. Reid, *The Lives of Roger Casement* (Yale University Press, 1976), p. 139.
3 Jeffrey Dudgeon, *Roger Casement: The Black Diaries* (Belfast, 2002), p. 30.
4 Mark Tierney, *Eoin MacNeill: Scholar and Man of Action* (Oxford University Press, 1980), p. 84.
5 Dudgeon, op. cit., p. 179.
6 Dudgeon, op. cit., p. 176.
7 Dudgeon, op. cit., p. 182.
8 http://www.northantrim.com/rogercasement.htm
9 Dudgeon, op. cit., p. 47.
10 Dudgeon, op. cit., p. 403.
11 Dudgeon, op. cit., p. 406.
12 Dudgeon, op. cit., p. 408.
13 *The Times*, 27 October 1913, p. 4.
14 Brian Inglis, *Roger Casement* (London, 1973), p. 241.
15 http://www.bbc.co.uk/history/society_culture/protest_reform/casement_06.shtml
16 http://www.bbc.co.uk/history/society_culture/protest_reform/casement_05.shtml
17 Roger Sawyer, *Roger Casement's Diaries* (Pimlico, 1997), p. 264.

Francis Joseph Bigger

8

FRANCIS JOSEPH BIGGER
HISTORIAN, GAELIC LEAGUER AND PROTESTANT NATIONALIST

Eamon Phoenix

> I think I see him now as in his prime
> A short-built, thick-set, brown-faced, eager man.
> Born of the seed of fighters,
> Who in time of old, had fought for love of man,
> And found their touchstone in the simple words
> 'Giving and Forgiving'.

These words of the Belfast poet Joseph Campbell recall one of the central figures in the establishment of Feis na nGleann in 1904: the Belfast lawyer, antiquarian, Protestant Nationalist, Gaelic Leaguer and generous benefactor, Francis Joseph Bigger (1863–1926). Bigger's name is now almost forgotten in his native city, but in the late nineteenth and early twentieth centuries he was something of a living legend. He was known throughout Ulster and, indeed, the whole of Ireland for his infectious enthusiasm for Irish history and the Irish language and for his personal contribution to the preservation of castles, high crosses and patriot graves throughout the country.

Francis Joseph's branch of the Bigger family originated in Nithsdale in the Scottish lowlands in the seventeenth century. 'It was no fear of religious persecution,' wrote their descendant, 'nor its result that induced them to cross Glenluce Bay and in their open boat to make Donaghadee. Their main inducement was the conviction that they were coming to a freer land where opportunities were wider and prospects likely to be more satisfying, all of which turned out as anticipated.'

Once in Ulster the family traded with energy and success and eventually acquired lands in the Carnmoney and Mallusk areas of south Antrim; indeed, so prominent were they in the life of district that the townland of Biggerstown still commemorates their residence. They quickly established themselves in business in the thriving town of Belfast. Their premises were in the High Street, and for many years part of the present Crown Entry was known as Bigger's Entry. The Biggers issued their own semi-armorial trade tokens and three of these, dated 1657, 1666 and 1667, have been preserved.[1]

From the original settlers in Co. Antrim, who had intermarried with Parkers, Abernethys, Findlays and MacNeillys, Francis Joseph Bigger sprang. He was born in Belfast on 17 July 1863, the seventh son of Joseph Bigger of 'Ard Righ', who was the seventh son of David Bigger of 'The Trench', Mallusk, who was also, by a curious coincidence, the seventh son of William Bigger of Biggerstown.

Francis Joseph's most famous nineteenth-century relative was undoubtedly Joseph Gillis Biggar, the colourful Home Rule M.P. for Co. Cavan during 1874–90, and a cousin of his father's. A prosperous pork butcher on Belfast's Hercules Street, this little hunchbacked figure, with his rasping Belfast accent, was a close ally of Charles Stewart Parnell and the architect of the Home Rule Party's policy of 'obstruction' in the House of Commons. But the ancestor whom 'F.J.B.' most admired was his grandfather, David Bigger, who had been a Volunteer in the heady days of Grattan's Parliament and had fought at the Battle of Antrim in 1798.

By far the greatest influence on Bigger was that of his mother, the former Mary Jane Ardery of Ballyvalley near Banbridge, 'a woman of great sweetness of character'. Francis Joseph was not a robust child and, for the sake of his health, he spent much of his boyhood with relatives amid the 'green fields and tonic breezes' of Carnmoney. There he learnt of the rural habits and customs of which he was to write so much, and first heard the tales and legends of the 'turn out' in '98 – still strong in that Presbyterian district.

Family business interests forced the Biggers to move to Liverpool for a period, and it was there that the young Francis Joseph received the rudiments of his education. The family returned to Belfast when he was eleven and he was enrolled at the Royal Belfast Academical Institution, the famous school founded by his grandfather. On leaving 'Inst' he matriculated at the then Queen's College, Belfast, and was articled for four years to Messrs Henry and William Seeds, then a leading firm of solicitors in the town. In 1884 he proceeded to Dublin to attend law lectures; while there he met his former school-fellow and future legal partner, George Strahan, LLD. Together, in their leisure hours, they used to explore the ancient sites and historic buildings of the city and surrounding area. In this way Bigger began to store up the archaeological knowledge on which he was to build. He began to haunt the old bookstalls along the quays and the antiquarian bookshops of Dublin, picking up many a rare volume to be long treasured; in this way, he built up a matchless collection of Irish books and manuscripts which now form the F.J. Bigger collection in Belfast Central Library.

Bigger was admitted a solicitor in 1887 and, two years later, commenced partnership with Dr Strahan in Rea's Buildings at the corner of Donegall Street and Royal Avenue. The partnership lasted until Bigger's death, but it seems clear that the cares and responsibilities of a busy legal practice were outweighed in his case by his zeal for historical and cultural pursuits. He joined the Belfast Naturalists' Field Club and for ten years served as its honorary secretary; for three years (1900–03) he was its chairman. At its discussions, he gained a readiness of speech that made him a popular and entertaining speaker on his favourite topics. Through its numerous field trips he broadened his topographical knowledge of Ulster and Ireland until, as his contemporary John S. Crone noted, 'it is hardly an exaggeration to say that he knew something of every parish in Ireland and his name was known to them'.

Through his close friendship and lengthy correspondence with such leading historians as Monsignor James O'Laverty and Rev. George Hill, he formed the connecting link between the great circle of antiquarians like George Petrie, John O'Donovan and Sir Samuel Ferguson and those of his own day, and faithfully carried on their tradition of research and scholarship.

He was elected a member of the Royal Society of Antiquaries in Ireland in 1888 and a Fellow in 1896. In 1895, he helped to resurrect – after a gap of 30 years – the *Ulster Journal of Archaeology* and, together with Robert M. Young, a prominent local historian, became joint editor. A few years later, Young resigned and Bigger assumed sole control for the next 17 years of the series' existence. During that period he contributed to every single edition and, by his example and encouragement, stimulated other workers in making their researches into the history and antiquities of the province more widely known.

'FJB' was steadfast in his love for Ireland, its people, its history, its monuments and its folk-customs. In common with many other Protestant landed and professional figures in the 1890s and early 1900s, he became a firm supporter of the movement to preserve and revive the Irish language – then still spoken in the less accessible parts of Ulster such as the Glens of Antrim. In April 1894 he delivered a paper on 'Local Gaelic placenames' to the Celtic class of the Naturalists' Field Club, and he was a constant attendant at the Irish language classes conducted in Belfast by P.J. O'Shea. He became a member of the Coiste Gnótha of the Gaelic League – founded in 1893 by Dr Douglas Hyde, the son of a Church of Ireland rector in Co. Roscommon, and Eoin MacNeill, a historian and native of Glenarm – and president of its Belfast Council. As a lecturer on Irish archaeology at the Irish School ('Coláiste Comhaill') in Bank Street, he was brought into close contact with the leading Gaelic scholars of the time such as Hyde and MacNeill. In June 1904, he was involved with a number of prominent individuals in North Antrim, including Miss Margaret Dobbs of Portnagolan, Miss Ada McNeill of Cushendun and Miss Rose Young of Galgorm Castle, John Clarke (the writer 'Benmore') and Andrew Dooey of Dunloy in the founding of the Glens Feis – a colourful festival of Irish language, culture, crafts and games.

In addition to all this feverish activity, Bigger was a member of the Royal Irish Academy, a governor of his old school, Inst, and an enthusiastic contributor of articles on all aspects of Irish history and folk-life to a host of newspapers and magazines. He gave lectures throughout the province on the same theme, all the while trying to preserve old customs and to encourage people to restore historical buildings.

1910 marked the centenary of the birth of a famous Belfastman, Sir Samuel Ferguson, equally distinguished as a poet, writer and antiquary. 'FJB' played a leading part in the celebrations. At the ceremony in Donegore churchyard where

Ferguson is buried, he placed a wreath of bays from his own garden on the grave, while his friend, the educationist, Alfred Perceval Graves, delivered an address on the poet's life and work.

In the same year, Bigger performed one of the most notable of his many laudable acts, and the one of which he was proudest, when he rescued from destruction Jordan's Castle, one of the five Norman castles that guard the Co. Down port of Ardglass. The Beauclerc estate was being sold to the tenantry under the Land Purchase Act, and the old tower-house was earmarked for demolition. Such a golden opportunity to preserve a historic building was not to be lost. Bigger at once purchased it, renamed it 'Castle Sean' ('Shane's Castle') and set about furnishing it from his vast collection of antiquities. The transformation that he effected at Jordan's Castle may be gleaned from the following contemporary account by J.K. Owen:

> Here we are now in sight of Ardglass and behold, looming up above the houses in the centre of the town, Castle Sean with flagstaff planted on its loftiest tower supporting an immense flag on which is blazoned the Red Hand of the O'Neills … A fire of faggots blazes on the hearth, a large oak table stands in the centre of the floor, a great dresser against the wall, a bronze chandelier filled with candles is suspended from the ceiling. It is an Irish kitchen of the olden times … Continuing the ascent, we stand on the garden roof in the open air … Here the beacon fire is lighted on occasions and Irish dancers foot it to the skirl of Irish war-pipes.[2]

At 'Castle Sean', the Belfast antiquary entertained a host of Irish literary and cultural figures while he lived there in the manner of an Irish chieftain, complete with a retinue of bards and uilleann pipers. At his regular *céilithe* at the castle music would be provided by the South Derry-born uilleann piper, Francis McPeake, whose talents Bigger encouraged. On Bigger's death, the castle passed into the care of the state, one of the conditions being that 'the red right hand of Ulster should be raised on its battlements every 17 July' – Bigger's birthday.

The restoration of Jordan's Castle was only one of the many altruistic tasks undertaken by the Belfast antiquarian out of his own purse. Some of his heritage projects, however, are open to criticism and betrayed his tendency to interweave history and legend. It was he that had the huge slab of Mourne granite placed on the reputed grave of St Patrick at Downpatrick Cathedral. In the same locality, he restored the ruined church at Raholp and the tenth-century high crosses at Downpatrick and Dromore, as well as the old wooden 'termon' cross at Cranfield on the shores of Lough Neagh near Randalstown. As his friend and biographer, Dr John Crone, recorded: 'Whether it was a monumental cairn on a mountainside, a mighty chieftain like Sean the Proud, a mural tablet to a humble man of letters in a village churchyard, or the recutting of the inscription on the defaced tombstone of a deceased scholar, he was the active agent, the guiding spirit and, not infrequently, the sole paymaster'.

In the period following the centenary of the 1798 rebellion, he was responsible for marking the graves of many of the leading actors in the insurrection including those of Mary Ann McCracken, sister of the executed Henry Joy, and the Rev. William Steele Dickson in Belfast's Clifton Street Cemetery. And when, in 1902, bones thought to be those of McCracken were unearthed in Church Street, they were secured by Bigger and reinterred by him in the United Irishman's sister's grave in Clifton Street. He was also interested in the career of Robert Emmet, and in 1913 he assisted Emmet's grandnephew, Thomas Addis Emmet, in an unsuccessful attempt to locate the executed United Irishman's grave in St Peter's Churchyard in Dublin.

Some of Bigger's discoveries seem inspired by a kind of historian's intuition. One day in 1908, while going into the clubhouse at Ardglass Golf Links, his attention was attracted to an unusual marking on the doorstep. He had it unearthed and to his boundless delight discovered it to be a medieval statue of a Madonna and Child, carved in freestone and buried face downward in the earth. He had it restored and it now adorns the east wall of Dunsford Catholic Church in Co. Down.

During the early decades of the twentieth century, 'FJB's' spacious, ivy-clad home 'Ard Righ', on the shores of Belfast Lough and under the shadow of Cave Hill, was a power-house of learning, culture and conviviality. To his 'ceili' evenings around the cheery log fire in the vast library flocked the aspiring poets, writers and musicians of the day, among them Shane Leslie, the writer and cousin of Churchill; Alice Stopford Green, the passionate historian; Lord Ashbourne, the aristocratic Gaelic Leaguer; the talented Morrow brothers of the 'Ulster Literary Theatre'; Joseph Campbell, the Belfast poet; Cathal O'Byrne, the writer and folklorist; Alice Milligan, the Nationalist poetess; Herbert Hughes, the arranger of Irish folk-songs; and Canon James Hannay, the Belfast-born novelist 'George A. Birmingham'. 'No searcher after historical truth or local "colour",' Dr Crone has written, 'appealed to him in vain.' His great knowledge was distributed as liberally as the contents of his purse to any truly deserving object. His house included a ''98 room' containing mementoes of the United Irishmen whom he admired so much.

A regular visitor to 'Ard Righ' in those halcyon days has left us with the following vivid pen-picture of the house and its occupant:

> To walk into that house was a thrilling experience, you were almost certain to meet an established or rising celebrity. Even if you didn't, there was the vast army of books in the library, the relics of McCracken, Orr and Jemmy Hope in the little museum; and if you strolled out into the garden, you could feast your eyes on the parterres of flowers or inhale the scents of musk, thyme or sage or gaze in wonder at the little shrine dedicated to St Francis and the birds.
>
> In a corner of the library, you might surprise a whimsical clergyman poring over a dusty tome – never guess that he was the Rev. Mr Hannay of Westport known to fame as George A. Birmingham. In the garden, you might encounter Shane Leslie meditating on his projected novel *Doomsland* wherein he was to describe his host as 'a Protestant with Franciscan leanings'. You might find Joseph

Casement and Bigger with entertainers outside 'Ard Rígh'

Campbell browsing ... or come upon Alice Milligan in the throes of a new historical pageant. If there was nobody in the house but Brigid [Bigger's faithful housekeeper] herself, it would be best just to sit down in the kitchen and have a 'crack' with her for she had the gift of laughter and was 'great value entirely'.[3]

Nor should the purely philanthropic side of 'FJB' life be overlooked. On the hall-table at 'Ard Rígh' was a small dish that he called 'St Anthony's Tray' and which contained pennies for the poor who called there; adults were usually given food but for mothers and children, pennies were added. He always showed an anxiety to improve the lot of his less fortunate fellow-man. Thus, in 1907 he drew up imaginative plans for labourers' cottages and argued that they could be built of better materials and more cheaply than those being provided by the government. Bigger's ideal cottage would be adorned with 'Irish pictures and Gaelic mottoes' but would not include a kitchen sink, reflecting his blend of practical ideas and romanticism. To prove his point, Bigger erected a row of houses at his own expense in pleasant surroundings at Carnmoney and named them after Yeats's poem, 'The Sally Gardens'.

He was also active in the cause of temperance and, as the founder of the 'Ulster Reformed Public House Association', he embarked on a one-man crusade to improve the standard of local public-houses, many of which were little more than drinking dens. He was instrumental in the conversion of 'The Crown and

Shamrock' at Carnmoney in 1901. Bigger chose the name carefully in a symbolic attempt to merge the two political traditions in Ireland. He later acquired several more pubs including 'The Mermaid' at Kircubbin, Co. Down and the 'Dunleath Arms' in Ballywalter. Both were transformed into pleasant 'refreshment houses'. The venture was not a commercial success, however, and Bigger eventually wound it up.[4]

An active member of the Church of Ireland and a High Churchman, he was honorary secretary of St Peter's Church committee for nine years. He was also an active Freemason, drawn by the organisation's pomp and ritual.

As a young man, Bigger became an ardent Irish separatist, although he was always careful to keep his cultural and political activities separate from his professional work as a solicitor. This was important as his clients included some of the leading Belfast Unionist merchants and entrepreneurs including the Baird family, owners of the *Belfast Telegraph*. Like Arthur Griffith, the founder of Sinn Fein in 1905, Bigger was deeply influenced by John Mitchel's *Jail Journal* and the national ceremonies to commemorate the United Irishmen in 1898. As his brother, Colonel F.C. Bigger, noted in a posthumous tribute, he was a keen supporter of the Sinn Fein campaign to encourage Irish home industries, by using only Irish-made products.

Bigger's strong Nationalist views surfaced publicly in 1907 in a lecture that he delivered to the Belfast Linen Hall Library. It bore the innocuous title of 'The Hills of Holy Ireland', but shocked the largely middle-class Unionist audience by its anti-British sentiments. As a result, the lecture committee of the library left Bigger in no doubt as to their feelings: 'Without expressing any opinion on Mr Bigger's statements as to English government in Ireland, the committee is of the opinion that any lectures calculated to rouse party and religious bitterness are not in the interest ... of the society; and had they been aware that the title ... was to be used as a pretext for ventilating political prejudices, they would not have given their sanction to such a lecture.'[5]

Bigger shared Patrick Pearse's vision of a Gaelic-speaking Irish nation-state that would embrace both Protestants and Catholics in a united national identity. It was in this context that he joined the organising committee of the first Glens Feis and participated in the festival at Glenariff in June 1904.

Bigger's involvement in the Feis was unwelcome to at least one local luminary, however. Miss Barbara McDonnell of Monavert, Cushendall, the president of the Feis and a representative of the McDonnells of Antrim, resigned from her post in October 1904 in protest against what she saw as a 'take-over' of the event by the Belfast solicitor and his friends. She complained to the Feis Committee that the Feis was 'emphatically not our own. It was entirely undertaken, controlled and carried through by a person who has never been a resident in the Glens of Antrim.' She acknowledged Bigger's selfless commitment to Feis na nGleann, adding: 'It was a day enjoyed by a great many, but in truth, it was not a Feis of the Glens but a Feis in the Glens ... I ... have said it to no one more plainly ...

Alice Stopford Green
Irish historian and close
friend of Bigger

than to Mr Bigger himself; he is a whole-hearted Irishman ... but we ought to be Glens people also ... No one would object to the kind help of Mr Bigger himself or even that of his friends, but to have the whole thing run by outsiders, I for one do object to.'6

Bigger served as joint treasurer of the 1904 Feis and two years later launched a campaign to preserve Irish on Rathlin Island. This was to result in the establishment of an Irish language summer college, St Malachy's College, on the island in 1913.

The Belfast lawyer's political sympathies surfaced once more in the following year when a young Nationalist activist, Stephen Clarke, was arrested in Ballycastle for distributing anti-recruitment pamphlets. When Clarke was sent for trial for sedition at Belfast Assizes in 1905, Bigger took charge of organising his defence behind the scenes. He engaged a leading Unionist barrister, James Chambers, K.C., on Clarke's behalf. As Bulmer Hobson, a Protestant IRB figure and associate of Bigger's, records, the Belfast solicitor's range of personal and social contacts was invaluable. 'In all political trials it was the practice of the government to pick the jury carefully; so Bigger, who had an extraordinary knack of knowing nearly everybody, very genially went about talking to men whose names were on the panel from which the jury would be selected. In the result we were sure of five members … when the trial started … Their verdict was guilty but with no seditious intent.' Stephen Clarke was duly discharged.[7]

During the decade and a half before the 1916 Rising, Bigger's home was a power-house of Irish music, cultural renaissance and revolutionary politics. His regular *céilithe* attracted the leading figures in the new Nationalism, among them Hobson, Denis McCullough and Ernest Blythe of the Irish Republican Brotherhood, Cathal O'Byrne, Joseph Campbell, Alice Stopford Green, Desmond and Mabel Fitzgerald, and Sir Roger Casement. Casement used 'Ard Righ' as a base during his frequent visits to Belfast after 1904, once describing Bigger in a letter to Mrs Green as 'a pipe and banner maniac'.

As early as 1904 Bigger had played a key background role in the formation of the Republican 'Dungannon Clubs', which served to revitalise the IRB in Ulster and throughout Ireland. He also funded the movement's newspaper, *The Republic*, and secretly supported its propaganda campaign against recruitment to the British army. A year later, in 1905, Bigger was largely responsible for the election of the northern Home Rule leader, Joe Devlin in West Belfast in the general election. His contribution was to sponsor an Independent Liberal Unionist, Alex Carlisle, who split the Unionist vote enabling 'Wee Joe' to win by the narrow margin of just 16 votes.[8]

By this time Bigger's activities were attracting the attentions of the police. In 1907 he confided to Mrs Green that Dublin Castle's spies in Belfast were 'ghosting people in a very Russian way'. This followed a motor tour of the Irish-speaking areas of west Donegal by Bigger in the company of Pearse, then headmaster of Scoil Eanna, a bilingual school in Dublin. In a letter thanking Bigger for the use of his motor-car, the future leader of the Easter Rising jocularly referred to the R.I.C. mutiny in Belfast, asking: 'Are you at the bottom of the police strike?'[9]

In March 1912 Bigger helped to launch Countess Markievicz's Fianna Éireann in Belfast. Hobson and McCullough hoped to use the new Nationalist boy scout movement as a recruiting ground for the IRB in the north. Addressing the Fianna in west Belfast, Bigger urged the young men present 'to take as models for themselves the youthful heroes of Irish history'. The chairman, the Republican priest Fr Robert Fullerton, paid tribute to the guest speaker: 'Mr Bigger knew of the virtues of nationality and had done his part in endeavouring to keep it alive'.[10]

By the outbreak of the First World War the R.I.C. had no doubts about the subversive leanings of the Antrim Road lawyer-historian. A secret police report of November 1914 noted 'a Francis J. Bigger whose associates are all extremists … Mr Bigger is constantly visited by leading Sinn Feiners [such as] Bulmer Hobson, John [Sean] MacDermott [later executed for his role in organising the Easter Rising], Denis McCullough, E. Blythe … He has also been seen with James Connolly of the T.W.U. [Irish Transport and General Workers' Union]. He does not bear a good moral character and is said to hate British rule.'[11]

Bigger's political ideals were mirrored in his historical and literary activities in the 'crease in time' between the death of Parnell in 1891 and the 1916 Rising. The United Irish uprising of 1798 in Antrim and Down fascinated him. In all, he completed six lives of the Ninety-Eight leaders including William Orr, Henry Joy McCracken and Jemmy Hope, but he published only one volume, a biography of William Orr in 1906. As Roger Dixon has observed, Bigger wrote these lives as works of propaganda. His overriding aim was to remind the Presbyterian descendants of the United Irishmen of their patriotic past and thereby win them over to Irish Nationalism.[11] In 1910 he published *The Ulster Land War*. This told the story of the 'Hearts of Steel', a secret agrarian society of Presbyterian farmers, formed in Co. Antrim in the 1770s in reaction to landlord excesses. Bigger welcomed the Land Purchase Act of 1903 and saw the creation of a land of peasant proprietors as vital to the emergence of an independent Irish nation state.

He threw his weight behind the Irish Volunteers on their formation to uphold Home Rule in 1913, and played a minor role in the Howth gun-running by the same force in July 1914, hiring two Donegal fishermen to man the *Asgard*.[12] He was shaken, however, by the Easter Rising and the execution of his friend and house-guest, Casement, on 3 August 1916 for his role in the insurrection. Casement's last letter from his condemned cell in Brixton was addressed to Brigid Matthews, Bigger's faithful housekeeper, and recalled nostalgically happy days spent at 'Ard Righ' in the run-up to the Great War.

Though Bigger gloried in the heroic deeds of the ancient O'Neills or the men of Ninety-Eight, he does not seem to have considered the bloodshed and human loss that would inevitably follow any revolutionary attempt to gain Irish independence. The young Belfast separatist and future Irish cabinet minister, Joseph Connolly, readily acknowledged the central importance of 'Ard Righ' as a meeting place for the IRB but he was surprised by Bigger's reaction when, as a precaution before taking part in the 1916 Rising, he asked him to draw up a will. Bigger was dumbstruck by the idea, as Connolly records: 'Frank shied away from the whole business, told me to have sense and not to be worrying about a will or anything else. His attitude stunned me …' Connolly did not see Bigger until the release of the internees some months after the insurrection, and 'realised that the whole period must have been a nightmare of shock and apprehension to him'.[13]

After the Rising the Belfast solicitor largely withdrew from political activities.

He was shattered by the violent events that followed, and especially by the Belfast sectarian violence of 1920–2, in which 450 people died, and by the Civil War of 1922–3. The Rising resulted in the execution of two regular visitors to 'Ard Righ', Casement and Sean MacDermott, while the Civil War divided his friends into the pro- and anti-Treaty camps.

Bigger was outraged by the partition of Ireland and seems to have refused to cross the border after 1921, preferring to pursue his intellectual pursuits in Scotland or on the continent. He welcomed the Anglo-Irish Treaty of 6 December 1921 as giving Ireland 'the freedom to achieve freedom'. As his brother, Colonel F.C. Bigger, a retired British officer, recalled after FJB's death: 'he saw that with the withdrawal of the English troops, the "goodbye" of the Lord Lieutenant, and Dublin Castle empty, the tide of Anglicisation had been successfully rolled back. The future of Ireland … lay entirely in her own hands.' He continued to hope that economic forces would force the North to merge with the rest of Ireland in a federal arrangement such as that envisaged by the Treaty terms.

The 1916 Rising marked the end of the cultural evenings and animated political discussions at 'Ard Righ'. One of those who had visited that house often in the years before the insurrection was Denis McCullough. McCullough, who had been president of the IRB's Supreme Council at the time of the Rising, had moved to Dublin after partition, becoming a pro-Treaty member of the Dáil. In 1924, a year before Bigger's death, McCullough wrote his old friend a letter tinged with sadness at 'the scattering of the company' at 'Ard Righ' as a consequence of political events. The letter referred to 'Benmore', one of the stalwarts of the Glens Feis two decades before, and the song written by Joseph Campbell, 'The Blue Hills of Antrim':

> As Johnny Clarke used to say, 'The Clouds are darkening over the hills of Ulster again, but yerra! What's the good of talkin?' I hope you are as well as usual and that you will look me up when you are in Dublin as I cannot look you up. Much as I would like to do so. I get lonely for the Blue Hills and for the auld times whiles. Give my love to Brigid …With every good wish as always, your friend, Denis McCullough.[14]

Apart from his abiding love of Ireland in the broadest scene, Bigger's great devotion was to his mother and her memory. From the time of an infant illness, he became his mother's most cherished son, and after her death they seemed to share an almost mystical relationship. Two features always attracted attention in his dining room; his mother's vacant armchair where no one was permitted to sit, and her favourite flowers, which he renewed and placed at her place every day.

He delighted in his beautiful garden at 'Ard Righ' and in the birds that chose to build their nests there, and in May 1921 he published *The Birds of Ard Righ* – a source of wonder to his naturalist friends.

Bigger was never *persona grata* with the new government of Northern Ireland. However, in July 1926 Queen's University conferred on him an honorary M.A.

Eoin MacNeill, Cardinal Logue, Francis J. Bigger and Rev. McNally at Omeath Summer School, 1912

in recognition of 'a lifetime of enthusiasm to researches in Irish archaeology and local history'. That same summer, before leaving to trace the footsteps of the Irish missionaries through Britain to the continent, he published his last book and one of the strangest he ever penned – *Crossing the Bar*. It deals with Irish legends concerning death and the hereafter, and its principal illustration depicts a nineteenth-century funeral at Mallusk, the burial-ground of the Bigger family. Might it have been a premonition of his fast approaching death that prompted him to write it? He took ill after a visit to the Low Countries in November 1926. He passed away on 9 December that year after a short but painful illness and, 'on a lovely December afternoon when all nature was still as if in sympathy', he was laid to rest among his kinsmen beneath the High Cross that he had erected at Mallusk. Sadly the cross was destroyed in a bomb explosion in 1970, but the Gaelic inscription on the base has survived. It is a verse from psalm cvii: 'Then they are glad, because they are at rest; and so He bringeth them into the Haven where they would be'.

A lover of Ireland in the broad sense, a tireless worker and a generous benefactor, Frank Bigger died lamented by his talented circle of friends. In his enthusiasm to preserve customs and traditions, it is true that he was often too quick to interweave legend with historical fact. His friend, Mrs Stopford Green, stressed his real contribution to preserving Ireland's heritage. 'He had what is far from common, a sense of the dignity, the value and the wide range of the history that lies behind the people of Ireland … To him nothing of Ireland was dead. There must have been many who felt a new life kindled [by him] … In this generation …we miss an Irishman whose range, if not scientific, was large and true.'

Colm O'Lochlainn, a Dublin 1916 activist and regular caller at 'Ard Righ', described Bigger as 'a noble figure in that far-off time' (before 1916) and recalled 'those countryside meetings where he spoke of Ireland's glorious past'.[15]

Bigger's cultural impact in the Ireland of his day was freely acknowledged by the Unionist press. As the *Belfast Telegraph* observed in a tribute, he was 'a great loss to a widespread community and his memory will long remain fragrant in the land he loved so dearly'.

1 J.S. Crone and F.C. Bigger, *In Remembrance: Articles and Sketches by Francis Joseph Bigger* (Dublin, 1927), pp. vii–xxxviii.
2 Ibid., p. xxiv.
3 Hugh McCartan, in *Capuchin Annual* (Dublin, 1943), pp. 176–8.
4 Roger Dixon, 'Francis Joseph Bigger: Belfast's Cultural Don Quixote', in Jonathan Bell (ed.), *Ulster Folklife*, vol. 43, pp. 40–8.
5 John Killen, *A History of the Linen Hall Library 1788–1988* (Belfast, 1990), pp. 86–7.
6 Letter from Miss Barbara McDonnell to the Committee of Feis na nGleann, 8 Oct. 1904 (in possession of Mr Seamus Clarke, Ballycastle).
7 Bulmer Hobson, *Ireland Yesterday and Tomorrow* (Tralee, 1968), p. 25.
8 J.C. Beckett and R.E. Glasscock (eds), *Belfast: Origin and Growth of an Industrial City* (London, 1967), pp. 135–6.
9 S. Ó Buachalla, *The Letters of P.H. Pearse* (Gerrards Cross, Bucks, 1980), pp. 110–11.
10 *Irish News*, 13 March 1912.
11 Jeffrey Dudgeon, *Roger Casement: The Black Diaries* (Belfast, 2002), p. 194
11 R. Dixon, 'Heroes for a New Ireland: F.J. Bigger and the Leaders of '98', in T.M. Owen (ed.), *From Corrib to Cultra: Folklife Essays in Honour of Alan Gailey* (Belfast, 2000), pp. 32–6.
12 F.X. Martin, *The Howth Gun-running, 1914* (Dublin, 1964), p. 68.
13 J.A. Gaughan (ed.), *Memoirs of Senator Joseph Connolly* ((Dublin, 1996), pp. 95–6.
14 Dixon, op. cit., p. 37.
15 Crone and Bigger, op. cit., pp. xxxvi–xxxviii.

9

BROTHERS IN ARTS
JOSEPH AND JOHN CAMPBELL AND THE FIRST GLENS FEIS

Jack Magee

> Tomorrow thou shalt hold jubilee, with harps and songs and dancing.
> (from a Joseph Campbell poem)

In 1904 the young and talented Campbell brothers were two of the stalwarts in the planning, preparation and successful operation of the first Festival of the Glens. They were born in Belfast – Joseph in 1879 and John in 1883 – and they were to become artistic partners in a number of projects that still resound today. The poet, Joseph, and artist, John, were also both fine singers, and their love of drama and opera had prompted their first artistic partnership: they wrote an unsuccessful opera when they were still in their teens. Already managers of manpower and materials due to their father's death in 1902, which had left them prematurely in charge of the family business, their experience and organising ability, combined with their artistic genius, was utilised by the *Feis* organising committee.

The Campbell family was Catholic and Nationalist. They lived in Loretto Cottage, at the corner of today's Castlereagh Road and Ravensdale Street. A blue plaque bearing Joseph's name marks the location today. Their Parnellite father, William, was a builder and their gentle, sophisticated and well-read mother, Catherine, who fostered an interest in Gaelic culture in her offspring, was from Presbyterian stock. Her family, the Canmers, was a well-known Belfast family from Co. Antrim. Joseph later told of visiting Granny Canmer, née O'Hara, of Ballymena. Gathering her grandchildren around her and like a traditional *seanchaidhe*, she would begin 'tracing' their family ancestry and lore. The influence and identity of Co. Antrim was thus indelibly stamped on the eight children – five sisters and three brothers – of this musically and artistically gifted family.

One of the sisters, Josephine, who adopted the stage name 'Seveen Canmer', was to become a well-known actress with the Ulster Literary Theatre. She married Samuel Waddell, brother of Helen Waddell, the Latin scholar and author. He became famous as Rutherford Mayne, the playwright, of *The Drone* fame, and she acted in his plays, which were among the most successful produced by the Ulster Literary Theatre. Joseph Campbell wrote the third play produced by the group, *The Little Cowherd of Slainge, a Dramatic Legend*. Joseph and John were also accomplished actors, and all three siblings appeared in the group's productions.

Cushendall

The eleven founding members of the Ulster Literary Theatre included Samuel Waddell, Fred Hughes, brother of Herbert Hughes the musician, and Joseph and John Campbell. Josephine was the only woman in the group. They regularly met at Loretto Cottage and at Francis Joseph Bigger's 'Ard Righ' home for evenings around the piano and for poetry readings. Supping around the fire they soon acquired the nickname of the 'Firelight' school, a tongue-in-cheek reference to the numerous reports in the press relating to the 'Twilight' school of literature inspired by the book *The Celtic Twilight*, by W.B. Yeats, who had shown an early antipathy towards the Belfast group's theatrical efforts, which he later modified.

A short-lived but highly acclaimed quarterly periodical, *Ulad* (Ulster), was launched almost at the same time as the formation of the theatrical group. This venture was to be their official publication. John Campbell was one of the five members who donated the required capital of £5 by subscribing £1 each. Contributors to *Ulad* included many that were later to become famous: James Connolly, George Russell (Æ), Pádraic Colum, Forest Reid, Roger Casement, Robert Lynn, Alice Milligan and Herbert Hughes, the musician.

Joseph Campbell was one of the three co-editors and his name also appeared under some of the articles. John Campbell designed the beautiful cover of intricate Celtic design and contributed other drawings. Despite the best intentions of its founders, *Ulad* appeared for only four issues and was discontinued due to lack of capital; financial priority was possibly given to another publication that simultaneously deeply involved both Campbell brothers, the *Songs of Uladh*. The songs published in this work were the result of the merging of the talents of the Campbell brothers, the Hughes brothers, Herbert and Freddie, and the extraordinary drive, encouragement and monetary support of Francis Joseph Bigger, who was also the driving force behind the success of the first memorable Feis na nGleann in Glenariff, on 30 June 1904. Bigger was the personification of the reawakening of Irish culture and tradition in Ulster. The camaraderie initiated by the events and activities of the 1904 Glens phenomenon proved to be the catalyst for the cultural and literary renaissance that blossomed during that remarkable year.

Concurrently with their theatrical and related artistic commitments, the Campbell brothers were excited by the scale of the planned event, which had

Benmore

captured the imagination of everyone interested in the Nationalist revival that was sweeping the country. Joseph's eager anticipation of and preparedness for the Feis na nGleann was demonstrated by the special poem he wrote, appropriately on St Patrick's Day, 1904, which appeared in the Feis programme. He interweaved the Gaelic names of the Glens into his verses.

The Nine Glens
There is fire in the heart of the Nine Glens within,
That Oisin[1] the ardent-souled would live again to light:
The seed of fire that moulders there in darkness chill and dim
Must blow to bloom flame-bright.

Gleann-taise sings the faery-songs she knew of yore;
Thro' Gleann-seasg exalting the blue-streamed runnels leap;
And stirred by the seaborne breath that fills her bosom hoar
Gleann-Duine looks up from her sleep.

Strange sounds of shrilly music are rift in the wind
That breathes down Gleann-arif from the long-forgotten years;
'Tis the pipes of Sohairle Buidhe[2] leading out his Gaelic kind
That ring in her wondering ears.

Gleann-corp marks the cry, and Gleannann green
Takes up the quickening ether within her zone of hills;
And Gleann-baile-Eamain looks like a battler's queen
When her pulse at his piobroch[3] thrills.

Gleann-gorm[4] is out to meet the risen dawn
In summer busk of purple broom and lichen grey;
And swift as the phantom-ships of Manannan[5]
The shadows of Gleann-cloiche fleet away.

There is fire in the heart of the Nine Glens within,
That *Oisin* the magic-tongued is come again to light:
The seed of fire that moulders there in darkness chill and dim
Will blow to bloom flame-bright.

Seosamh Mac Cathmhaoil, St Patrick's Day, 1904

The young poet's imagery of the reincarnated Oisin igniting the spark of Gaelic fire that mouldered, or flickered, in the Nine Glens at the start of the twentieth century was symbolic of the resurgent state of the Irish language and culture. It

JOSEPH AND JOHN CAMPBELL AND THE FIRST GLENS FEIS

Seaġan mac Caṫmaoil — Cushendall

was well and truly fanned to a bright flame by the first Feis na nGleann, the momentous event that brought many notable and unknown enthusiasts and supporters of everything Irish to Glenariff. The poem shows that Campbell had an intimate knowledge of the topography of the Glens and of Irish folklore and legend. During childhood visits to his grandfather Campbell's farm near Flurry Bridge in Irish-speaking south Armagh he had discovered and developed his love of Hidden Ireland's past and language. There he also acquired a deep appreciation of nature; his educated uncle showed him the local antiquities and told him the Cuchullain country lore, tutoring him in the botanical and Irish names of the local flora.

At 16 years of age, Joseph developed a nervous illness that required a period of rest. It was a formative time for the future poet and he immersed himself in reading, walking, folklore, nature and history. His favourite walk was along the Lagan River towpath at Shaw's Bridge, near Belfast. He started to collect and record folklore at this time, which was to become the raw material of many of his songs and poems. When he subscribed to the *Ulster Journal of Archaeology*, which had been revived and edited by Francis Joseph Bigger, it was a defining moment for the youngster. He and Bigger became good friends and the sensitive adolescent, later joined by his younger brother, John, became one of the many friends, admirers and companions that met regularly at 'Ard Righ', Bigger's open-door home in north Belfast under the lofty MacArt's Fort, or Cave Hill. At this miniature university of Irish ethos, with Bigger's collection of Irish antiquities and his unique library of books on Ireland, he met a catalogue of writers, singers, musicians, linguists and other luminaries that were to have a significant influence on the national scenario and in the formation and shaping of Irish history.

Since the founding of the Gaelic League by Douglas Hyde, Eoin MacNeill and others in 1893, the relationship between the groups of Belfast and the Glens Gaelic enthusiasts had been very close. Between 1895 and 1904 the Gaelic enthusiasts and artistes of Belfast, led by the dynamic Bigger, travelled to visit Gaelic League branches established in the Glens and to Irish days at Glenarm, which attracted great crowds, to witness and partake in the piping, singing, dancing, hurling and kindred events. During such trips Bigger made the home of John 'Benmore' Clarke, one of the most famous of Glensmen, his headquarters. Doubtless, the Campbell brothers would have been members of

the Belfast contingent. Joseph would have used the opportunity to expand his already considerable prowess and expertise in speaking the Irish language.

In 1903 Joseph had over 20 items – poems and prose, related mainly to legends – published in *The United Irishman*. The weekly paper was edited by Arthur Griffith, the father of Sinn Fein, who gave new writers a voice. However, when Lurgan-born George Russell (Æ), who delighted in discovering new talent, excluded Joseph from his anthology called *New Songs*, the emerging poet was shattered. Later in life his temperament was to react to adversity by withdrawing into a somewhat recalcitrant and morose state, and it was probably the disappointment of this exclusion that led to him declining to take part in a field expedition to north Donegal. The trip was suggested and led by Bigger, who likely financed the venture. He had been inspired by his experiences in the Irish-speaking Glens of Antrim. The small group included John Campbell, the fine singer, Frederick Hughes, and his brother, Herbert. Their objective was to record the fast disappearing Gaelic culture of that region, especially the unrecorded airs and folksong. Joseph was afterwards to regret his decision, as his fluency in Irish would have complimented the bountiful harvest reaped by the group.

The Campbell brothers had met Herbert Hughes at 'Ard Righ' a number of years previously. The young Belfast-born son of a flour miller was a musical prodigy, later to become an internationally known composer and arranger. He was back in Ulster on leave from his studies at the Royal College of Music, London, at the behest of Bigger, who had alerted him to the importance of rescuing the dying oral folksong tradition of the northwest region that had been ravaged and depopulated by the Great Famine and its aftermath. On his return from Donegal, with his notebook filled with a treasure trove of previously unrecorded airs and fragments of songs, Hughes suggested to Joseph that they collaborate by listening to the musical raw material and writing new lyrics sympathetic to the timbre of the airs. While having a unique ability to create arrangements for piano without impairing the subtleties of the peasant music, Hughes spoke only a little Irish and was unable to record some of the fragments of the original words, but noted some of the songs' provenance. Joseph's knowledge of the native language and Irish folklore was the perfect match for such a task, and he leapt at the opportunity to redeem himself from his recent disappointment.

At Loretto Cottage they sat at the piano while Hughes repeatedly played the almost-forgotten airs that had been on the verge of extinction to the inspired poet, who wrote his sympathetic new words. Thus they created 'My Lagan Love', 'The Garten Mother's Lullaby', 'The Ninepenny Fiddle' and 'The Blue Hills of Aon-druim [Antrim]', probably the best known four of the 18 songs written by Campbell in the collection. His fondness for the 'blue hills' is evident in the new lyrics he penned for the last of these; Hughes noted it was originally a ballad called 'The Sweet County Antrim', now lost. The complete work contains 30 items, with reels, jigs and cotillions in addition to the songs.

Some of these jewels of songs were destined to be sung on concert stages across the world, and it has been suggested that 'My Lagan Love' is a strong contender for the greatest song written in the twentieth century by an Irish poet. John Campbell illustrated the song collection with his superb drawings of mountain scenes, images from Irish legend and peasant figures. They called their collection *Songs of Uladh* and dedicated it to Francis Joseph Bigger, whose ever-open purse financed its publication. It was published in August 1904. In the meantime the talented trio turned their attention to the imminent Glens Festival.

In 1903 it had been decided to establish the GAA in Glenarm and throughout the Glens. Bigger presented the first hurling team formed, the S. O'Neill Club, with its first set of jerseys and with a banner of pure Irish linen. This was followed by a decision to encourage the native language and culture, and at a meeting in February 1904 it was resolved to hold a Feis of the Glens that summer. Bigger was chairman and he called for the stimulation of the Irish language, pastimes and literature, and the propagation of rural industries. Subscriptions and donations of special prizes poured in, with Bigger sparing no expense to ensure that the pageant was a colourful and memorable success.

Joseph Campbell was co-opted as a member of the Co. Antrim committee and John Campbell drew the design for the cover of the Feis programme. He also designed the banners of the Clans and Glens used in the grand opening parade and during the Feis, and sketched the pipers and hurl-carrying players at Red Bay. The hundred or so categories on the programme covered every aspect of Irish lifestyle: native industries, vocal and instrumental music, dancing, history and literature. Bigger's archival hand-written notes estimated that the total entries for the events reached over 600. Women's industries, toys and general work accounted for more than half of the participants; Gaelic, dancing, literature and music made up the other categories.

Bigger listed the names of the principal judges for some of the main events; they read like pages from the history of Ireland for the following few decades. Judging well over a hundred entries for the Gaelic-speaking prize were Eoin MacNeill, scholar and patriot, and Thomas Concannon, the Irish language teacher and author of Irish textbooks. Concannon was the Gaelic League's first appointed organiser and husband of Helena, née Walsh, sister of the Ballycastle lawyer and writer Louis J. Walsh. Ulster Literary Theatre playwright David Parkhill (alias Lewis Purcell) and Bulmer Hobson, writer and co-founder of the Dungannon Clubs, plus William MacDonald, co-founder of the Protestant Nationalist Society and Joseph Campbell pooled their talents to select the winner of the recitations competition. Joseph also partnered Stephen Gwynn, MP and author, to judge the literature competition. John Campbell and Denis McCullough, Dungannon Clubs co-founder and IRB figure, were two of the four Irish dancing judges.

Robert J. Welch, photographer extraordinaire, and Jack Morrow, repoussé

metal worker, one of the very talented Morrow brothers who were the backbone of the Ulster Literary Theatre, selected the winners of the Wood/Art exhibits.

The 'Prince of Irish Pipers', Richard Lewis O'Mealy of Belfast, and Herbert Hughes were the adjudicators of the singing and music category. Five other people were involved in assessing the singers and instrumentalists. Three of these were William Reynolds, later music critic of the *Belfast Evening Telegraph*, Herbert Hughes brother Freddie and his sister, Lena. In addition to his participation in the Ulster Literary Theatre, Freddie was a talented tenor and had formed an ensemble with his piano-playing brother, Herbert, and their friend, violinist Leslie Alexander Montgomery, who became famous as Lynn Doyle, the author of the *Ballygullion* stories. Lena, with their father, Frederick, was a member of the Belfast Philharmonic Society chorus.

Spinning & weaving and butter & eggs were additional categories listed by Bigger, but unfortunately he omitted the names of the judges for these obviously strongly contested and artisanal pursuits of the Glens people. He did, however, note that the baking competition, which doubtless would have included cakes, sponges, tarts, oatcakes, griddle cakes, oven breads and potato breads, was judged by John Andrews, who was probably a member of the Andrews flour milling company in Belfast. Roger Casement, who had enthusiastically supported the whole event, was an umpire at the hurling match that was the culmination of the festival. A beaten copper trophy, 'The Shield of Heroes', specially commissioned by Francis Joseph Bigger and made by Jack Morrow in his studio at Hanover House, Clifton Street, Belfast, was presented to the winners.

Joseph Campbell, as an actor and singer, had a voice that was much admired, but he records that when he carried out his duties as the announcer, at a time when no form of artificial amplification existed, he was hoarse for days afterwards. At the Feis he met another poet who was to be a lifelong friend and his artistic soulmate. They both acclaimed the noble peasant in their work. Joseph had read Pádraic Colum's poems before they met and, from the rustic phrases and images of strong farmers and the smell of the beasts in his poem 'A Drover', he had expected the writer to be a sturdy young countryman 'with the hands of a ploughman'. On one of the evenings during the Feis, Joseph was sitting with his back to a rock 'under the green hill of Luirgeadan' reviewing and marking essays when he saw a red-haired *leaprachán* running towards him. Colum turned out to be a book-carrying 'small, eager city youth with a high brow and pallid complexion'. They became friends at once and the diminutive Colum became a regular favourite visitor at the Campbells' Belfast home.

On the final night of the Feis, when Joseph's responsibilities as judge and announcer were ended, he went for a stroll through the warm summer night accompanied by his new friend and Herbert Hughes, his *Songs of Uladh* partner. They were a formidable artistic trio. Hughes was later to collaborate with Colum in arranging one of his poems, which was destined to become one of the most loved Irish songs: *She Moved through the Fair*.

They wandered and talked the night away. In the brightening all-night twilight of a beautiful Irish summer morning they drifted into the small still-sleeping village of Waterfoot at 3.00 a.m. Colum announced that he was hungry and suggested they seek a hearty breakfast somewhere behind one of the blind-drawn and shuttered windows of the hamlet. They selected the post office, which was the only two-storeyed building in sight, and Colum threw pebbles at an upper window. The clatter succeeded in wakening a drowsy postmaster who partly opened the front door and pushed a rare Sebastian Erard concert harp in its heavy case out to them. The trio were intrigued. Colum was touched by the symbolism of asking for breakfast and being given a harp.

Owen Lloyd had attended the Feis, evidently to play at the prizewinners' concert, at the invitation of Herbert Hughes. He had left his harp at the post office for forwarding to his home, and the half-conscious postmaster thought they were there to collect it. It would have made an interesting topic of conversation over the bacon and egg breakfast they promptly received. The incident seemed a happy and fitting one to wind up the Feis. The three young men were to achieve international acclamation for their work later in life; they each recalled their 'harp' adventure in their writings.

As part of the Irish Revival in Ulster, the events preceding, during and following the inspiring 1904 Feis produced a remarkable burst of creative work in all aspects of Irish life, in which Joseph and John Campbell played a central role. Doubtless many of those who organised and took part in the 1904 Feis attended the Glens Feisanna that followed over the years, but the stories of the splendour of that first occasion, which drew people irrespective of class, politics or creed, still echo down the years.

Notes on illustrations
The drawings of Glen scenes included in this article are by John Campbell. The illustrations are by his brother, Joseph, and are taken from his book of poems entitled 'The Rushlight' (Maunsel & Co., Dublin, 1906). He signed his drawings 'c-m'. The photograph of Loretto Cottage is used by permission of Mr and Mrs W. H. Emerson. The Emerson family, who also owned the close-by Emerson's Dairy, occupied the cottage after the Campbells.

Further reading
'Benmore', 'Founding the Glens Feis', *The Glensman*, Vol. 1, No. 9, June 1932, pp. 30–2.
    Or Fifty Years Ago (Glens of Antrim Historical Society, Cushendall, 1982).
Francis Joseph Bigger Archives, Belfast Central Library.
Seamus Clarke, *Feis Na nGleann, A History of the Festival of the Glens* (Priory Press, Holywood, Co. Down, 1994).
John Killen (ed.) *Rutherford Mayne, Selected Plays* (Institute of Irish Studies, Queen's University of Belfast, 1977), pp. 2–18.
Margaret McHenry, *The Ulster Theatre in Ireland*, English Literature Thesis, University of Pennsylvania, Philadelphia, 1933.

Jack Magee, 'An East Belfast poet, Joseph Campbell (1879–1944)', *Journal of the East Belfast Historical Society*, Vol. 1, No. 3, September 1983.

Sr Assumpta Saunders (ed.), Joseph Campbell Special Issue, *The Journal of Irish Literature*, Vol. VIII, September 1979.

Norah Saunders and A.A. Kelly, *Joseph Campbell, Poet & Nationalist 1879–1944. A Critical Biography* (Wolfhound Press, Dublin, 1988).

1. Poet son of Fionn Mac Cumhaill. Romantic legend claims he was buried at Lubitavish, Glenann.
2. Sorley Boy McDonnell.
3. Piping.
4. *Gleann-gorm*, 'the blue glen', appears to have evolved into the modern Glenarm, 'the glen of the army'.
5. Sea god of the pagan Irish; he ruled *Tir Tairngiri* – 'The Land of Promise'.

10

EOIN MacNEILL (1867–1945)
GLENSMAN, LANGUAGE REVIVALIST AND STATE BUILDER

Rev. Professor F.X. Martin, OSA

Early years

Eoin MacNeill was born in Glenarm, in the Glens of Antrim, on 15 May 1867, one of eight children of a Norse-Gaelic family deeply rooted in the area. His father, Archibald, a tall, strongly-built man with a red beard, had, after an early career at sea as a ship's carpenter, settled in Glenarm as a general merchant and building contractor. He built the present Glenarm Catholic church. Eoin's mother, Rosetta MacAuley, was the daughter of the local doctor and a descendant on her mother's side of the O'Neills of Clandeboye. On his father's side, MacNeill was related to William Orr, the Presbyterian United Irishman executed at Carrickfergus in 1797. An uncle of Eoin's, Rev. Dr Charles MacAuley, was Professor of Rhetoric in Maynooth.

Young Eoin MacNeill first attended the local Protestant school in Glenarm, the manager of which was the village rector. There he received private tuition from the teacher in the Catholic girls' primary school and, according to himself, this was sufficient to put him in the lead when he went to St Malachy's College, Belfast, in the autumn of 1881. The Intermediate Education Act of 1877, with the regular annual examinations and valuable scholarships it provided, was a great fillip to Catholic secondary education; the young MacNeill got the full advantage of it in St Malachy's College.

Though Irish was a subject under the disguise of 'Celtic', he did not take it in school. In 1885 he took his matriculation in the Royal University, which had been established in 1879. The Royal was an examining body, not a teaching university, and students could get tuition for it wherever they chose. St Malachy's, like many another school, had its university class, numbering only six or seven students, but these were of picked quality and the standard was high. All MacNeill's classmates – men like Brian Moore (whose sister he was to marry), Alexander Blayney, Joseph MacNabb (known in later life as Fr Vincent MacNabb OP) and John MacErlean – were to achieve distinction. There was a full Arts course up to degree level, and good scholarships to be won at all stages. MacNeill got a scholarship in Modern Languages at matriculation. In 1887, when working for his Second Arts, he secured a nomination that entitled him to compete for a Clerkship in the Dublin Four Courts. This he did, and he was awarded first place and an appointment in the Accountant-General's office. The

Eoin MacNeill
– first professor of Irish and Medieval History at University College Dublin

same summer he sat for his Second Arts and in the autumn of 1888 finished his degree with honours in economics, jurisprudence, and constitutional history.

MacNeill was at the parting of the ways. Now, guided not by knowledge, experience, or the advice of others, but acting on a firm instinct, he decided to study Irish. His decision is by any average standard inexplicable. The language was a closed book to him, except for a few phrases that were in common use in the Glens of Antrim. There were then no societies for the teaching of Irish in Dublin, and acting on the advice of Fr Eoghan O'Growney, who had been recommended to him by a mutual friend, he went to Inis Meán in the Aran Islands in the summer of 1891. He returned fired with enthusiasm for the dying national language.

Foundation of the Gaelic League, 1893
In March 1893, MacNeill published a historic article in *The Gaelic Journal*. The article was entitled 'A plea and a plan', with the subtitle, 'For the extension of the movement to preserve and spread the Gaelic language in Ireland'. The hard core of MacNeill's article was a proposal that a new organisation be established, centred in Dublin but with its main activities throughout the provinces. The article has sometimes been described as the trumpet-call heralding the Irish cultural revolution.

On 31 July a group of nine gathered in a classroom for civil servants at 9 Lower O'Connell Street, Dublin. Of those present, the only two names that would now command attention are Douglas Hyde and Eoin MacNeill. MacNeill's proposal for a new organisation was accepted: the new body was named 'The Gaelic League', *Cunnradh na Gaedhilge*, and MacNeill was appointed honorary secretary. At a subsequent meeting Hyde was elected president; he continued so for 22 years. He was an ideal choice; the League was professedly non-political and undenominational, and Hyde was a Protestant with no personal interest in politics. But while Hyde deservedly enjoyed the limelight, Eoin MacNeill was the stage-manager working persistently but unobtrusively in the wings. It was he that arranged the foundation meeting of the League, and for its first six formative years he acted as unpaid secretary.

All had to be done during the weekends or after his working day in the Four Courts. He became a frequent traveller on the night mail-trains. One of the many lecturing invitations he accepted in 1897 was to address the New Ireland Literary Society in Dublin. The president of the society was a serious seventeen-year-old student, Pádraig Pearse, who on MacNeill's recommendation joined the Gaelic League.

The Gaelic League became a revivifying force in the cultural life of the people. The young generation learned to look on Ireland with fresh eyes, each recruit to the league declaring, *Is Gael mise, nac uasal san!* ('I am an Irishman/Irishwoman and proud of it'). Pearse wrote of the League in February 1914: 'the Gaelic League will be recognised in history as the most revolutionary influence that has ever come into Ireland. The Irish Revolution really began when the first Gaelic Leaguers met in O'Connell Street … The germ of all future Irish history was in that back room.' A very different point of view was expressed by the *Derry Sentinel*, that resolute organ of Unionist opinion. While stating quite bluntly that the League was at bottom nothing better than a Fenian organisation, and a society for the wholesale desecration of the Lord's Day, it exhorted all good men and true to repeat the words of the prayer – 'Good Lord, deliver us from all these abominations'.

Revolution in historical studies
Meanwhile MacNeill had become engaged in another branch of learning – Irish historical studies – in which he was to introduce revolutionary changes. It was

Birth place of Eoin MacNeill in Glenarm, Co. Antrim

no surprise when the National University was established by an act of parliament in 1908 that MacNeill was deservedly chosen as the first professor of early (including Medieval) Irish History at University College Dublin.

Yet for all his preoccupation with academic work, MacNeill still gave generously of his time to the Gaelic League. It was because of his Gaelic League interest that he was drawn into politics and the dramatic events that led on to the Easter Rising.

The Ulster question
MacNeill was an Ulsterman, and it was the Ulster Protestant agitation against Home Rule that induced him to lead an Irish armed national movement. On more than one occasion in later life MacNeill declared that the revolution in modern Ireland was brought about mainly by Sir Edward Carson and the Orangemen. After the general election at the end of 1910, the Irish Party held the balance in the House of Commons, and the Liberal government under Asquith agreed perforce, in order to stay in office, to put through a Home Rule Bill for Ireland. The House of Lords had killed the Home Rule Bill in 1893, but this right of an absolute veto was shorn from them in August 1911 by the Parliament Act. Nothing but the unforeseen could prevent an Irish parliament meeting with British consent in Dublin before the end of 1913, with the Home

Rule leader, John Redmond, as its first prime minister.

The rank and file of the Orangemen were led to believe that Home Rule would certainly mean direct rule by the Pope of Rome and the destruction of those Protestant liberties so dearly bought since the Ulster Plantation of 1607. Instead of the popular slogan 'Home Rule for Ireland' they substituted 'Home Rule is Rome Rule', and Lord Randolph Churchill's challenge, 'Ulster will fight and Ulster will be right'. They induced Sir Edward Carson, an M.P. for Trinity College Dublin who was a brilliant lawyer, neurotic in character and dramatic in mob oratory, to lead the Ulster resistance to Home Rule.

The overwhelming majority of the Irish people had voted in favour of Home Rule, and Redmond, who still fondly believed that democracy would triumph, summoned a vast Home Rule demonstration to meet in O'Connell Street, Dublin, on 31 March, 1912. Redmond spoke from one platform, Devlin from another, MacNeill from the third and Pearse from the fourth. At this stage MacNeill and Pearse were Home Rulers, as were the vast majority of the Irish people, believing not that Home Rule was the ultimate solution, but that it would be the first stride forward towards self-government. Redmond confidently assured his optimistic audience – 'Trust the Old Party – and Home Rule next year'.

The Ulster loyalists began to talk in terms of war and to prepare for it. In January 1913 the Ulster Volunteer Force was founded as a military body. The question in many Irish nationalist circles now was – if the Orangemen can arm and defy the government, thwarting Home Rule, why can we not take a leaf from their book and arm to ensure that Home Rule becomes a reality?

Foundation of the Irish Volunteers, 1913

There was, indeed, one body, the IRB, ever vigilant, waiting for its opportunity to arm and strike. As the Brotherhood was a secret, oath-bound and illegal organisation, and had no more than 2,000 members throughout the country, it could not give the lead publicly. It was now largely gingered up by a group of men born or trained in Ulster – Tom Clarke, Denis McCullough, Bulmer Hobson, Sean MacDermott and Pat McCartan.

On 1 November 1913, the hour struck and the man appeared. An article, written by Eoin MacNeill and entitled 'The North began', appeared in *An Claidheamh Soluis* ('The Sword of Light'), journal of the Gaelic League. The brunt of the article was plain. The Orangemen in Ulster were setting an example by successfully arming and defying the British government. There was nothing to prevent the rest of Ireland following suit, enrolling, drilling and reviewing a national volunteer force. But in that case, MacNeill pointed out, the national volunteer force should take care not to disband until it had obtained full self-government from England. No sooner had the article appeared than MacNeill was asked by Bulmer Hobson and The O'Rahilly if he would lead the new movement. MacNeill agreed. He was aware of the IRB's revolutionary agenda but hoped to lead a force that would include both Home Rulers and Republicans.

The Irish Volunteers was launched in the Rotunda, Dublin on 25 November 1913 and soon numbered 170,000 members throughout Ireland.

MacNeill's policy now and right up to the Easter Rising was clear-cut. The Volunteers were there to guarantee freedom and self-government for Ireland – for all Ireland. MacNeill, the Ulsterman, was very conscious of the danger of partition – more so than the younger men on the Volunteer committee who favoured an armed confrontation with England and the coercion, if necessary, of the Ulster Unionists. For him that was an unreal policy that might well dismember the country. He believed in toleration and persuasion, combined with a firm stand on principles.

The split with Redmond, September 1914
In September 1914 Redmond and MacNeill came to a sharp parting of the ways. When the Home Rule Bill was ready to receive Royal Assent on 18 September – though to be suspended until after the war – Redmond threw discretion to the winds and issued a declaration that it was now Ireland's duty to keep faith with England and supply her with recruits for the war in Europe.

Four days later MacNeill and the members of the original committee of the Volunteers issued a public statement repudiating Redmond, and calling on the Volunteers to remain united in order to ensure that a national government be established without delay for all Ireland. Of the 180,000 Volunteers, only 11,000 remained with MacNeill; the rest decamped with Redmond to form a rival organization, the Irish National Volunteers.

While the Irish Party began to lose support over its association with recruitment after 1914, MacNeill's greatest problem as head of the Volunteers centred on an IRB conspiracy within the organization. In May 1915, the IRB's Military Council – composed of Pearse, Plunkett and Ceannt – decided to launch an insurrection using the Volunteers as a 'strike force'. MacNeill, a cultural nationalist, rejected the IRB's argument on the pragmatic grounds that a Rising during the war would be crushed by British forces. In any event, he argued, Ireland's nationality was not in danger of extinction.

When MacNeill discovered that a Rising was imminent following Roger Casement's capture at Banna Strand in April 1916, he issued an order countermanding the Volunteer manoeuvres planned for Easter Sunday. This forced Pearse and his associates to fall back on the 'Dublin Plan' for a more limited uprising in the capital, beginning on Easter Monday. The scene was thus set for the 'blood sacrifice' of Easter Week and the execution of 15 of the revolutionary leaders by the British authorities.

> WOODTOWN PARK,
> RATHFARNHAM,
> CO. DUBLIN.
>
> 22 Apl 1916
>
> Volunteers completely deceived. All orders for tomorrow Sunday are entirely cancelled.
>
> Eoin MacNeill

The order by MacNeill calling off the Volunteers' mobilisation on Easter Sunday

Career in Dáil Eireann, 1918–25

After the Rising, MacNeill was arrested in the general round-up and sentenced to penal servitude for life. At his court martial he spoke of those who had deceived him as truthful and honourable men, and gave strict instruction to his counsel that they were not to be inculpated in any way.

It was a measure of his stature that in the 1918 election he was, like de Valera, returned for two constituencies, Derry City and the National University. He became Minister of Finance in the First Dáil ministry of 1919.

With the reconstitution and transformation of Sinn Fein, MacNeill was in the fullest sympathy and declared himself in favour of a Republic as the most appropriate national aim. MacNeill was never doctrinaire and never shared the romantic mystique that saw the Republic as something indefeasible. When the Treaty came, MacNeill recognised it as giving Ireland substantive freedom, with a few concessions to the Empire that were no more than formalities. As Speaker of the Dáil during the Treaty debates he was in a better position than most to understand what was at issue in that extraordinary conflict.

MacNeill made a great contribution to the success of the first Free State government, in which he was Minister for Education.

The Boundary Commission (1925)

MacNeill's retirement, first from the cabinet and a year later from all political activity, was caused by the Boundary Commission. He became the Free State representative on the Commission set up under the Treaty of 1921 to make adjustments in the boundary between the Free State and Northern Ireland. Since the Treaty, the position of the Nationalist side had of course gravely worsened.

There was no longer a powerful united national movement in the south. MacNeill did not make regular reports to his cabinet colleagues because he regarded the proceedings of the Commission as confidential. When a premature report of the Commission's findings, which recommended only minor changes, was published in the English press, MacNeill took the opportunity to resign from both the Commission and the cabinet.

Though his handling of his brief evoked strong criticism, particularly in the nationalist north, he regarded his membership of the Commission as 'the most disagreeable duty I had ever undertaken' involving as it did the stereotyping of partition 'on a basis of religious differences'.

Last years
He was only 60 years of age and had nearly 20 years of scholarly activity before him. During these years he carried on his historical work, founded the Irish Manuscripts Commission, lectured in the United States and became President of the Royal Irish Academy (from the roll of whose members his name had been struck off in 1916), visited Rome and had audiences with Pius XI. His health remained perfect until the year of his death, 1945.

Few men of MacNeill's stature have cared less than he did for the criticisms of others. He was never eager to rush to his own defence, and always ready to admit mistakes whether in scholarship or in action. During his active years he was in the centre of many controversies and suffered a great deal of criticism. Yet he retains the unique distinction in modern Irish history of having successfully launched three revolutions: the revolution that he ushered in with the foundation of the Gaelic League in 1893; the revolution in Irish historical studies that became evident in his 1904 lectures; and the revolution that began with the foundation of the Irish Volunteers in 1913. Therefore, MacNeill the 'scholar revolutionary' must rank as one of the chief architects of modern Ireland.

11

JOHN CLARKE
'BENMORE' (1868–1934)

Eamon Phoenix

John Clarke was born in Ballycastle on 11 August 1868, the son of John Clarke and Eibhlin McCluskey. His father's family were steeped in the Nationalist tradition of the period. The young boy had a deep admiration for his uncle, James Clarke, who had founded the Land League in the Ballycastle district in 1879 and was a loyal follower of the Home Rule leader, Charles Stewart Parnell. In his youth James had been a member of the Fenian movement along with the leading Ballycastle separatist, Dan Darragh. It was in this strongly Nationalist atmosphere that John Clarke grew up in the 1870s and 1880s.

Like most children in the Victorian era, he received only an elementary education. As he later recorded: 'Six years at the old Chapel School in Ballycastle gave me an elementary start, after which I took to the reading of works by eminent Irishmen whose writing filled me with inspiration to seek for still more knowledge of my country'. On leaving school, he served his apprenticeship to Charles McLoughlin, a local publican, and then went to Belfast to find work.

The young North Antrim man's arrival in the city coincided with the Gaelic Revival that followed the creation of the Gaelic League by his fellow Glensman, Eoin MacNeill, in 1893. Passionately interested in Irish history and culture, John Clarke became business manager of the *Northern Patriot*, a nationalist literary journal published weekly at 8 North Street, Belfast by Alice Milligan, the Protestant nationalist poetess, and Anna Johnston ('Ethna Carbery'). Clarke penned numerous articles for the paper on historical topics, often using the pen-name 'Benmore'. He was particularly interested in the United Irishmen, and in the June 1897 edition he contributed an article on the Battle of Antrim in 1798.

By this stage John Clarke was being drawn into the Gaelic League and the national commemoration of the 1798 Rebellion. He joined the Henry Joy McCracken Literary Society in Belfast in 1895 and, on 19 November of that year, delivered an address on the life of Wolfe Tone. He was also active in the Belfast Branch of the Gaelic League, founded by P.T. McGinley ('Cú Uladh') in 1895, and was a regular attender at the weekly language classes in its Queen Street premises.

Not surprisingly, 'Benmore' joined the rapidly expanding GAA, helping to lay the foundations of Gaelic games in Belfast and Co. Antrim. As he recalled in an article in *The Glensman* in 1932: 'A few of us – we were young then – set the O'Neill Crowley Gaelic Club agoing in 1895. Our meeting-place was in

John 'Benmore' Clarke

Donegall Street, adjacent to the *Irish News* office ... Other clubs such as the 'Red Hand', the 'Brian Oge' and 'Tir-na-nOg' followed in quick succession. The national game became firmly established.'

Around 1902 Clarke left Belfast for Glenarm, where he bought the Seaview Hotel. Around this time he married Miss Isobel Campbell of Ballycastle. Once in the picturesque coastal village he founded a branch of the Gaelic League and helped to form the Shane O'Neill Gaelic Athletic Club in 1903. It was in Glenarm that 'Benmore' first became acquainted with the Belfast nationalist and language revivalist, Francis Joseph Bigger. In 1904, Clarke joined with Bigger, Miss Margaret Dobbs, Roger Casement and others to organise the first Feis na nGleann in Glenariff.

Over the next 30 years, 'Benmore' was a central figure in every attempt to

Irish eviction scene

promote Gaelic culture in the Glens of Antrim. He was a strong Irish separatist. A firm supporter of Parnell, he transferred his allegiance from the Irish Party to Sinn Fein after the 1916 rising. He was a keen amateur archaeologist and published several books and myriad poems and ballads set in his native North Antrim.

John Clarke was instrumental in the erection of statues to practically every Irishman of note except himself; often, when funds were not forthcoming for his purpose, he would pay the balance for a particular monument of memorial out of his own pocket. That is one of the many reasons why 'Benmore' died a poor man.

One of his works that tends to stir Celtic blood is that on Daniel Darragh, an 1867 Fenian belonging to Ballycastle. Here 'Benmore' gives a very touching scene of the eviction of some 200 families in Carey and district under the landlord scourge. Darragh's family was among those turned out of their homes. At the suggestion of 'Benmore' a fund was raised and a Celtic cross was erected over the grave of Dan Darragh. Such was the spirit of 'Benmore' and many will find his works most interesting, for they remind us of stirring times in Ireland.

'Benmore's' career spanned the tempestuous period of Home Rule, the Gaelic Revival, the Easter Rising and partition. His death in 1934 removed one of the key architects of the Glens Feis and the language revival in Ulster.

12

THE FOUNDERS OF FEIS NA nGLEANN 1904
Eileen McAuley

President: Miss Barbara McDonnell, Monavert, Cushendall
A descendant of the McDonnells of Antrim, Miss McDonnell was interested in the improvement of living standards for the local people. With her friend Miss Sturge, she established the toy factory in Cushendall in 1901. This not only provided employment but also encouraged the promotion of traditional wood skills. Examples of the work, including a Georgian-style dolls' house, can be seen in The National Museum in Dublin. The factory closed in 1914, though the work was still profitable; it is believed the lack of a suitable workforce was one reason for the closure.

Secretary: Miss Ada McNeill
Born in England in 1860 but brought up in Cushendun, she was known throughout the Glens as 'Miss Ada'. She was a first cousin of Ronald McNeill – Lord Cushendun, a staunch Unionist. Miss Ada was an early member of the Gaelic League and, along with Miss Dobbs and Rose Young, was a strong supporter and promoter of the Gaelic revival. She was a lifelong friend of Roger Casement and visited him in Brixton jail in 1916 before his execution. Throughout her long life she worked tirelessly for the promotion of the Irish language and the folklore of the Glens. Miss Ada died in 1959 and is buried in the Church of Ireland graveyard in Cushendun.

Assistant Secretary: Daniel McAllister, Mill Street, Cushendall
Born in Cushendall in 1878 into a well-known Glens family of tradespeople, McAllister spent all his life in the Glens apart from a few years away learning 'business skills'. He married Ellen McSparran from Carnlough and settled in Mill Street, Cushendall, where she ran a general store and boarding house and he was an auctioneer and, for a while, a JP. Noted for his sharp tongue and ready wit, Daniel was fiercely loyal to the Glens and its people until his death in 1965.

Treasurer: Francis Joseph Bigger, 'Ard Righ', Belfast
Bigger, a Belfast solicitor born in 1863, was intensely interested in the preservation of the language, history and folklore of Ireland. He was a member of Coiste Gnótha of the Gaelic League and president of its Belfast Coiste Ceantair, a member of the Belfast Naturalists' Field Club, its Chairman from 1900 till 1903, and a governor of his old school, Royal Belfast Academical

Institution. He was one of the prime activists in getting the first Feis up and running and, at the first committee meeting set out the aims: 'the stimulation of the Irish language, pastimes and literature in our midst not forgetting the propagation of rural industries, these aims to be in accordance with purely National sentiment irrespective of class or creed.'

F.J. Bigger was known for his personal generosity to his many causes, and his home at 'Ard Righ' in Belfast was a meeting place for all the literary figures of the time. He died in December 1926 and is buried in Mallusk cemetery, where a large Celtic cross marks his grave.

Treasurer: Joseph Duffy, Cushendall
Born in Co. Mayo in 1840, Duffy was a teacher and headmaster of Knocknacarry Primary School from 1875 to 1902. He had a good knowledge of Irish, and won a prize at the 1904 Feis for a comprehensive collection of Irish place names and their meanings. He was interested in all aspects of Irish culture and in local and national history, and wrote several poems of local interest. He died suddenly in Kilnadore House, Cushendall on 28 January 1905.

Members of the committee representing each of the nine glens were as follows:

Glentaisie
Mrs Frances Riddell
A native of Ballycastle, with the help of F.J. Bigger in 1903 she set up the Irish Peasant Home Industries in Ann Street, Ballycastle. This initiative was to help boys from poor backgrounds to acquire a skill or trade, to help them get employment or set up in a trade in their local area, and especially to help stem the need to emigrate. Mrs Riddell gave her services voluntarily and no private profit was made; boy workers irrespective of class or creed reaped the benefits. It proved so popular that a similar scheme was set up to assist girls, and to improve the standard of embroidery, crochet, knitting and also homespun yarn-making for socks. The premises was called 'An Tuirne Beag' (The Little Spinning Wheel), and was fitted out in the style of an old Irish kitchen.

Dominic Maguire (also known as Denis)
Maguire was a teacher in Carey and lived at Ballyvoy; he originally came from the Coleraine area. He and a Master Moore, who also taught in Carey, were the original sponsors of the Carey hurling team of 1903.

Glenshesk
Roger Casement
Roger David Casement, born 1 September 1864 at Doyle's Cottage, Sandycove, Dublin into the Irish landed gentry, was the third son of a Protestant father and a Catholic mother. By the age of 13 he was an orphan boarding at Ballymena

Academy and spending his holidays with his Uncle John (Casement) at Magherintemple, Ballycastle. On leaving school he worked for Elder Dempster Shipping Co., trading with West Africa for a number of years. He then joined the British Foreign Office and went on to become consul in the Congo. There he became famous as an emancipator, and received a knighthood in 1911 for his public service there and in Putamayo in South America.

Thoughout his period in the Foreign Office Casement continued his deep interest in Irish affairs and became committed to the cause of Irish independence. He joined the National Volunteers and actively canvassed for support in America and later in Germany, where he was involved in the shipment of arms to Ireland. He was put ashore from a U-boat at Banna Strand, Co. Kerry on 21 April 1916, and was immediately captured. He was taken to the Tower of London and convicted of treason and espionage against the English Crown. He was hanged at Pentonville Prison on 3 August 1916. His final wish was to be buried at Murlough Bay, Co. Antrim; this wish was not granted and he was buried at Pentonville Prison. His remains were repatriated from England in 1965 and he was reburied at Glasnevin cemetery in March of that year.

Stephen McGeown
McGeown is believed to have been a teacher in the local school; little other information about him is available.

Neale McAuley
Born in Teoghs, Glenshesk, McAuley was one of at least seven children. He and his sister, Catherine, (both unmarried) ran the family farm; records suggest that the rest of the family emigrated to Scotland, the U.S.A. and Australia. This brother and sister were remarkable human beings who took on the responsibility of raising no fewer than six orphan children. Their Christian example was an inspiration to all who knew them.

Neale died about 1930 and Catherine in 1949.

Glendun

Denis Black
Born in 1864, Black lived in the townland of Ballure on the family farm. He represented the area as a councillor on Ballycastle Rural District Council, and later became a Justice of the Peace. He sold his farm at Ballure to Hugh Sharkey in 1917 and moved to Dunurgan, where he died in May 1929.

Margaret MacGonigle
MacGonigle was a teacher who taught in Glendun school for about three years before returning to her native Toomebridge. When teaching in Glendun she resided with the MacLaughlin family at Shannish, Glendun.

THE FOUNDERS OF FEIS NA nGLEANN

William McLaughlin
McLaughlin was a native of Glendun, living on the family farm at Shannish. The farm was later sold to the McCormacks; the McLaughlins purchased College Farm, Carnlough, where William's descendants still farm.

Glenann

John MacNamee
A teacher in Glenann school, MacNamee originated in Co. Derry. He was renowned locally for his teaching ability, and ran night-classes in navigation skills. These classes were very popular and well attended.

Glenballyeamon

Hugh Flatley
A teacher by profession, Flatley was to become principal of the primary school at Mill Street, Cushendall. He was a keen promoter of the Irish language, which he taught locally with great enthusiasm. His great passion was cycling, and in 1905 he and Dan Delargy set out from Cushendall to cycle round Ireland. Both were hurling enthusiasts; they are believed to have introduced a new design of hurl that they discovered on their travels round the country.

Daniel MacAllister
Also Assistant Secretary – see above.

John Higgins
Born in 1880, Higgins was an only child and lived on the family farm at Tate's Lane, Newtowncrommelin. A teacher by profession, he taught in the Old Chapel school in Ballymena. Each weekday morning he would cycle from his home to the crossroads, where he boarded a train to Ballymena. On Sundays after Mass in Glenravel he would cycle all the way to Ballymena to take Sunday school and then cycle home again. He was a founder member of the Con Magee's GAA club. He had nine children, including three sets of twins.

Higgins died in the 1930s as a result of injuries received when his bicycle was in collision with a lorry.

John Higgins, Glenravel, represented Glenballyeamon on first Feis committee

Glenariff

Thomas Moorhead
Moorhead was a teacher in the school at Drumnacur, Glenariff, which was known as a Bible School because of its concentration on teaching the bible through the Irish language; children paid from one to two shillings per quarter to attend. The school closed in 1914 when the children moved to the new school in Waterfoot.

John Mackillen
Mackillen was Clerk of the Petty Sessions and worked from an office in High Street, Cushendall. He lived at Main Street, Waterfoot, beside the present Costcutter Supermarket.

Glencloy

Bernard O'Donnell
O'Donnell was born in 1851 and lived at Waterfall Road, Carnlough. He represented the Carnlough area on the Larne Rural District Council and the Larne Board of Guardians for 15 years. He died in 1933, aged 82.

Miss Johnston
She was born Netta Jane Nicholl Johnston in 1876. The family owned a grocery/hardware shop and funeral undertaking business at the premises now occupied by Brendan Killough's Pharmacy. She was a keen musician, and organised the Carnlough flute band. At one point she was believed to be the only female uilleann piper in Ulster. She died in 1953.

Patrick Hamill
Hamill owned the licensed premises at the junction of High Street and Harbour Road, now owned by the Diamond family. He was a representative of the Carnlough area on the Larne Board of Guardians for many years. He died in 1908; his name lives on in the well-known ballad 'Sweet Carnlough Bay'.

Glencorp

Miss Rose Maud Young (Róis Ní Ógáin)
Born in 1865, the daughter of Colonel Young of Galgorm House, Ballymena, Miss Young was deeply interested in the Irish language and literature, having studied Irish under Bishop Reeves before the formation of the Gaelic League. She later joined the League and was an outstanding member for many years. She also edited a choice collection of Irish poetry, which was regarded as a valuable literary work. In her later years she resided with Margaret Dobbs; she died in 1947 and is buried in the Presbyterian churchyard in Ahoghill.

John McCambridge
Born in 1866, McCambridge was an only son and ran the family farm at Laney, Cushendall. Known as 'The Laney Man', he was reasonably well educated and helped people write letters and fill forms. He was a member of Ballycastle Rural Council at the turn of the century, and once represented the Council at a conference in Belgium. He was sometimes called on to help settle family feuds, and was thought to have had a hand in several matchmakings. He was a noted storyteller and was interviewed several times on radio.

Along with G.B. Newe and Canon Sharpe, the local Church of Ireland

'The Laney Man', John McCambridge, represented Glencorp on first Feis committee

minister, McCambridge founded the Cushendall agricultural show. It was held during the 1930s but ceased at the start of the Second World War.

Glenarm
John ('Benmore') Clarke
Clarke was born in Ballycastle in 1868 and came to Glenarm around 1898 as manager of the Seaview Hotel. Deeply interested in Irish history and all things Irish, he helped found a branch of the Gaelic League in the village in 1903. He was a founder of Shane O'Neill's GAC in the winter of 1903, and was chairman and secretary of the GAC for many years.

Clarke was always deeply involved in the running of the Feis, and was a proud man when Feis na nGleann was held in Glenarm for the first time in 1932. He was also the author of a number of historical publications and poetry books.

Mrs Annie McGavock
Annie was the daughter of Glenarm shop owner Archibald MacNeill, wife of William McGavock (Glenarm), mother-in-law of Senator Joseph Connolly and grandmother of Archie Irvine, Shane O'Neill's and Antrim hurler in the late 1940s. Her brothers Eoin and James were well known in politics in the South: Eoin was co-founder of the Gaelic League in 1893 and later of the Volunteers; James was at one time Governor-General of the Irish Free State. Annie died in 1923.

James McRann
McRann, a Co. Sligo man, was appointed national schoolteacher at Seaview School in 1902. He was closely involved in the founding of the Glenarm Gaelic League and Shane O'Neill's GAC in 1903. He left Glenarm in 1905.

The Committee issued the following instructions to the general public referring to the dress and behaviour expected on Feis Day 1904.

The Feis will be opened by a procession from Cushendall at 9 o'clock sharp, led off by the pipers and bearing the Feis banners. All wishing to take part in the procession should be in Cushendall before that hour. The Feis colours are green and saffron which should be generally displayed. All horses and machines should be decorated with flowers, foliage and the Feis colours. All costumes worn should, as far as possible, be of Irish material and manufacture. Hurlers should be in costume bearing their camans to march in the procession. The choirs should be prepared to sing in the procession and be decorated with flowers. The stewards will wear rosettes and Gaelic buttons and will be on duty all day. The procession will arrive at Glenariff about 10 o'clock, when the competitions will at once commence.

Every competitor should apply to, and receive from, the Honorary Secretary, a card giving the exact place and hour at which their competition will take place; if such instructions are not complied with, no responsibility will rest on the officers.

A board in the Feis grounds will display general notices or alterations.

In addition to the dancing competitions throughout the day suitable places will be provided for general dancing to the pipes and fiddles; only Irish dances will be permitted.

The athletic sports will be held on the sand hills at 1 o'clock, the hurling match on the strand at 3 o'clock.

In the Literary and Industrial Competitions the adjudications will take place before the 30th and made public at the opening of the Feis; in the other competitions the prize winners will be declared immediately after adjudication.

The principal prizes in each section will be distributed in the evening by Sir Horace Plunkett and the others will be distributed through the day; time would not permit of all being formally presented.

The meeting in the evening in the large hall will commence at 6.30.

When the prizes have been distributed there will be a full programme by harpers, pipers, singers, fiddlers and dancers, contributed by the prize winners and others.
– Admission: 2s. 6d and 1s.

After the other meeting the hall will be devoted to Gaelic dancing, open to all.
– Single tickets 1s; Double tickets 1s. 6d.

All the publicans in Waterfoot have generously promised to sell no intoxicants on the day in honour of Ireland. It is the earnest and particular desire of all interested in this great Gaelic movement for the upraising of our native land that there should be absolute temperance, especially on such an occasion as the day of the Feis, when so much can be done to prove that our race is capable of a noble effort to do all that in them lies to advance on the upward path of national regeneration. Any Glensman who fails in this duty will bring disgrace on himself and the Glen he comes from and degrade the common cause so dear to everyone.

An té nach ólann ach uisce ní bheidh sé ar meisce.
(He who drinks only water will never be drunk)

Gaelic league gathering on Rathlin Island, 1904, Sean Greene addressing the crowd with Feis na nGleann members seated on the bank

13
IRISH IN THE GLENS
FROM DECLINE TO REVIVAL (1890–2004)
Eileen McAuley, Eamon Phoenix and Pádraic Ó Cléireacháin

The Glens of Antrim and Rathlin Island formed one of the last Gaelic-speaking areas in Ulster, outside the Donegal Gaeltacht, until the early 1900s. The state of the language in the district, its gradual decline in the late nineteenth century and the attempts to preserve and revive it in the early 1900s are graphically charted in a series of fascinating documents from the 1890s to the 1980s.

In August 1897 the Belfast branch of the Gaelic League, led by its secretary, P.T. McGinley ('Cú Uladh'), made a visit to Glenariff to meet its remaining Irish speakers. McGinley (1856–1942) was a native of Glenswilly, Co. Donegal, and worked as a Customs and Excise officer in Belfast. The first meeting of the Belfast Gaelic League was held in his home at 32 Beersbridge Road in the city two years earlier, in August 1895.

The Belfast Gaels took the train to Parkmore before walking down the glen to Waterfoot. It is clear from McGinley's report of the excursion in the *Irish News* of 9 August 1897 that Irish, while clearly in decline, was still spoken by some of the older people in Glenariff.

Pádraic Ó Cléireacháin
(Leaschathaoirleach)

> On Saturday we opened the season by a visit to the Irish speakers of Glenariff. We had only a small muster, probably because of the threatening character of the morning, but as our president and our piper turned up we considered ourselves fit and strong for the work before us. We arrived at Parkmore about noon and proceeded down Glenariff. We were soon greeted by Irish speakers who recognised us and remembered our visit from last year. Henry MacAuley, of Cloneragh, a good Irish speaker, came from his turnip field to bid us welcome. He is quite enthusiastic about the future of the language, and is willing and anxious to teach it to his friends and neighbours. His little four-year old girl talked some sentences to us with a very good pronunciation. Henry is unfortunately without any literary knowledge of the language, but is a very intelligent man, and could be of the greatest use to any person seeking to acquire the spoken language.
>
> Another MacAuley of the same district, a much older man, whom we found in bed, and who bade us a hearty welcome, spoke Irish as one 'to the manner born' and is also a reader of the language. He repeated for us the parable of the Prodigal Son in English and Irish, and gave us other illustrations of his power over both languages. Lower down near Waterfoot, an elderly man named Mr McKissock recognised the strains of the Gaelic League pipes, and came forth to welcome us. He has a literary knowledge of Irish, is an ex-teacher and has taught Irish to several generations of students. He is still an ardent lover of the language, and would be glad to teach it to willing students. His neighbour is a worthy

shoemaker named McLernon who has also a fair knowledge of spoken Irish. He was glad to hear that an effort is being made to restore the old tongue and undertook that his family (one of whom is a monitress at Waterfoot National School) should take up the study of Irish and also intimated that he himself should at least recover the power of saying his prayers in Irish.

At Waterfoot we called on Mr James MacAuley, of the Post Office, a brother of Henry's who acquired a knowledge of written Irish from Mr McKissock. He would like to see the Irish language restored but was afraid the rising generation at Waterfoot would hardly take the matter up. At Waterfoot a very pleasing incident occurred. A Scottish fisherman, hearing the pipes, approached us and asked Mr Martin's leave to play upon them. This was readily accorded and the Scottish man handled his national instrument with consummate skill. But, what was of more interest, he proved to be a Gaelic-speaking highlander and appeared to be even more delighted to find that we could converse together without calling in the aid of Saxon speech.

At Waterfoot also, we were accosted by a Munster pedlar with a familiar 'Go mbeannaidh Dia dhaoibh' and an offer to sing us a gaelic song, which just then we had not time to listen to. We next proceeded to Cushendall where we were joined by a noted gaelic 'Seanachie', James McNeachtin, who related many things to us in our native tongue. We called on Fr Convery, PP who received us kindly and offered encouragement to the future of the movement, saying that when classes are started he will himself become a student.

Before leaving Cushendall, a piper played a number of selections and as a number of people collected on the bridge, a member of the league took occasion to explain our aims and objects. We found the people everywhere favourable to our movement and we returned to Parkmore in the evening having, as we believed, done a good day's work for Ireland.

The second document on the state of Irish in the Glens was written by Joseph Duffy, the principal of Knocknacarry National School, in July 1900.

'Master Duffy' (1840–1905) was a native of Co. Mayo and had a good knowledge of the language himself. In his report, entitled 'Reflections on the state of the Irish Language in the Glens of Antrim in 1900', the author ascribes the dramatic decline of Irish in the district in the nineteenth century to two factors: the building of the Glendun Viaduct (1835), which introduced English-speaking workers into the area, and the hostile attitude of the Catholic clergy to Gaelic following the establishment of Irish medium 'Bible schools' in the district by the General Assembly of the Presbyterian Church in the late 1830s. Duffy neatly summed up the dilemma facing the local people at the time: 'When Irish schools and teaching were denounced by the priests, the great majority looked upon it almost as a sin to speak Irish. Hence English – if at all known – became the conversational language.'

Duffy estimated that in 1875 around 20 per cent 'could converse freely in Gaelic' but by 1900, only five per cent could 'with some difficulty' understand Irish while a mere three per cent could speak it. Morning and night prayers, he noted sadly, were no longer repeated *as Gaeilge*. He concluded: 'Virtually the vernacular no longer exists here as a living language. It is gone, I fear, forever.' If the language was to be revived in the Glens, he felt, it would require the support of the clergy and the gentry: 'Nothing can rescue it from extinction except the work of restoration is set about at the right end. If the clergy and gentry go into the work with a will, there is still some hope of its revival; otherwise, it can never return as the speech of the Glens.'

Interestingly, the foundation of Feis na nGleann in June 1904 was partly a response to Joseph Duffy's timely warning. The Feis committee witnessed the involvement of a cross-section of the gentry of North Antrim including notably Miss Rose Young of Galgorm Castle, Miss Margaret Dobbs of Portnagolan, Miss Ada McNeill of Cushendun and Sir Roger Casement, as well as local clergy. The involvement of Miss Young (Róis Ní Ógáin), a liberal Unionist and Ronald McNeill, a British Conservative M.P. and strong Unionist, showed that the preservation of the Irish language in the Glens at that time was regarded as an issue that transcended creed and politics.

Joseph Duffy's comments on the decline of Irish were drafted in pencil in an exercise book in July 1900 – four years before Feis na nGleann was founded. Joseph Duffy became joint treasurer of the first Feis Committee in 1904. These are his thoughts, written during the month of July:

12 July 1900
Strenuous, and I must say, noble and patriotic efforts are being made by a few zealous Irishmen to re-establish the tongue of the Gael as a living spoken language. That it should be permitted to utterly perish would be a national loss and a great misfortune. So far as I can learn, it is a cultured language, abounding in elegance of expression, richness of utterance, and remarkably well adapted to all practical purposes of intercourse. It has lived for many centuries and has survived ancient languages of more recent birth. Coming down from the earliest ages, it is no conglomerate, but remains as pure and unadulterated as it was in the days of St Columba.

14 July 1900
Up to the beginning of the Nineteenth Century, Irish, exclusively almost, was the commercial and the domestic language of the Glens. During the Seventeenth and Eighteenth Centuries English, of course, was used by government officials and those of necessity were forced to acquire a knowledge of Gaelic, and more especially so if they became residents.

English became fashionable in Glendun at the building of the viaduct ('Big Bridge') about the year 1835. This building brought in skilled workmen who spoke nothing but English. The National schools were called into being about the same time; and the teaching was carried out in English alone. Hence it was that the old tongue was despised, looked upon as a sign of ignorance, and was not attempted by the young people who let them know it or not, did all their conversation in English.

15 July 1900
One of the most powerful agents in the suppression of the vernacular was the opposition of the R.C. Clergy during the years 1835–40 when instruction in Irish was substantially encouraged by the General Assembly of the Presbyterian

Church. Under the patronage of the Assembly schools were started, teachers paid and prizes awarded to scholars, with a view of qualifying the peasantry to read the Scriptures, i.e. in Gaelic. This means of proselytism amongst a R.C. people was open and clear. The Priests denounced the schools in strong language, pointing out the insidious snares for the undermining of the faith. The Assembly cared nothing for the language.

Presbyterianism and its spread were their only objects. Thus the death blow came. It was looked upon as a sin to say a word in Gaelic if one could at all avoid it.

In the year 1875 about 20 per cent – mostly advanced in years – could converse freely in Gaelic, but as to book knowledge of the subject, they had none. In the present year (1900) there may be about 5 per cent of the population, who could with some difficulty partly understand Gaelic, and about 3 per cent who might venture to speak in it. Morning and Night Prayers are no longer repeated in Irish. Virtually the vernacular no longer exists here as a living language. It is gone I fear, never to return.

If this ancient form of speech is to be revived, the movement must commence, where all improvements are to be looked for, from the higher social ranks, from the clergy and from the gentry. Except this be accomplished, the prospect for the revival and the extension of Gaelic is not of the brightest character.

21 July 1900
We may well deplore the decadence of our ancient tongue, but there is little use in crying over spilt milk. There are still amongst us a solitary few who would willingly aid in the work of restoration. Why not invite and encourage them in the start of the good work and something of a practical and sustaining nature may yet be done?

The Feis Cheoil has achieved something in the preservation of ancient music; and the Feis Uladh promises well for the dissemination of Gaelic book knowledge, including writing, oratory and poetry. To these and kindred societies we heartily wish success.

Three causes have operated almost simultaneously in the decadence of the vernacular in the Glens. These are, the introduction of the National Schools, the attempts to proselytism through the medium of the Irish language by the General Assembly of the Presbyterian Church, and the building of the Glendun Viaduct ('Big Bridge'). The Assembly established Irish Schools for the purpose of teaching to read, so as to understand the Scriptures. The Irish schools were coequal with those of the National Board, but their span of existence was very limited. The ulterior view of the Assembly was quite apparent. When Irish schools and teaching were denounced by the Priests, the great majority looked upon it almost as a sin to speak Irish. Hence English – if at all known – became the conversational language.

25 July 1900
So far as I can learn, previous to the establishment of the National School system, there were some schools of a temporary nature kept open mostly during the winter months, in which the rudiments of English were clumsily taught. Semi-hedge in type and management, these schools aimed at imparting instruction in reading, spelling, writing and a little arithmetic. Spelling held the foremost place

The Glendun Viaduct, opened in 1839

in the programme, and an English dictionary (Walker's) was an essential textbook, and the pupil was forced to plod his way, time after time, in a language foreign to him (English), just as well as he might, from A to Z. The teacher considered it ungraceful and undignified to use Gaelic in elucidating any school subject, and the old tongue was looked upon – if at any time used by a pupil – as a sign of deplorable ignorance.

The building of the Viaduct was commenced about 1834. Skilled workmen were employed in its construction, and these were English men, who understood no Gaelic. The natives in the immediate neighbourhood used their best efforts to acquire a knowledge of the strange language, so as to come on a level socially with the strange men who were much better dressed and more sumptuously fed. Hence Gaelic became inelegant and unfashionable. Disused in every quarter, it was doomed to perish.

In 1875 about 20 per cent of the population – all advanced in years – understood, and could hold conversation in Gaelic; now in 1900 about 5 per cent could partly understand it, and about 3 per cent might attempt to speak it.

We may well mourn its fate. Nothing can rescue it from extinction, except the work or restoration is set about at the right end. If the clergy and the gentry go into the work with a will, there is still some hope of its revival; otherwise, it never can return as the speech of the Glens.

Roger Casement's first involvement in the language revival in the Glens is chronicled in a remarkable letter from Mrs Annie McGavock of Glenarm to her brother, Professor Eoin MacNeill, in Dublin in March 1904. Mrs McGavock, who ran the MacNeill family bakery in Glenarm, described Casement's dramatic appearance at a meeting in Cushendall to discuss arrangements for the first Glens Feis. The letter is dated 8 March 1904 and is of considerable historical significance. The 'Mr Clarke' referred to was John Clarke of Glenarm, or 'Benmore'. The meeting inspired Sir Roger to compose his best known poem on the decline of the Irish language, 'The speech of our sires': 'It is gone from hill and glen – The strong speech of our sires.'

The letter from Mrs McGavock to Eoin MacNeill (8 March 1904) reads as follows.

> Mr [John] Clarke told me that at the meeting on Sunday week in Cushendall he said a few words about the movement and when he had finished a tall, soldierly looking man came over to him and said: 'I agree heartily with all you have said; these have just been my own thoughts for years' Mr Clarke thought no more of the incident but on Friday last he got a letter from the gentleman telling him he had heard of the little manuscript paper that had been started and enclosing a couple of verses on the Irish language for the March number. He is greatly interested in the Feis, hopes he will be here at the time, but as he is going to South Africa soon, he fears he may have to leave before 30 June. He subscribes £5. Mr Clarke says that he can hardly believe that a Casement of Ballycastle (they were considered tyrants in the old days) could hold such views.

Francis Joseph Bigger, the Belfast solicitor, historian and Gaelic Leaguer (1863–1926) was one of the most influential figures in the campaign to preserve the language in the Glens and Rathlin Island after 1904. In November 1906 he was instrumental in an effort by the Gaelic League to 'preserve and encourage the use of the Irish language' on Rathlin, where it was still spoken. To this end, Bigger proposed to send an instructor to the island. This notice was issued by Bigger from his Belfast residence, 'Ard Righ' in November 1906:

> A number of representative Members of the Conradh na Gaedhilge are most anxious to preserve and encourage the use of the Irish language, which is largely spoken on the island of Rathlin, off the coast of Antrim. With this object in view, it is proposed to send a Gaelic Instructor to the island, a warm welcome having been promised for him on behalf of the islanders.
> The Coiste Gnótha has already been approached for pecuniary assistance, and the whole scheme will be under the direction and approval of the Dáil Uladh. Liberal promises of support from individuals have already been received. It is desired to have the list of subscribers as large as possible before a public appeal be made in the press.
> Subscriptions may be sent to the Honorary Treasurer for this fund.

Another Protestant nationalist deeply committed to the Gaelic Revival in the Glens and Rathlin was Bigger's friend, Roger Casement (1864–1916), who attended the first Glens Feis at Glenariff in 1904. Following a visit to the island around 1906 Casement recorded the details of its Irish-speaking population in a letter to a friend:

> The population of Rathlin, by the way, was taken by our teacher, Mr Green. He

Gaelic League gathering at the Chapel on Rathlin Island in 1904 (the man standing on the bank with outstretched arms is Sean Greene of Ballycastle)

found it (above two years of age) to be 325 persons. Of these 218 were Irish speaking and 107 spoke English only, having no Irish at all, but of these 107 English speakers, 35 belonged to the lighthouses, public works, etc. – all imported people for special work – so that of the island population itself – native born – only 72 had no Irish. Of these 218 who spoke Irish only 10 were non-native born – Irish from other parts of Ireland. So there is a good big residuum of Irish speaking still in Rathlin to keep alive.

In February 1907, Dr Beatty, the Inspector of Schools on the Ballymena Circuit, noted the introduction of Irish as a subject in a number of schools in the Glens:

> Irish is taught in a large number of schools; mathematics, with fair results, in somewhat less than 30; French in three, to a small number of pupils.

Mr Heron (School Inspector) writes:

> About half-a-dozen schools in the district have taken up mathematics as an extra subject with success. About the same number in the neighbourhood of the Glens of Antrim have taken up Irish, and have been inspected by Mr Manager. One teacher taught mathematics with fair success. Irish is taught in a few schools in the Londonderry uplands, under the inspection of Mr Manager.

One consequence of the interest of both Bigger and Casement in the prevalence of Irish on Rathlin was the establishment of St Malachy's College of Irish on the island in 1913. During 1914–18 it was not possible to hold the annual Summer College on Rathlin owing to wartime restrictions. Instead the classes were held in Ballycastle. The success of the college, known as St Malachy's College of Irish, was reported in the *Irish News* in July 1918 as follows:

> A meeting of the Coiste Malachi was held last week in the Irish College, Bank Street, Belfast. The secretary and registrar of the Summer College submitted a report on the work of the past year, of which the following is a brief summary: The fifth session of St Malachy's College of Irish began on July 1, 1918, and ended on August 31.
>
> The session was divided into two four-week terms. There were no classes held on Rathlin owing to war restrictions. At Ballycastle the work was continued as usual. The attendance was excellent and beat all previous records.
>
> Included in the large number of students enrolled were University graduates and undergraduates, Gaelic League teachers and King's scholars. The College was under the charge of Michael Maguigan. The assistant teachers were Tomas Ó Suilleabhain, Miss Rosin Ní Dhochartaigh, Miss Nora Grange, and Miss Cait Ní Bhriain, BA.
>
> The thanks of the Coiste Malachi are due in a special manner to Very Rev. E. Murphy PP, VF, for his very deep interest in the classes at Ballycastle and for the facilities afforded there, and to Rev A McKinley PP Rathlin; and Rev. Professor Clenaghan, BA, BD, BCL, Principal of Rathlin College, to whose zeal, ability and energy the marked success of the College is chiefly due.

The Irish language movement in North Antrim was greatly disrupted by the 'Troubles' of 1919–22. During the Truce of 1921, however, an Aeridheacht was held in Glenarm. The following report appeared in the *Irish News*:

> The Gaelic day at Glenarm gives every promise of being most successful, given good weather. An amount of enthusiasm so necessary to make a success has been thrown into the work. A large number of entries have been secured for the field sports, and keen contests are expected in the notable events. The five-a-side hurling has brought in a number of Glens teams; exciting contests are expected. The football struggle gives promise of good play. St Mary's Larne; Eire Ogs, Glenarm, and the Pearse Club, Cushendall, have entered. Gaelic dancing and singing, recitations and dialogue in Gaelic, will prove very interesting features of the day. Competitions in Glens history and art have induced not a few scholars to enter. Another feature which will enliven and brighten the proceedings will be the attendance of a number of rare pipers from the Ballycastle Pipe Band, travelling specially for the day. Felix Devlin, GAA, Belfast, will act as official starter and handicapper, assisted by a number of capable officers from local clubs. All arrangements are complete. The admission to grounds is 1s. Surplus funds go to help the Irish White Cross. Tournament starts sharp at O'Neill grounds 2 o'clock.

The Irish dialect spoken in the Glens and Rathlin bore striking linguistic similarities to the Scots Gaelic (pronounced 'Gallic') of the Western Isles. The historic ties between the Glens and Gaelic Scotland were symbolised at the 1946 Feis in Glenariff when the oration was delivered by Rev. J. MacKechnie, a

Preparing the ground on the eve of the first feis, 1904: Roger Casement, Margaret Dobbs, Ada McNeill, Annie McGavock, Rose Young, John ('Benmore') Clarke, Francis J. Bigger, Pádraic Mac Cormaic, Harry Scally, Andy Dooey, Joseph Duffy, Denis Maginnis, Stephen Clarke, Rev. Tom Toal, Rev. McGrattan

minister of the Church of Scotland and Director of the School of Scottish Studies in Glasgow. The theme of Rev. MacKechnie's address was the state of Gaelic at the end of the Second World War (as reported in the *Ballymena Observer*, 5 July 1946):

> The time has now happily passed when the very mention of the word 'Gaelic' led people to think at once of revolutions, riots, disputes and political and religious wranglings. The eyes of those people of narrow outlook have been turned to the wider world beyond the bounds of Britain and Ireland, and they have seen Gaelic in its true place and perspective. It is the language which has preserved and, we firmly believe will preserve, all that is best in the culture and civilisation of the Celts.
>
> Gaelic today is on the verge of a great awakening. The follies and cruelties of the past are past, and may well be forgotten. The future lies before the Gaelic speakers, and the names of the Gaels found among all the great nations of the world testify to the fact that the Gaelic people are still the bearers of culture and civilisation to all nations everywhere …
>
> Scotland and Ireland have many things in common in connection with Gaelic, but most important it is that once again the fellowship of letters, of music and of other precious things that once existed between the two lands shall be renewed.

A vote of thanks to Rev. MacKechnie was proposed by Rev. T. Toal, PP,

Carnlough and seconded by Miss Margaret Dobbs, Portnagolan.

The Irish language declined dramatically in the Glens from the 1920s onwards. A few native speakers remained, however. The last speaker of Antrim Gaelic was Seamus Bhriain Mac Amhlaigh ('Big Jim' McAuley), who died in February 1983. The late Jack McCann, the well-known Ballymena solicitor, paid this tribute to him in the *Irish News*:

> As the French fairies were leaving Glenariffe for the last time they met a great procession of white lights coming down from Ballymena. When they looked back the lights had turned red.
>
> Not a fairy tale.
>
> What has passed in the night was the funeral cortege of the man on whose lips the fairies had lived for so long. To us who sadly have not the Irish he was Jim McAuley, but to the wee folk he was Seamus Bhriain Mac Amhlaigh, last native Irish speaker in the Glens of Antrim who died on February 25th 1983.
>
> His tale of a troop of fairies all astride benweeds riding off to France every night, 'Big Jim' learned from his father, Briain Mac Amhlaigh, who gave Glenarm's Eoin MacNeill, founder of the Gaelic League, his first lesson in Irish.
>
> Thanks be that another great Glensman, and collector of folk tales, Hamilton Delargy, beat the reaper to Brian's door, for the old man is nigh 45 years dead.
>
> We, in our time, are indebted to Alex McMullan of Glenariffe for having recorded Big Jim's re-telling of his father's stories; of stilkin the grugach, of the pieste who carried off a baby boy to its nest near Killarney, of an enchanted town at Coill Bheag, of the man who shod the devil's horse for a bottomless hat of gold, and so on.
>
> The old tongue is hushed now in a glen where 150 years ago numberless legendary and fabulous tales and songs were recited and sung in the Irish round the fire and where 'many neither spoke nor understood English but all spoke the Irish'.
>
> The last Irish storyteller in the Glens is stilled. For some, a statistic. For us, a reminder that we scarce paused in our pursuit of pence to mark the passing of a centuries-old oral tradition, or long enough to realise that the man laid to rest was the last of a people from whom we got our family names, the names of our townlands and of every field that's in them.
>
> I have no words to properly express my sense of loss for I have not the tongue. Let this translation from the Irish say it for me: 'What shall we do for timber? The last of the woods is down …'

People like Casement, Bigger, M. Dobbs, R. Young, Ada McNeill and others saw in the Feis another vehicle for the advancement of the language. It was another opportunity to show people that without a living language, and especially a spoken language, their culture and history had no meaning. This today remains a principal aim of Feis na nGleann.

Language competitions were an important element in the first Feis. In this and in all the early Feiseanna there were junior and senior competitions in conversation, storytelling and recitation. Prizes usually consisted of books. There were also at times competitions for best short story in Irish, best poem in Irish, best play in Irish, best list of placenames with meanings, etc.; some of the prizes were presented by donors and others were given by the Feis committee.

When the Feis was revived in 1928, scholarships to the Donegal Gaeltacht were introduced. Several colleges had been opened during the 1920s. During the 1950s and 1960s up to 20 scholarships were awarded each year. The Feis funded most of the scholarships, but others came from Comhaltas Uladh (the Ulster Section of the Gaelic League) and donors such as the *Irish News* and the GAA When the late Miss Dobbs was alive, she gave a scholarship each year out of her own money.

In May 1971, buses taking children to the literary and history competitions in Ballymena came under attack in Harryville. In the interests of safety it was decided to suspend these competitions indefinitely and scholarships were allotted to schools that had traditionally sent entries. This continued until single-day competitions were renewed in 1992 at the Feis in Carey, where they have been held each year since. Over the years, the number of applicants for Gaeltacht scholarships had decreased, and the Feis committee have also given grants for intensive A-level Easter courses and to the Tír-na-nÓg Irish Summer School for beginners which is based in Garron Tower and run by Comhaltas Uladh. Fewer secondary school children are following courses in Irish, due mainly to the proliferation of other subjects in the curriculum. The cost of a three-week stay in the Gaeltacht has also increased considerably, so that grants towards the cost rather than full scholarships are now awarded. It should be noted that local branches of the Gaelic League also give grants to students attending Gaeltacht colleges, and several local GAA clubs have done the same.

History competitions at the first Feis involved written work only. At present the competitions cover both oral and written history and are held along with the language competitions.

Early in 1988 a meeting was held in Cushendall under the auspices of Feis na nGleann to consider how best to continue promoting Irish as a spoken language in North Antrim. The meeting was the brainchild of Fr John Moley, then Parish Priest of the Braid and a member of the Feis Committee. It was addressed by Caoimhin Patton and Seán de Búrca from Teach Comber in Claudy, Co. Derry, where very successful Irish classes were and still are being held. They stressed that intensive classes over a relatively short period were much more effective than one-evening-a-week classes over longer periods. Later that year classes were started in Dunloy, inspired mainly by Michael Breslin who had attended the meeting in Cushendall. Classes lasting three hours were held on three evenings a week from September to Easter. They were an immediate success, attracting students, mainly adults, from a wide area and from across the community.

After two years four classes were necessary, and in 1990 it was decided to start a naíscoil for pre-school children. Several years later a bunscoil (primary school) was also started and both operated in the Teach Cheoil and in an attached mobile in the GAA grounds. The facility suffered a serious setback in 1998 when it was

A group of Irish Language students in Donegal

attacked by arsonists. The damage was repaired and the schools continued for two more years. They are no longer functioning, but some students who had started there now continue at an all-Irish bunscoil in Maghera, Co. Derry.

In 1989, after the commencement of the classes in Dunloy, Comhchoiste na Gaeilge Aontroim Thuaidh was set up to try to co-ordinate the work of the different bodies involved in reviving the language. It included representatives of Feis na nGleann, *Comhaltas Ceoltóirí Éireann* and branches of Conradh na Gaeilge in Cushendall, Ballycastle and Dunloy as well as other interested individuals. An important achievement was the setting up of a video-conferencing link between the classes in Dunloy and Rathlin Island, whereby classes on Rathlin can follow the teaching in Dunloy by video link. This has been running successfully for the past four years and Rathlin now has its own branch of Conradh na Gaeilge.

In the mid-1990s also, a number of people from Ballycastle and Carey who had been attending classes in Dunloy decided to organise classes in Ballycastle. They formed a working body called Glór na Maoile, the name being selected as a result of winning a Glór na nGael competition. This very active body, which is part of Comhchoiste na Gaeilge, still runs classes including an intensive course each February and a week-long summer school in Carey that attracts up to 100 participants.

A naíscoil and a bunscoil now also operate in Ballycastle. They were set up and organised by a body called Pobal an Chaistil which is separate from and unconnected with Glór na Maoile. An attempt by some parents associated with the Ballycastle schools to start a naíscoil in the Middle Glens has so far failed because planning permission to erect a mobile on a proposed site has been refused. Irish classes have now started in the Glenariff GAA clubrooms.

For most of the 1990s the Comhchoiste received funding from bodies such as the Ultach Trust and the Community Relations Council, which allowed the appointment of a Development Officer. This position has been held in turn by Pádraig Ó Coileáin, Donncha Ó Broin and Deaglan Ó Doibhlin. The position is vacant at present.

In 1992 the Comhchoiste organised the first Éigse na nGlinntí. This was a high-profile exercise opened in Dunloy on Thursday 14 May by John Wilson, the Minister for Education and Tánaiste in the Fianna Fáil government. The Éigse moved to Loughgiel on the Saturday and to Glenariff on Sunday 17 May, where a plaque was unveiled at the birthplace of the writer Seán Mac Maoláin. Speakers included Dr Brendan Ó Doibhlin from Maynooth and Dr Micheline Kearney Walsh from U.C.D.

The 1993 Éigse was in Glenariff and was opened by Éamonn Ó Cuiv, Minister for the Gaeltacht and grandson of Éamonn de Valera. In 1993 a plaque was erected in Dunloy in memory of Aindreas Ó Dubhaigh and in 1994 a plaque was erected at the birthplace of Professor James Hamilton Delargy in Cushendall. His daughter, Mrs Catriona Miles, carried out the unveiling. The 1995 Éigse was held in conjunction with the Co. Antrim Fleadh Cheoil in Cushendall. Éigse events were held in a marquee in the garden of the house where Dr James McDonnell was born in 1763. Jean Kennedy Smith, United States Ambassador to Ireland, unveiled a plaque commemorating his life; Janet Harbinson and harpers from the Belfast Harp Orchestra gave a recital. Dr McDonnell had been responsible for the original Belfast Harp Festival of 1792 as a result of which Edward Bunting was to collect and publish three volumes of old Irish tunes, many of which would otherwise have been lost.

The Éigse each year included a trip to places of historical interest. The 1998 trip was to Antrim town, where a huge crowd had gathered for a re-enactment of the Battle of Antrim in 1798. It was a truly cross-community spectacle in which politics were forgotten. The 'rebels' arrived in Antrim carrying pikes, firing muskets and beating drums, some of which bore the names of local orange lodges. Each year also the Éigse concluded on the Sunday with an ecumenical service in Irish. Regular Irish-speaking participants included Dr Bill Boyd, retired Presbyterian Minister, Dr Donald Caird, former Church of Ireland Archbishop of Dublin, and Fr Eddie Coyle, PP Culfeightrim, and a native speaker from Donegal.

During the early and mid 1990s there was also an October weekend in Kilmore House, Glenariff, consisting mainly of intensive language courses. The autumn weekend in 1997 was in Ballintoy and featured visitors from Cairdeas Chloich Cheann Fhaola in Donegal. This very useful contact has been maintained and is being actively developed. At the 2001 Éigse in Dunloy a book containing a collection of the writings of Aindreas Ó Dubhaigh (Andy Dooey) was launched. Most recent Éigsí have been in Ballycastle, Rathlin Island and Ballintoy.

Monthly get-togethers for Irish speakers were at least until recently taking place in both Cushendall and Waterfoot. The Glens Choir which has a repertoire of hymns in Irish was chosen to sing in Aifreann Feirste which was performed for the first time in St Mary's Chapel, Belfast on Sunday 18 May 2003. Belfast musician, Patrick Davey, composed the music for the Mass and a special orchestra of classical and traditional musicians was assembled. Éamonn Ó Faogáin as a soloist joined the Glens Choir for what was a truly historic occasion. Aifreann Feirste, with the Glens Choir, was later celebrated in the Pro-Cathedral in Dublin and live on R.T.E. 1 on St Patrick's Day 2004.

An Bealach Romhainn
Gan amhras sí an aidhm is deacra a bhaint amach agus a bhfuil an obair is treise de dhíth air ná an Ghaeilge a chaomhnú mar theanga bheo. Tá litríocht saibhir ilchineálach i nGaeilge faoi láthair ach ní hionann an focal balbh ar leathanach lámhscríbhinne agus an focal beo i mbéil na ndaoine.

Without a doubt the most difficult aim to achieve and the one requiring the greatest effort is the preservation of Irish as a spoken language. There is today a vibrant and varied literature in Irish, but the dead word on the page of a manuscript is no substitute for the living word on the lips of the people.

Traditional Gaeltacht areas are contracting due to the influence of English-language media and the proliferation of holiday homes whose owners are almost exclusively English-speaking. When planning permission was granted for these developments, no consideration seems to have been given to the disastrous effect it would have on the last remnants of an ancient culture. Gaeltacht areas are now largely English-speaking due to the sheer numbers of imported Béarlóirí.

Each branch of *Comhaltas Ceoltóirí* plays a small part by using Irish names of tunes where possible and by incorporating Irish phrases in the general business. Each branch appoints a Treoirí na Gaeilge to help promote the language. GAA and camogie clubs are also charged with promoting the use of Irish by using the Irish form of names etc., but progress beyond this point is slow. Better co-ordination between the different organisations might prove to be worthwhile.

The most promising development is the growth of the Gaelscoileanna – both naíscoileanna and bunscoileanna and, more recently, meánscoileanna (secondary schools). It is a proven fact that pupils from these schools continue to speak Irish among themselves long after leaving the all-Irish environment. As numbers increase, better use of the Fáinne would identify these students to each other and to anyone else willing to speak Irish. It has the potential to transform the restoration of Irish as a spoken language.

The Feis committee will endeavour to follow in the footsteps of those who have worked hard over the years to protect and preserve the most important aspect of our native culture – the living language. That is what sets us apart as a nation. In this duty we must not fail.

Sé bunú na nGaelscoileanna an fhorbairt a bhfuil an gealladh is mó faoi i láthair na huaire, idir naíscoileanna, bunscoileanna agus, ar na mallaibh, meánscoileanna. Is deimhin go leanann daltaí ó na scoileanna seo ar an Ghaeilge a labhairt eatarthu féin i bhfad tar éis dóibh an chomarsanacht lán-Ghaelach a fhágáil. Do réir mar a théann na huimhreacha i méid, thiocfaí úsáid níos fearr a bhaint as an Fháinne chun go gcuirfeadh na daltaí iad féin in aithne dá chéile agus do dhuine ar bith eile a mbeadh toilteanach an Ghaeilge a labhairt. Tá sé ar a chumas thar aon tionscadal eile an Ghaeilge a thabhairt ar ais mar theanga bheo.

Tá sé leagtha amach ag Coiste na Feise leanstan ar lorg na ndaoine a d'oibrigh go dícheallach i rith na mblianta chun an ghné is tábhachtaí den ár gcultúr dúchasach a choiméad agus a chaomhnú – an teanga bheo. Is mar sin a aithneofar muid mar náisiún. Níl sé ceadaithe faillí a dhéanamh sa dualgas seo.

Among those with roots in the Glens is the Auxiliary Bishop of Down and Connor, Dr Donal McKeown. This is an extract from his address to mark the centenary of Feis na nGleann in June 2004:

Cuirim fáilte romhaibh uilig chun an aifreann seo tráthnóna inniu agus sinne cruinnithe ins an áit iontach seo, ag bun banríon na naoi Gleann – no na nGlinntí, mar a deirtear anseo is ansiúd. Ceiliúraimid an t-aifreann seo mar chuid dena ceiliúraithe ar son céad blain i stair Feis na nGleann. Bhí sport agus craic agaibh an deireadh seachtaine seo chaite agus bhí dinnéar mor agaibh cúpla mí o shin. Anois tugtar cuireadh theacht thart ar bhord an Dé a chruthaigh sinne agus an áit iontach seo, an tobar domhan óna thagann ceol agus sport agus cultúr an chinne daonna. You are very welcome here tonight whatever cultural or religious tradition you come from and whatever your own role may have been in the culture of this part of our island.

Ní as an cheanntar seo mé – ach ní stráinséar anseo mé uch oiread! Seo an áit mar a rugadh agus a tógadh mo mháthair mhór. Baisteadh an seisear a bhí sa teaghlach sin ins an sean-theach an phobail a bhí ins an reilig in aice linn agus a raibh ainm Naomh Cilian air. Agus chaitheamar ár laethanta saoire ar fad ins an Ghleann – suas go dtí go raibh me aosta go leor chun mí gach samhradh a chaitheadh sa Ghaeltacht. Agus ansin nuair a bhí me ar scoil i gColáiste Mhic Naosa, ghlacamar páirt gach blain i gcomórtais Feis na nGleann – agallaimh, scéalaíocht agus dánta. Mar gheall ar sin, tá mé an-sásta ar fad bheith anseo anocht chun obair na Feise a cheiliúradh agus chun onóir a thabhairt dona daoine a bhunaigh agus a chothaigh an Fheis ar feadh céad bliain.

Because of my long-standing family and educational connections both with the area and with the Irish language, I am happy and honoured to be here this evening for this part of your celebrations of one hundred years of Feis na nGleann. We give thanks for the work of people of all faith traditions and none who have worked here – and elsewhere – to enable communities to celebrate their cultural heritage in a way that enriches all and impoverishes none. Francis Joseph Bigger and his colleagues were not concerned with theological issues when they founded the first Glens Feis. They wanted to celebrate the great cultural tradition of the area – when my granny was born in 1890 – so that the lives of the people could be enriched.

Culture is not easy to define. It is not just about certain cultural expressions. Such expressions – like dance, music and stories – can be removed from their cultural context and exploited for financial rather than human purposes. The culture of the Glens involved language, dance, storytelling, customs, music – and of course hurling. But the culture of the Glens could not simply be reduced to these cultural expressions. The culture also involved neighbourliness, solidarity despite hard times, the importance of celebration and fun, a belief that this life was to be understood in the context of eternity, that there was the possibility of forgiveness for everybody, that life was a gift and love was a virtue. Such a culture is a pervasive atmosphere, how we do things round here, the things that we take as normal that others view differently – rather than an articulated system.

Thus this evening, we celebrate the cultural achievements of so many people here and the rich cultural life that they have been encouraged to appreciate – after long periods when they had been told that their practices were savage and uncultured, and that they should drop their silly old language. The whole history of the Gaelic League and the GAA sprang from a concern with getting communities off their knees and able to be proud of what they did and who they were. That contribution has helped many local communities throughout the country to take pride in themselves and in their unique contribution to the rich God-given tapestry that is the world.

That is why people of faith have always been keen to get into the heart of a culture, not to enslave but to enrich it. Certainly, there is always the temptation to use cultural features in a way that closes people off from others, rather than opening up horizons. There has been the assumption in some quarters that to be Irish and Catholic meant the same thing, and that was indeed the case since the time of the Reformation and the Plantation. Much of the great Irish poetry of the seventeenth and eighteenth centuries was inspired by religious imagery and a deep spirituality. Such an excessive link may have been understandable in a time of conflict. But it limited horizons. It meant that many from the Protestant community did not feel particularly welcome where there were expressions of Irish cultural identity. And there were Unionist leaders who despised Irishness. Thankfully, that has been changing – in the model of both the United Irishmen and people like Francis Joseph Bigger.

The celebrations have been about celebrating the great richness of gifts that people in the Glens have had over the generations. Cut off, as they were, from much of the island and with strong links to their Scottish brothers and sisters in the Highlands and the Islands, they developed their own unique version of the cultural traditions of these islands. Many people – teachers and local leaders – encouraged that and sought to hand it on to a new generation. We thank God for those gifts and for the giftedness and generosity of so many people. That great tradition of the Glens Feis was about a positive celebration of identity and achievement. It was not based on an assertion of victimhood or self-pity. It was an attempt to assert that we are somebody because we are not somebody else. It was a proud statement of what people were and are and an invitation to others to share in that culture. It was thus about encouraging confidence. And where people were confident about their own identity and achievements, they are to be open to others to share in that culture. It was thus about encouraging confidence.

This specific culture can be salt to the earth and light to the world. But it brings all the more light and flavour to life when it does not retreat behind barricades but rather moves out into the world, aware of its own strengths and keen to engage with others and with their culture. Here I hope that we will have increasing opportunities to do that in the context of the peace process and of the increasing number of people from other countries and cultures who are coming to live and work in this island of ours. Cultural diversity will enrich us all here, just as our Irish culture has travelled the world and has been received with great enthusiasm elsewhere.

14
GAEDHILG AONDROMA
Brian Mac Lochlainn

Cuirfidh sé iongantas ar chuid mhór daoine a fhoghlaim go bhfuil Gaedhilg Aondroma beó beathach indiu san aonmhadh linn fichead, agus ar a shon sin tá buidheachas tuillte do Alex Morrison as Inis Reachrann. Chum Alex lasair na teangan beó ón a óige ar an oileán sna 1920aí go ruige an lá indiu. Anns na 1930aí, chomh math, bhí sé ina fhear tagartha ag an Ollamh Nils Holmer, Sualainneach cáileamhail a rinn sár-obair sna Glinn, Reachraidh, Ceann-Tíre agus Árainn. Thóg agus d'fhoillsigh Holmer graiméar cuimsitheach de Ghaedhilg Reachrann (tugadh 'Gáidhlig' agus 'Gaedhilg' uirthi ar an oileán), ach cha d'fhuair sé ach iarsmaí ar thírmór na nGleann. Bhreac Holmer síos na fuaimeanna san fhoghraidheacht, agus mar sin de, tá fhios againn ar riaghalacha na guthaidheachta ar Reachraidh agus ar thírmór Aondroma. Ár ndóighe, thig linn cainnt Reachrann a dhearbhughadh le Alex.

Tá dóigheanna áirighthe le sonnrughadh ina rabh an t-oileán agus tírmór Aondroma mar an gcéadna lena chéile, ach eadar-dhealaighthe ó Thír Chonaill. Mar shampla: bhí an fhuaim 'v' in áit 'w' le 'bh' nó 'mh' agus iad a' dol le guta leathan. Tá sin le feiceáil sna h-ainmne áite mar 'Ballyvaddy' (Baile a' Mhadaidh in aice le Carnlach). Bhí an guta 'u' ní b'fhuide chun tosaigh sa bhéal mar a tá sa Gháidhlig Albannaigh (dálta 'p<u>u</u>t' sa Bhéarla chaighdeánaighthe), seachas mar a tá i dTír Chonaill, agus ó thaoibh na bhfocal mar 'deas', 'seas', 'easán', srl. bhí an guta mar 'e' goirid (dálta 'dr<u>e</u>ss' sa Bhéarla) seachas 'a' goirid. Cleachtadh 'có?' seachas 'cé?' anns an dá áit, agus 'cha' in áit 'ní' le briathar a dhéanamh diúltach.

Ach ar dhóigheannaí eile bhí siad eadar-dhealaighthe óna chéile; mar shampla, dubhradh 'char chuir mé', 'ar chuir mé?' srl. ar tírmór, ach 'cha do chuir mé', 'an do chuir mé?' ar an oileán. Dar leis go rabh 'bhí' agus 'bhá', an dá chuid, ann ar tírmór mar aimsir chaithte (saoilim 'bhá' ma gcuairt ar Bhaile a' Chaisteil), ach 'bhá' amháin a cleachtadh ar Reachraidh, maille ri 'é', 'í' agus 'iad' mar tuiseal ainmneach. Ar Reachraidh bhéadh an uimhir iolra a' criochnughadh in '-an' (dálta na h-Alban) an áit a mbéadh 'í' nó '-aí' ann ar tírmór.

Ó thaoibh struchtur na gramadaighe de, bhí teangaidh Reachrann go minic ní ba chosamhla le cainnt na h-Alban, ach bhí an blas cosamhail le blas na nGleann. Chuaidh a' ghramadach sna Glinn le tírmór na h-Éireann. Chan Gáidhlig Albanach amach is amach a bhí ann i Reachraidh. Bhí gnéithe na gramadaighe 'Éireannach', mar shampla 'cuidigh' seachas 'cuidich' mar a bhíos de ghnáthach in Albain, ach b'amhlaidh sin in Íle, Ceann Tíre, Árainn agus Gigha (féach *The Gaelic of Islay: A Comparative Study* le Seumas Grannd).

Rinn Alex cuid mhór foclóireachta a thaithmheadadh do Sgoil Eólais na hAlbann i 1975, agus tamall ina dhéidh, thug sé ceithre chéad ainmne áite Gaedhilge domh fhéin. Ainmne Gaedhilg Reachrann a bhí ionnta ar fad, ach amháin corr-cheann Bhéarla, agus is bealach eile sin isteach sa Ghaedhilg áiteamhail, staidéar a dhéanamh ortha. Ba ainmne iad, ar a' chuid a ba mhó, nar sgríobhadh síos riamh roimhe agus nach rabh ar léarsgáil ar bith. Thug mé anonn iad don Ulster Place Names Society, agus foillsiughadh iad san iris aca, 'Ainm' (imleabhar IV, 1990). Bhí ainm ag Alex fiú ar ghrinneall na fairrge eadar tírmór agus an t-oileán — 'Coiscéim Bhairr'. Dar leis go dearn an Naomh Barr céim anonn annseo ar a bhealach as Corcaigh (na Mumhan) go ruige na h-Innse Gall.

Ba chainnteóir dúthchais duine eile a casadh orm uair nó dhá, ná Séamus Mór Mac Amhlaigh ('Big Jim') a chaochail, ar an droch-uair, i 1983 agus a bhí ina chomhnaidhe ar a' Chluain Riabhaigh i nGleann Airimh. Ba é an cainnteóir dúthchais deireannach sna Glinn Séamus Mór. Bhí mé ró-mhall a' cur aithne air agus mar sin de, char thóg mé mórán uaidh, ach is cuimhin liom go rabh sé go fíochmhar cosantach do na h-ainmne áite, go h-áirighthe 'Allt na Gamhna', easán a dubhairt sé, a bhí na coimhthighigh ag iarraidh 'The Grey Mare's Tail' a thabhairt air. Is easán beag é seo, feiceálach ó lár a' ghleanna ach chan chomh mór le Easán na Lárach thuas ag bárr a' ghleanna.

Bhí athair Shéamuis Mhóir cliúiteach mar seanchaidhe. Rinn sé taithmhead den sgéal as a' Bhíobla, 'An Mac Straoidheamhail' nuair nach rabh de ghléas ortha ach ceiríní bunadhasacha. Tá na ceiríní ann go fóill ag Ollsgoil na Banríoghna ach tá an inbhe go dona. Ina theannta sin tá siad i riocht digiteach anois mar dlúth-dioscanna i Leabharlainn an Acadaimh Ríoga, Baile Atha Cliath.

Tá an t-eólas is cruinne ar Ghaedhilg thírmór Aondroma le fagháil anns na 'breac-leabharthaí' a d'fhág an t-Ollamh Delargy, agus tá sgrúdadh agus anailís ortha foillsiughthe ag an Ollamh Seosamh Watson (féach *Zeitschrift fur Celtische Philologie*, 1984). Rugadh Delargy sna Glinn ach ghluais sé go h-óg go deisceart na tíre agus ar an droch-uair d'fhoghlaim sé Gaedhilg na Mumhan in áit Gaedhilg Uladh. Tháinig sé arais a thógáil Gaedhilg na nGleann ach gan dian-oileamhaint aige san fhoghraidheacht. Dar leis go bhfuil a' chuid is mó dar thóg sé a' teacht ó Bharney Mac Amhlaigh.

Sgríobhthar ainm athair Shéamuis Mhóir ag na sgoiléaraí i gcomhnuidhe mar 'Barney Bhriain', ach thug muinntear na h-áite 'The Bhréin' ar a' mhac sa Bhéarla, mar ainm comharsanachta, agus tá mé a' creidsinn go bhfuil sin a' taispeáint a' ghinidigh a bhí ar an ainm 'Brian' sa cheanntar (ar nós Niall/Néill).

Aistidheach go leór, tá an bóthar fhéin a ruitheas suas an gleann luaidhte san fhoclóir (faoin fhocal 'boillscean') ag an Duinníneach mar 'An Bóthar Boillsceannach' — i bhfad níos cruinne na an 'Glen Road' mar a tá air anois.

Fuair an t-Urramach Ó Duinnín a chuid eólais ar Ghaedhilg Aondroma ó 'Aoidhmín Mac Gréagóir' de réir na h-admhála ag toiseach an leabhair. Ba duine diamhair an Gréagórach céadna. Tá taighde déanta air ag an Dochtúir Ciarán Ó Duibhín, Béal Feairsde – McMillan an fíor-sloinneadh a bhí air – b'as Conndae an Dúin a athair agus as Sasain a mháthair. Bhí sé tráth ina mhac léighinn le Léigheas ag Ollsgoil na Banríoghna i mBéal Feairsde ach tá cuma ar an sgéal nar chríochnaigh sé an céim. Thóg sé sgéaltaí i nGaedhilg Reachrann, a nocht faoina ainm i 1910, agus 'Criomáin Aondroma' a nocht in 'An tUltach' (1927). Tá a chuid abhrais ar a h-ath-fhoillsiughadh ag an Ollamh Gearóid Stockman agus ag Gearóid Mac Giolla Domhnaigh mar 'Athchló Uladh' (Comhaltas Uladh, 1991). Luaidheann Mac Gréagóir cuid de na daoine a thug adhbhar Gaedhilge dó, ach chan iad uilig, agus tá amhras ar na h-eagraitheóirí thuas luaidhte gur chuir sé leis an méid a thóg sé in amannaí. Go dearbhtha, chuir sé iongantas orm fhéin go dtiocfadh leis sgéal chomh fada le 'Alastair na mBróg Buidhe' a thógáil as cainnteóir dúthchais sna Glinn chomh mall le toiseach na ficheadmhadh linne. Gan amhras bhí Gaedhilg na h-Alban ag Mac Gréagóir chomh math, agus is doiligh oibriughadh amach caidé a' bhuaidh a bhí ag sin ar a chuid sgríobhaidh agus ar an dóigh ar thóg sé lena chluais. Dar liom-sa go bhfuil buaidh thírmóir na h-Éireann ar chuid den adhbhar Reachlainneach a sgríobh sé, mar shampla 'd'éirigh' in áit 'dh'éirigh'.

Ba é duine eile ar a dearn Ciarán taighde, John McCambridge as Cois Abhann, duinne a fuair bás i 1873 ag aois ochtó bliadhan. Shaoil Eoin MacNeill (féach *The Scholarly Revolutionary*, lch. 323) gurab é McCambridge a sgríobh an t-abhrán cliúiteach Áird a' Chuain nó Áird a' Chumhaing – an t-aon abhrán Gaedhilge atá fágtha againn sna Glinn. Bíodh sin fior nó ná bíodh, tá sé soiléir go mba duine oilte é, díleas don Ghaedhilg. Ba Phrodustanach McCambridge (tháinig a shinsearacht ó Cheann Tíre corradh is dhá chéad bliadhan roimh a bhreith) agus bhí sé gaolta troimh chleamhnas a dheirbhshiúr, Sarah, leis an teaghlach mor-le-radh Dixon i Latharna. Bhí sé ina fhear ranna le gnaithe plúir agus cartadh leathair i Latharna, agus bhí feirm aige tráth, in aice le Gleann Arma. Ba mhac a dheirbhshiúr Sir Daniel Dixon, a rinn a' Bhanrioghain Victoria ridire de, agus a' chéad 'Lord-Mayor' de Bhéal Feairsde. Mo bhuidheachas do Chiarán as an eólas sin a thabhairt domh ar Mhac Greagóir agus McCambridge.

Cha dtig linn Gaedhilg agus Aondroim a luadh san aon alt gan iomrádh a dhéanamh ar Seán Mac Maoláin a rugadh i mBun na h-Abhna ag deireadh na naomhadh linn déag. Ghluais an teaghlach go Béal Feairsde agus Seán ina bhuachaill óg. Ina stócach agus é ag obair in Oifig a' Phuist thoisigh sé a dh'fhoghlaim Gaedhilge, agus tamall ina dhéidh sin fuair sé amach go mba chainnteóir dúthchais a athair! D'fhoghlaim sé agus d'fhoghlaim sé ar fóghnamh, agus chaith sé bunadhas a shaoghail ag obair ar son na Gaedhilge i mBéal Feairsde, agus i mBaile Atha Cliath. Ba Ghaedhilg Thír Chonaill a chleacht sé ina chuid sgríobhaidh agus bhí a' chanamhaint sin ar a chomhairle aige. Is é an saothar is luachmhaire aige an leabhar tagartha *Cora Cainnte Thír Chonaill*, ach ina theannta sin sgríobh sé dornán úr-sgéaltaí, ina measg *Corr Éan*, a nocht i 1937. Baineann an sgéal le Cogadh na Saoirse in Éirinn agus bheir sé radharc ar dearcadh an úghdair ar a' choimhlint. Tháinig a bheath-fhaisnéis, *Gleann Airbh go Glas Naíon*, amach sa litriughadh nuadh i 1969 agus ó thaoibh a bheatha fhéin agus stáir na tíre de, tá an leabhar seo ar leith suimeamhail.

Chuir Mac Maoláin spéis sa Ghaedhilg mar bheitheá a' dúil leis, agus dúthchas na nGleann aige. D'fhoillsigh sé leabhar beag gramadaighe a chuir síos ar na difridheachtaí eadar Gaedhilg na h-Éireann agus Gàidhlig na h-Alban, agus tá alt da chuid in *An tUltach* (1926 3:5) a' déanamh comparáid eadar Gaedhilg na nGleann agus Gaedhilg Reachrann. Saoilim fhéin go dearn sé amach iad a bhith ní b'fhuide ó chéile ná mar bhí. Mar shampla, thug sé an focal 'coinfheasgar' mar teóranta do Reachraidh, gidh go bhfuil sé le fagháil fiú i litridheacht Thír Chonaill. Cha chreid mé ach oiread, nach rabh 'toigh' seachas 'teach' mar tuiseal ainmneach da chleachtadh ar tírmóir agus ar an oileán.

Bhí teagmháil ag Mac Maoláin, ár ndóighe, le cainnteóirí dúthchais na nGleann, agus ba mhór an truaighe nach dearn sé iarracht ar rud éigineacht a sgríobhadh le blas a cheanntair air. Bhreac sé síos nótaí ar ainmne na h-áite agus ar a' chéill a bhain sé asta, agus tá eólas ceilte a' teacht amach as na nótaí sin. 'Sé an rud is suimeamhla go n-abair sé nar chuala sé trácht ar 'Red Bay' ag na sean-chainnteóirí dúthchais. Cha dearn siad iomrádh ach ar 'an fhairrge', ach thugadh siad 'Tráigh Amhairc Dheirg' ar a' chladach sin. Tá cuid mhór oibre le déanamh ar an adhbhar seo sna Glinn.

Ár ndóighe, chuaidh Gaedhilg Aondroma chun meatha ina laethanta deireannacha eadar ghramadaigh agus fhuaimeanna. Mar shampla, d'éirigh aimhréidhe eadar 't' agus 'c' go minic, rud a thug 'cimire ceallaigh' sa chainnt ar tírmóir in ait 'timire teallaigh', agus 'coistéim coiligh' ar Reachraidh in áit 'coiscéim coiligh'. Rud saoitheamhail eile, a' guthaidheacht 'airm' fá choinne 'ainm'. Ach is iongantach liom an méid atá ar a choimhéad ceart cruinn ag daoine dálta Alex Morrison nach d'fhuair lá teagasg Gaedhilg lena bheó.

Mar focal sguir, ba mhath liom foinse eile a luadh atá thar a bheith tábhachtach ó thaoibh Gaedhilg Aondroma de, agus 's é sin an Béarla 'Albanach' a labhras a' chuid is mó de na daoine i dtuaisceart agus i meadhon na conndae – 'Beurla Ghallda' mar deirtear in Albain fhéin. Nuair a bhí a' Ghaedhilg ina teangaidh ach aon lae ag na daoine anios go aimsir na Gorta Móire bhíodh eadar-éadan aice leis a' Bhéarla Ghallta. Da tairbhe sin, thóg an Béarla Gallta cuid mheasardha de fhoclóireacht na Gaedhilge, agus d'fhan an fhoclóireacht sin reóidhte sa chanamhaint Albannaigh mar a chuaidh a' Ghaedhilg díobhtha. B'urra le seo tachairt os rud é go rabh (agus go bhfuil) an Béarla Gallta fhéin faoi thoirmisg anns na sgoileanna, sgoileanna a ghlan a' Ghaedhilg as béal na bpáistí. Tá an saidhbhreas seo le fagháil indiu i mBéarla Aondroma, go h-áirighthe sa tuath. Cluinidh tú trácht, mar shampla ar: 'a *lachtar* o' eggs/birds', 'a wee *eireóg*', 'to *sgaoil* dung', 'a *maoile* o' *preatas*', ' a wild *pracas*', ' to *clad* your heid', 'a damned *spailpín*', 'a wee *sgraidín*', ' a big *goilpín*', 'a big *spág*', 'a *brat* o' sna', 'to cut a *sgrath*', 'to come *i gcionn* a day's time', 'to be oot on your *céilidhe*', 'the *stoich* o' the fire', 'there's nae *faic* left', ' niver thocht *a shéad* o' it', 'cannae see a *stoim*', ' a dark *sgead*', agus cuid mhór eile.

'Sé mo ghuidhe ar son na nGleann sa bhliadhain seo nuair a táthar a' comóradh na chéad Fhéise, go mbéadh na daoine atá a' teagasg Gaedhilg anns a' cheanntar a' cur fearta ar a' Ghaedhilg atá ann cheana féin, agus do na h-ainmne áite, siúd a's nach mbídh siad a' teacht salach ar na foinsí luachmhara seo agus a' críochnughadh le Ghaedhilg choimhthighigh, an rud a toisigheadh leis a' Bhéarla.

15

EALAÍONA AGUS CEIRDEANNA
(ARTS AND CRAFTS)

Introduction
Pádraic Ó Cléireacháin

It was Francis Joseph Bigger's idea to have a Local Industries Section at the first Glens Feis in 1904. He was almost certainly inspired by the Russian peasant arts exhibit at the Paris Exposition of 1900. Bigger had been planning how best to revive the ancient native Gaelic culture of Ireland and he regarded native crafts as an essential part of this culture. Joseph McBrinn, in his section 'From Moscow to the Moyle' below, tells of the close links between the Russian exhibit and the craft section at the 1904 Feis.

In the 1904 Feis the local industries section was one of the largest, with 46 competitions. Among the activities covered were spinning, weaving, knitting, embroidery, lace-making, garment-making, quilting, butter-making, baking, shoemaking, metal working, furniture-making, basket-making, woodcarving, toy-making, drawing and painting. Skills among the local population were well defined. The founding of the toy factory in Cushendall in 1900 had helped to raise and improve standards, especially in wood-carving, sewing, knitting, embroidery and associated skills. The section on Cushendall's toy-making industry by Rosemary O'Rawe Brady tells us that the items produced were in high demand due to their excellent quality. The home industry workshop founded by Mrs Riddell in Ballycastle at the turn of the century had also helped to improve the standard of traditional skills, especially among the young.

Over the centuries, spinning, weaving and needlework to make family clothing and furnishings were part of the daily ritual in most homes in Ireland. In an article written for *The Glynns* in 1975, the late Rose Emerson of Cushendall remembers the variety of crafts at the

Cathal McNaughton demonstrating wood craft at the Feis

Costume designed by John Campbell for the first Feis
(Courtesy Ulster Museum/MAGNI)

first Feis and especially the patchwork quilt display. She recalls how the women came together to make a quilt, and how it was quite a social occasion. In the nineteenth and twentieth centuries the introduction of the large weaving and spinning mills was to revolutionise this craft. By the mid twentieth century the custom of spinning and weaving in the home was largely extinct. The availability of ready-made clothing and the improvement in living standards made the purchase of off-peg items more appealing and fashionable. In the section 'The story of flax from seed to linen', Moira McNeill tells how these traditional skills moved from the countryside to the factory.

In recent years, due mainly to the increase in tourism, the arts and crafts industry has enjoyed a revival throughout Ireland. This section continues to be a popular feature of the Feis weekend and over the years other crafts have been added such as pottery, leatherwork, rug-making, calligraphy, flower-arranging, jam-making and photography. There is also a group heritage project, open to both primary and post-primary schools. It can be on a locality, an ancient monument, etc., and the winning school is awarded the John Turnly Memorial Trophy.

In 2004 there were 68 competitions in four main sections: art; kitchencraft; needlecraft; and wood, metal and other craft. The exhibition was held in a marquee over two days in the field at Glenariff, and attracted over two thousand visitors.

From Moscow to the Moyle:
Arts and Crafts at the first Feis na nGleann
Joseph McBrinn

The 'Art and Industrial Exhibition' at the very first Feis na nGleann in 1904, although little acknowledged today, was one of the most significant exhibitions in Irish cultural history. It flowed directly, in its championing of rural craft traditions, folk art and National Romanticism, from the éclat of the Russian peasant arts (the *kustar)* in the 'Russian Village' at the 1900 Paris Exposition Universelle. The link between the 1900 Russian exhibit in Paris and the arts and crafts exhibition at the 1904 Feis is much closer than is generally thought. There had, in fact, been a direct and conscious cross-pollination of the Moscow *style moderne* to the shores of the Moyle. This Russian–Irish correspondence first occurred in *fin de siècle* Belfast, where Russian craft-worker and proselytiser Anna Pogosskaia, who became well known through her work for Princess Tenisheva at Talashkino in Russia, came to promote her William Morris-inspired rural handicrafts, encouraging a group of young local women to set up the Portrush-based Irish Decorative Arts Association in 1894.

Also in Belfast, following the success of the 1798 Centennial, Francis Joseph Bigger, local solicitor, antiquary, folklorist and Celtic Revival polymath, first formulated the idea to found a more permanent celebration of local Gaelic culture. Bigger was looking beyond Belfast and was already visiting the Glens of

'Interior of Russian Pavilion', Paris Exposition Universelle, 1900
L'Illustration, 280, 5 May 1900

Antrim, where he found a rich repository of ancient native culture. As elsewhere during the nineteenth and early twentieth century, industrial revolution, famine, linguistic obliteration, urban migration and economic depression had blighted the Glens' population but their irrepressible ingenuity and artistry, in poetry, song, dance and craft, revealed remnants of an ancient folk civilization. This culture, which stretched far back to the dawn of Ulster, was, Bigger saw, not moribund but vital; with his help the Glens traditions, once so full of colour, vibrancy, fluttering banners, dancing and pipe music, came alive again.

At a meeting in Cushendall in February 1904 a group of Glens folk devised the idea of a grand Feis, which would not only promote language and literature but also aid languishing rural industries and local crafts. Bigger, like others such as Horace Plunkett and Standish O'Grady, saw the revival of rural crafts as central to ensuring not only the preservation of native traditions but also a sense of national, and regional, identity. From the outset Bigger saw arts and crafts as a central element of the structure of the Feis, stating clearly in early 1904 that *'a prominent place will be given to peasant industries'*. Bigger hoped that the production of furniture, toys, textiles and other handicrafts by Glens folk would evoke 'old times, old customs, old ways'. These Glens crafts were expressly designed as souvenirs, and, as Bigger noted, 'Sentiment is thus encouraged in a healthy way, and at the same time full advantage is taken of it for the primary object of the industry'. Making toys, and more importantly instructing children in such activities, would for Bigger breathe life into the ancient proverb, 'mould the boy and make the man; make the man and build the nation'.

In organising the 'Arts and Industrial Exhibition', Bigger was assisted by the recently established Department of Agriculture and Technical Instruction (D.A.T.I.) in Dublin. The principal contribution of the DATI was a display of 'Russian peasant toys', which its representatives had purchased at the 'Russian Village' at the 1900 Paris Exposition. They had been especially impressed by the Russian revival of toy making, especially the collection of wooden toys made at Sergiev Posad, shown in Kostantin Korovin and Aleksandr Golovin's *l'izba des koustary* building. The D.A.T.I. saw the relevance of the '*kustarni* or cottage industries … carried on in every part of Russia' to Irish cottage industries and clearly hoped to encourage similar enterprises in Ireland by exhibiting an exemplary and commercially successful model, which had brought international attention and acclaim to Russia in 1900. At the Feis the press noted that the 'toys manufactured by Russian peasants … were placed in a prominent place in the hall and the eagerness in which they were studied and compared with the local display showed that the experiment was a happy one'. Bigger's young protégé, the artist, John Campbell, even created in his cover design of *An Clár* (programme), showing a pipe-playing figure engulfed in a sinuous swirl of music and lines, a Celtic equivalent of the Art Nouveau, *style moderne* and Folk Revivalism of the Russian *Mir iskusstva*.

The practical outcome of the 'Arts and Industrial Exhibition' was primarily to focus attention on local arts and crafts enterprises, which were already producing similar folk art designs for toys to the Russian *kustar*. Barbara McDonnell's 'Cushendall toy-making industry' had been founded in 1901, to teach first of all drawing and carving, and then toy-making, to local children. As her workshops swelled, the quality of products also developed, from stuffed toys to models made from cigar boxes to replicas of antique furniture for dolls' houses. In 1903, with Bigger's assistance, Frances Riddell opened a toy and furniture-making enterprise, the 'Irish Peasant Home Industries', in Ballycastle, in a shop called *An Tuirne Beag* (The Spinning Wheel). Like Bigger, the people at D.A.T.I. were acutely aware of the relationship between rural arts and crafts and economic and social regeneration, and they were keen to promote workshops such as those of the Glens at the upcoming St Louis World's Fair of 1904, which they perceived could act as the Paris 1900 Exposition had for Russia, as a world's stage, bringing Glens industry and artistry to international attention. Both the McDonnell and Riddell workshops showed in the 'Irish Village' at the St Louis fair, to much acclaim.

Although the Moscow–Moyle connection of the first show has been greatly undervalued, and remains an important chapter of Irish art history yet to be written, the arts and crafts exhibitions inaugurated at the first Feis have continued to be an integral element in its structure to the present day.

Cushendall's toy-making industry
Rosemary O'Rawe Brady

Back in 1900, long before government agencies such as Invest N.I. came upon the scene, an English lady called Miss Sturge made the suggestion for the establishment of a local craft industry. She was a friend of Miss Barbara McDonnell of Monavart, Cushendall and between the two of them, the Cushendall toy industry became a reality.

The remoteness of the Glens of Antrim meant that there was little contact with the inland towns such as Ballymena and Larne, and Miss Sturge provided the artistic talent to develop prototypes of wooden toys that could be manufactured. Miss McDonnell then enlisted two other instructors: Miss F.A. Hicks, who gave lessons in drawing, and Mr Arthur Spence, who later became manager of the factory.

The toy factory began operations in the coach house at Monavart, where lessons in art and wood-carving were given and Mr Spence examined each piece

Doll's house known as 'Domville Doll's House, exhibited at the Great International Exhibition at Crystal Palace in 1851

Furnishings were commissioned from the Cushendall Toy Factory

that was made, casting his expert eye over the work produced and making suggestions for improvement. The first year's operations resulted in a significant financial loss, but this was only to be expected as the fledgling company was training its staff and developing its product range. Before it became popular to recycle materials, the toy factory made use of cigar boxes to produce dolls' house furniture and mechanical toys.

In order to promote the business, Miss Hicks entered one of her creations in an exhibition in London; it won her a Gold Star. The superior quality of the other models produced by the toy factory at fairs in London and elsewhere resulted in an extensive order book. A new range of toys such as 'The Magic Mouse Trap', 'The Galloping Horse', 'The Mechanical Ostrich', and 'The Owl and the Pussycat Rowboat' were much in demand, with orders emanating from as far away as New Zealand and Philadelphia. This expansion necessitated a change in venue as the coach house was no longer large enough to accommodate the needs of the company.

As a result, the toy factory moved to High Street, Cushendall, to a house owned by James Whiteford, with another workshop further on down Shore Street in the village. The Shore Street workshop produced hundreds of soft stuffed animals under the supervision of Mr Spence's wife, who shared her husband's interest in the business. Miss Hicks left the company when she moved to Newcastle-on-Tyne but still represented it as a marketing agent, arranging for orders and putting on exhibitions of new toys. Her successor was Miss Eccles and, as the industry was gradually building up momentum, another move of premises was deemed necessary. This time the Toy Factory moved to a rather large house (owned by Miss McDonnell) called Dún-na-dTuar, directly opposite the police barracks in Cushendall (the house was later demolished).

I can remember seeing this house with its picturesque bay window. My grandmother, Mrs Mary Blaney, told me it had a wonderful assortment of toys in the window while a large workshop operated in the back and upstairs. It had a large sign proclaiming it to be the home of the 'Cushendall Toy Making Industry'. But the best was yet to come.

The National Museum of Ireland in Dublin was presented with a Georgian style dolls' house that had been exhibited at the Great International Exhibition at the Crystal Palace in 1851. The dolls' house became known as the Domville Dolls' House after its previous owners and, while it was beautifully handcrafted, it had no furniture. The Museum was keen to have native Irish workmanship and commissioned the manufacture of 44 pieces of furniture for the dolls' house in the styles of Sheraton, Hepplewhite and Chippendale at a cost of £10, with an additional Adams suite ordered later. A grand piano was even made for the house from a cigar box.

The dolls' house furniture was accentuated by a set of 22 miniature oil paintings, about the size of a postage stamp, all copies of famous masters in the Museum completed by Miss Mabel Hurst of Ranelagh. This dolls' house was a masterpiece, with a four-poster bed complete with curtains tied back with pink silk ribbons, inlaid wooden tables, fireplaces, carpets, everything done in perfect proportion to original antique furniture. It still exists, and is on display at the Museum in Dublin.

More orders rolled in from England and America, and the high standard imposed by Mr Spence meant employment for local people for the years from 1900 to 1914. The company was paying its way towards the end of its existence, and it is difficult to explain the demise of the factory. One of the reasons given was that workers fell away as they were needed to work elsewhere until eventually the only three who remained in the company were Miss Eccles, Mr Spence and Miss McDonnell. International recognition was given to a small place in the Antrim Glens where Santa Claus was going to see Miss McDonnell in Cushendall. According to a Christmas issue of the magazine *The Lady of the House*:

> Santa wanted to buy some Irish furniture for dolls' houses and some wooden toys which could not be had elsewhere. He bought settle beds at 8 pence because he thought them very Irish, jaunting cars at 5 shillings and 6 pence as well as several complete suites of furniture … as the objects were made by hand and not by machinery as in other countries.

It is a pity that there is no plaque at the site of Dún-na-dTuar to commemorate this unique initiative, this brave undertaking by forward-thinking individuals to provide much-needed employment in the Glens. Perhaps in the future, some local group will pay a long overdue tribute to Miss McDonnell and her intrepid and talented band of craftsmen.

Patchwork quilting
Rose Emerson[1]

My mind goes back seventy years to the first Feis in the Glens. One wonders about all the craftsmen and women whose work filled Holden's big hall at Waterfoot; everything from a set of horseshoes to a watch chain made from horse hair and from a pin cushion to a pair of homespun blankets. And the quilts – they were surely things of beauty – of every colour and many beautiful patterns. I wonder if there is a quilting frame left in the Glens.

The homemade wooden frame was like a bedstead without ends, with down each side laths perforated at equal lengths. Through these perforations the quilt would be fastened after being well stretched. This kept the quilt taut and made it easy for the needle-woman to ply her needle to and fro. The frame rested on four legs at a comfortable height for the women to sit at their work.

Usually four, but sometimes six women would work at one frame. Skeins of linen thread, perhaps bought from a traveling packwoman, needles and a piece of chalk to mark the half-diamond shaped sewing patterns were also provided. A young girl would be busily employed keeping the needles threaded, for all good needlewomen sewed with a short thread. As the women worked through the quilt it could be loosened from the laths and rolled, thus keeping their work close to them.

The women of the house always made the quilting materials ready for the frame. These consisted of a lining, an interlining and a cover. The interlining gave 'body' and warmth to the quilt, but the cover was always of greatest importance and could consist of stripes, waves or patchwork patterns. The final operation was binding the rough edges of the quilt with strips of material.

When Lady Longfield resided in Glenville she made visits to all the schools in the parish and left bundles of patchwork materials for the children to cut into squares which, when sewn together, made a cover for a quilt, as well as helping to make the children proficient in needlework. I believe you could find remnants of these patchwork quilts yet; they were made to last.

In the old days a quilting was second in popularity only to a lint-pulling as a social occasion. It was preceded by great activity and preparations in the house – oven-hot loaves, slim cake and griddle bread of various kinds and, of course fresh churning to ensure plenty of butter.

When quilting was finished and everything was ship-shape again, it was usual to have a *céilidhe* and a dance. Occasionally the night would end with the prospect of another quilting in the near future as two lucky people decided to 'go double harness'.

There were many traditions attached to quilting. The one I liked best was where, if the quilts were for a bride, those who took part in making them embroidered their names on a corner of the lining. Then there was the custom of 'tossing the quilt'. The boys, after many attempts, would 'capture' a girl, roll her in the quilt and toss her to each other. It was always said that the girl thus tossed would be the next bride.

Anne McCormick, Glendun, great-grandmother of Moira McNeill, reeling wool in her kitchen *(Courtesy Ulster Folk and Transport Museum/MAGNI)*

The story of flax from seed to linen
Moira McNeill

Linen made from the flax plant has been around for some 8,000 years; it is believed to have been first brought to Ireland by the Celts in the first millennium B.C. Legend has it that St Patrick was buried in a linen shroud.

The Irish climate and soil are well suited to the growing of the flax plant, especially in the northern counties of the country. We know that flax (known locally as lint) has been grown in the middle Glens for a long time. Records in the nineteenth century show it being grown extensively from locally grown seed. Small farmers grew plots of flax; it was spun and woven into linen cloth and sold to supplement the family income.

Flax was sown in the spring, and in midsummer the plant was covered in a beautiful blue flower. The crop was ready for harvesting when the stalk turned brown, about 100 days after planting. Lint was harvested by hand: the plant had to be pulled out of the ground, so that the greatest possible length of fibre could be obtained. This was back-breaking work, and the tough fibrous stalks cut deeper and deeper into the workers' hand as the day wore on.

After pulling, the lint was tied in bundles called beets and steeped in a water-filled dam or dub; this process was called retting. After about two weeks the dam

EALAÍONA AGUS CEIRDEANNA

This linen quilt was passed down to me by my grandmother, Ellen O'Neill, who died in 1956 in her ninetieth year. She had inherited it from her mother, Anne McCormick. The flax used to make it was grown, spun and woven on the family farm of my great-grandfather, Alexander McCormick of Brockaghs, Glendun. It was often used on the bed at family wakes. It was on such an occasion that I became aware of its history, and was informed that one day it would be left in my care.

gave off an obnoxious smell, indicating that the valuable fibres had separated from the inner core. Removing the lint from the dam was also back-breaking work, and the workers were often standing up to their waist in cold, stinking water. The beets were left to drain on the banks of the dub before being spread on the field for about two weeks to dry. The fibres were then ready to be cleaned, spun into yarn and finally woven into linen cloth. The linen process from plant to tablecloth comprised 27 steps.

The introduction of spinning mills for linen and cotton in the nineteenth century brought about a radical change in the industry. Now spinning was done in the large factories that grew up around Belfast and Lisburn, and spinning as a home industry gradually disappeared. Later, weaving factories were established and home weaving also became a thing of the past.

During the first half of the twentieth century flax growing was at its peak, and most farms in the Glens were growing one or two acres as a commercial crop. After the drying the flax was taken to a local scutch mill, where it was put through large rollers to remove the inner fibre (linen), which was then sold to the spinning mills. The local scutch mill in this area was owned and run by the

Sharkey family at Calisnagh, Cushendun; it closed in the early 1950s. From the end of the Second World War the demand for locally grown flax declined, as it was now possible to import better class flax from the continent more cheaply than to grow it. By then man-made fibres had begun to supplant linen, especially in the clothing industry. In recent years linen has again become fashionable in the world of *haute couture*.

Flax growing was a labour-intensive process, and it was the local custom for the farmer to have what was known as a lint-pulling day when all the neighbours would gather to harvest the crop or remove it from the dubs; sometimes a group of casual labourers known as a 'boon' would be employed. As well as hard work, it was an opportunity for a social occasion, and lint-pulling days were frequently followed by a lint-pulling dance or barn dance. As the name suggests, these were held in large barns; some of the best known locally were O'Rawe's of Tully near Cushendall, McKinley's of Ballyloughan Torr, and McFetridge's of Castlegreen in the Cushendun area, the last of which continued as a popular country dance-hall until the 1960s. The music was provided by local musicians with a melodeon (accordion) or a fiddle, and popular dances were 'The Lancers', 'The Waves of Tory' and fast reels such as 'The Rakes of Mallow'; these had taken over from the older kitchen set-dances of 100 years ago.

Unfortunately, as the popularity of growing flax declined, so did these pastimes, and as the older generation passed on so did many of the traditional skills associated with the home industries of spinning and weaving.

1 First published in *The Glynns*, 1975.

16

FEISEANNA REMEMBERED
REPORTS AND REMINISCENCES

Over the years since its foundation in 1904, the Glens Feis has been enjoyed by generations of Glensfolk and visitors. The following is a selection of reminiscences and newspaper reports of Feis days over the past century.

The 'Rathlin pipes' and Feis na nGleann
Augustine McCurdy

Following the foundation of the Gaelic League by Dr Douglas Hyde and Eoin McNeill in 1893, there was a great revival of language and culture which reached the Glens of Antrim and Rathlin Island over the next decade.

In 1904 the first Feis na nGleann was held in Glenariff, organised by a Feis committee that included many prominent Presbyterians. Francis Joseph Bigger, a well-known Belfast solicitor, was a leading figure together with Roger Casement, Margaret Dobbs, Ada McNeill and many more.

Rathlin figured prominently in their plans. The census of 1911 lists 213 Irish speakers on the island, i.e. 60 per cent of the population – a much higher percentage than anywhere else in Ulster.

Francis Joseph Bigger was well known to the islanders: he had taken their case successfully to the land court to have their rents reduced. He and Roger Casement chartered a large boat to take the islanders to the Feis. They landed at Red Bay pier and paraded to Glenariff, led by Neil 'the piper' McCurdy of Rathlin and John Scally of Ballycastle.

Neil McCurdy was born in Cleggan, Rathlin, in 1846. This year was at the height of an Gorta Mór (the Great Hunger). Neil would have gone to one of the three schools in this part of the Island, known as the 'Upper End' because it is generally upland in character. He probably attended the school in Ballygill South, whose foundations can still be seen. This was a private school, where Gaelic was taught and the pupils – 40 in number in 1835 – paid one penny per week; my grandfather, Joseph McCurdy, went to the same school.

Neil McCurdy grew up in a culture where the first language was Irish, and storytelling and yarning, music, song and traditional dance were the main way of passing a winter evening.

In 1834 Dr J.D. Marshall visited Rathlin and stayed a few weeks. He relates his experiences in the *Transactions of the Royal Academy*. He came to the island at 8 o'clock on a June evening with an island boat crewed by men from Kenramer; they rowed all the way with some help from a sail. When they arrived on Rathlin,

FEIS NA nGLEANN

Neil McCurdy known as 'The Rathlin Piper' won the uilleann piping competition at the 1904 Feis. His prize was a set of Mealy's pipes. *(Courtesy Ulster Museum/MAGNI)*

he was taken to the public house, just opened a few years. Here he found accommodation and then spent a congenial evening in the company of the boatmen, listening to songs in the Gaelic; he says that one song was sung as a duet by two men; it lasted 15 minutes, with everyone joining in the chorus. This is the *sean nós* or old style of singing in Gaelic, which can still be heard on the west coast of Scotland. This account gives a flavour of the culture of the 1800s and right up until the middle of the 1900s, which influenced Neil McCurdy and many others on the island.

Neil, in common with many McCurdys, had the gift of music. In nearly every house on the island there was at least one person who could play an instrument or sing a song or do a dance step. Neil was versatile; he could play the pipes or whistle and sing in the *sean nós* style.

At the 1904 Feis he entered the piping competition; other islanders entered various competitions including, singing, language and step dancing. Katie Glass was a noted island singer. Neil was tying with another piper on the same marks and number of times, when Katie Glass whispered to him to play 'The Foggy Dew' – not the well-known ballad, but a slow air played on the pipes. Neil did so and won first prize – a set of pipes.

Neil McCurdy was a stonemason and worked for the Commissioners of Irish Lights, carrying out construction work at various lighthouses. While working at the lighthouse on Aranmore island, off West Donegal, he met up with Roise na hAmhran (Rosie of the Songs), and taught her two Rathlin songs in the traditional style – 'Donal agus Morag' and 'Mo Choill'. Much later, both of these came to the notice of Donegal folk and traditional group, Altan, who recorded them on the C.D. *Harvest Storm* (1992).

The pipes won by Neil McCurdy at the first Feis eventually came into the possession of Kevin Black, a relative. Kevin could play the pipes and several other instruments; all the Black family were talented musicians and singers. Kevin told me the story of how he went to Dublin in the 1930s looking for work as a plasterer, taking the pipes with him. He settled in Dublin, got married and raised a family, who also have the gift of music. The best-known members are Mary and Frances.

Over the decades the pipes were forgotten. When I was researching my book on Rathlin a few years ago, I remembered the story told to me by Kevin of taking the pipes to Dublin. I asked his son, Martin, when he was visiting Rathlin if he had an idea of what happened to the pipes. A year or so later Martin told me that he had found a set of pipes wrapped in a hessian bag in the loft of the old house in Dublin. This find eventually led to the organising of a pipe festival on Rathlin in the summer of 2004 by the Rathlin Co-Op, at the suggestion of Paddy Burns. The ancient set of pipes was restored and was the centre of attention, having finally returned to Rathlin in the centenary year of Feis na nGleann.

Music, song and dance is still very much part of Rathlin culture. The younger generation have learned the dances, and have also learned the basics of accordion and whistle playing, although having to go to secondary school elsewhere works against the further development of their talent. Cumann Gaelach Reachtainn is working to restore the Rathlin dialect, which was a mixture of Irish and Scots Gaelic and was spoken by a number if island people up until the late 1950s. The last speaker with a good grasp of the language is Alex Morrison, who now lives in Ballycastle. We have collected several recordings of speakers using the dialects.

Excitement and expectations
Paddy recalls

Paddy Burns

My recollections of Feis na nGleann from over fifty years ago were of great excitement and expectations. After Christmas there were three big annual events in our lives; there was St Patrick's Day, Feis na nGleann and the 29th September sheep sales. Feis na nGleann was by far the most important, mainly because we knew a lot of the competitors and we could take part in it ourselves.

Our whole family looked forward to that weekend so much that even in later years after some of them went to work in England they still returned for the annual Feis.

Feis Sunday started early with first Mass for all of us. Then it was back home to help with the jobs around the house, water from the spring well, eggs gathered, milking, etc.

Our mother and sisters made an early dinner and of course sandwiches to take with us because it would be a long day.

We were warned to stay together and come home together. Then we set off to walk the three miles to Glenariff but it did not seem that long as we joined friends and neighbours along the way. Our grandmother gave us all a shilling each to spend, which got us a bottle of lemonade and a slider, with money left. As the day wore on the crowds grew bigger and bigger – or so it seemed. Then we would meet up with school pals and plan what races we would take part in. If we won a prize or medal it was important to ourselves and to our school. This was our Olympic Games.

After the children's races were over we would walk round the field watching the dancers and musicians on the platforms. Next to the arts and crafts, which was very competitive as each school and parish tried to outdo each other. We would be looking for something knitted, baked or woven by someone we knew. There were also some lovely walking sticks, little carved boats, Celtic crosses and many other products made from wood. It was a big plus if the gatemen or organisers asked you to do a message or help them in some way.

Then came the senior hurling match and how we clapped and called for our heroes as they made a good save or got a score. If we were lucky we would get a broken hurl and that was when the bean tin came into its own for the repair job.

When the match was over it was time to meet at a prearranged area and head for home. Funny, the road back to Cloughs seemed longer than when we were going to the Feis. Now the discussions started about who was the best runner, hurler, dancer or musician. What was best in the arts and crafts etc?

When we went back to school after the summer holidays the Feis was re-run, and if you won a medal or a prize that was replayed and re-run time and time again. This lasted up to the September sheep sales, but that's another story.

(Paddy Burns, Cushendall)

Winning a prize at Feis na nGleann
Kevin remembers

About 65 years ago, during an art class in school, Mr Hugh Blaney, our class teacher, suggested that we enter for the Feis in Glenariff. We had to submit an 'interlacing Celtic design'. We were given a blank, dark-coloured page about 12 by 16 inches and coloured chalks (the medium of the time).

We had two winners: a first and a second. Paddy McGarry, later to become Rev. Canon Patrick McGarry, got first and I received second, for which we won a book.

I fondly remember about ten years ago, winning a medal on the same day as my son, Patrick, rode back from a Dublin marathon cycle race, rode to Cushendall, donned a Ballymena club jersey and won a first prize medal in the hurling final.

(Kevin Neeson, Ballymena)

Kevin Neeson

Passing on the tradition
Peadar comments

In this age of commercialism and political correctness you might be tempted to ask, is there room left for a cultural explosion born 100 years ago? The short answer is a definite 'yes'.

The founding fathers of Feis na nGleann were far-sighted enough to see the importance of preserving the heritage, culture and language of the Glens, and their vision has borne fruit with the vibrant Feis of today. For those of us who witnessed the awakening of a pride in nationhood in the dark days of partition, feiseanna were an integral part in keeping that tradition alive.

Generations before this did their best to pass on the tradition, language and heritage, which was a bright new dawn at the beginning of the last century with the founding of the GAA and the Gaelic League.

Those who felt this was not for them and turned their backs on their roots sought refuge in an alien culture from across the Atlantic. But Feis na nGleann remained true to a heritage and language of one of the oldest cultures in Europe.

Those of us of a certain age can remember with pride the small feiseanna throughout the country, which benefited us in our language and history exams and were in many ways our passport to the Gaeltacht.

Long may Feis na nGleann thrive and prosper to serve each succeeding generation in the Glens and further afield in keeping alive the ethos of the Feis.

(Peadar Ó Ruairc, Larne)

Peadar Ó Ruairc

The *Ballymena Weekly Telegraph* reported in its edition of 9 July 1904 an 'interesting industrial and Gaelic festival at Glenariff':

> The Glens of Antrim have remained to this day practically untouched by the degenerating influences of the times, and except for the iron ore mines at their head and the little seaside villages fringing the shore the ordinary work day world

and the tourist had scarcely affected them. But for the building of a viaduct in 1846 over one of the glens it is quite probable that English would have been known there as an accomplishment fitted only for towns people. Even today a few native speakers remain, and many of the homely industries of the place have existed until quite recently.

Moira O'Neill had sung of the Glens in verse which came very close to the heart of the glens people, and Stephen Gywnn had described the scenic beauties of the coast in a volume of a series which has been read all over the world. However, none of these excellent people noted what, for an Irish district, must be counted somewhat unique; the fact that there is no sectarian jealously or strife in the Glens is surely a wonderful thing, and indicates how unspoilt the people are.

It only remained, then, to give them some outlet for native energy and native talent, and some time ago Miss Barbara McDonnell started a toy making industry in Cushendall, which, with the similar one in Ballycastle, started by Mrs Riddell has afforded employment and an excellent technical training to many boys and girls along the most approved lines of modern education and industrial equipment. It only remained to give the Irish language, music, literature, and the homely cults some inducement to flourish, and Mr F.J. Bigger, M.R.I.A., came along with the brilliant idea of a Feis of the Nine Glens, and set about organising committees and centres to make arrangements for the same.

It was a bigger undertaking than even its energetic originator thought, but hearty and sympathetic co-operation on the part of everyone brought the festival off with éclat and success, and it is safe to say that Waterfoot never in its history before had such a crowd of people along its streets and shore as on that memorable 30th June 1904, when the 'Feis na nGleann' was held. All the schools in the Glens were closed to enable the children to attend, cars brought in visitors and competitors from every part of the Glens, while motor cars and steam yachts conveyed the more wealthy observers to the place. The Raghery (Rathlin) folk were well represented. And Holden's Hall, a most fortunate erection, was crowded from 10 a.m. till the small hours of the next morning by excited, curious, homely, and fashionable crowds.

Athletic games, such as an caman, running, jumping, etc., were contested on the shore, dancing on the greens around the hall on specially erected platforms; while inside singing, fiddling (that's the pan-Gaelic way of it), whistling, story-telling , and reciting went on all day until six o'clock, when the competitions were concluded and the building cleared for the evening concert, at which quite a number of celebrities were present, including Sir Horace Plunkett, who distributed the prizes and made a hopeful speech on the industrial revival and the good work done by the Gaelic League.

It was stated that about 4,000 people came and went about the Feis during the day. The syllabus certainly afforded something for everyone's interest. This syllabus was like everything else, characteristically Irish in design, with good black and white work by Joseph Campbell, illustrating local places of interest, and conventional cut illustrating industrial sub-divisions. It contained no less than 102 competitions, literary, reciting, speech-making, story-telling in Irish, vocal and instrumental ('fidil' and pipe) music, dancing, spinning, knitting, weaving, crocheting, dress-making, ironwork, wood-carving, basket-making, decorative work and designing, toy-making, boat, and model boat building and so forth. How everything was got through in one day is what puzzled most thoughtful people. Some competitions were held over for decision, but an immense amount of work was done.

I shall only touch on some of the special features of the day's activities. In the solo singing for girls (junior), Anna MacDonnell, Glencloy, was first, and Mary McKendry second. Boys (senior): Hugh MacAulay, Glenariff, first, and Cornelius O'Donovan, Glendun, second. The latter sang the genuine old air to 'Fainne Geal an Lae' and is a native speaker of Irish. Girls (senior): Rosie McKay, Glendun, and Annie MacDonnell, Glentaise. In Choir singing (senior, unison), Miss Caulfield's Glendun Choir was first and Mr Dominic McGuire's Fairhead Choir second. School Choirs – Miss Eccles' Cushendall Choir sang most beautifully, and gave an example of good training; Glencloy Choir was second.

In fiddling, Mr O'Loan (first) and Mr Delargy (second) showed good talent. James McRann won the medal for flute playing, for whistling, Owen McNeill: and for war pipes, Neil McCurdy, who comes from Rathlin. At the concert, on this piper obtaining his prize (a fine set of O'Mealy's Uillean Pipes); a great shout went up from the crowd of the Raghery men – men of the sea, and with splendid lungs. The woodcarving section was especially good, one clever piece of work, by Mr Fife, of Glenravel, a chain of twisted links carved out of spade shaft, excited some wonder.

As a piece of good copper work, Mr Jack Morrow's 'Shield of the Heroes' shows what good talent can do with Celtic designs.

Cushendall won the toy competition, and displayed a variety of clever toys. For the best explanation of Gaelic names and places and objects in the Glens; Mr Joseph Duffy, Kilnadore cottage, Cushendall, won the prize. For historical notes on a group of ruins of Duns, Abbeys etc. Rev. Canon Dudley Janns, Glenarm, was successful. For the best collection of unpublished Glens' songs, Miss Rosina O'Neill Cushleake: special prize, Alexander McKay, Carnlough. Historical essay, Miss Mary McIlroy, Cushendall.

The Concert in the evening was crowded. Among the performers were Mr Owen Lloyd, Dublin (harpist), and Mr O'Mealy, Belfast (piper). The successful musical competitors also contributed to the programme. Sir Horace Plunkett's speech (already published in these columns) was full of happy ideas, and was received with great enthusiasm – Mr F. J. Bigger, who presided, also spoke, and Mr John McNeill, V.P., made a speech in Irish. On the conclusion of the concert and distribution of prizes, dancing was commenced in the hall, and carried on until an advanced hour.

What surprised visitors more than perhaps anything else about the 'outwardness' of the Feis na nGleann was the really admirable behaviour of the crowds on holiday and in festive mood; it was beyond compare the best behaved crowd I have ever seen. The arrangements for Press men were not all that could be desired, but that can be remedied next year if, as it is hoped, the Feis becomes an annual event. Toy-making and fiddling may seem rather slight methods of making people industrious; but if you consider for a moment the amount and the quality of the energies organised and let loose upon this Feis in these and similar activities, you must admit there is an educative principle at work somewhere. People went home to talk about what they had seen and heard and surmised, and brains and hands were set a working in many a quite hillside cottage and an interest and spirit brought into the lives passed there, so that no one can tell exactly where it may end or what evolution or genius it may bring forth. That perhaps is in a nutshell, the root idea of the Feis of the Nine Glens and I hope it will come to the richest fruition in the heart of those sea-echoing Antrim glens.

Sir Horace Plunkett outside the old Glens of Antrim Hotel, Cushendall, in 1904 *(Courtesy Ulster Museum/MAGNI)*

The following appeared under the heading 'Speech by Sir Horace Plunkett' in the *Ballymena Weekly Telegraph*.

A grand musical festival was held in Glenariff yesterday, organised by Miss Barbara McDonnell, Miss Ada McNeill, Mr D. McAllister, Mr Francis Joseph Bigger, and Mr Joseph Duffy. The proceedings opened at nine o'clock in Cushendall, where a procession was formed, and the march to Waterfoot began. Inside the hall were gathered exhibits to the number of over seven hundred. Their merit from both the artistic and the utilitarian standpoints is unquestioned, and they reflect much credit upon those who have manufactured them. Amid such an embarrassment of riches, one could only grasp a tithe of the work, and proceed somewhat composedly from the Irish yarns to the home-made wools and flannels to the crochet, Carrickmacross lace, or the best pair of boots made in the Glens.

Prominent amongst the exhibits, and attracting great attention, are several cases sent by the Department of Agriculture and Technical Instruction. In these are displayed well-executed objects from the Russian Peasant Industries shown at the Paris Exhibition of 1900, and these made by the people who have had no previous training are extremely creditable. At the Feis concert in the evening, Sir Horace Plunkett, who distributed the prizes, said – Before he made any remarks about the interesting event that had brought them there that day he would like to offer his sincere congratulations to the prize winners, who, as he had seen with his own eyes, had won against a measure of industry and zeal which it would be hard to find in any other part of Ireland. (Applause.) He wished also to congratulate those who did not get prizes, because they would look back upon this competition as one in which any Irishman might well be proud to have taken part. (Applause.) He could assure them that he had known old established institutions which had not got through a day's work of that kind with anything like the success which they had obtained.

The next reflection that he would lay before them was the extraordinary fact of the diversity of the men who has come to see the Glens folks of Antrim out for what to a superficial observer might appear to be a mere holiday. Since he had moved amongst them all he had met men who had come from Dublin, form Belfast, men who had come right across Ireland from Donegal, men who had all come to try and make that day's proceedings a success. (Applause.) What was the work they had to do? To develop Irish industries as other countries had developed theirs. They would have to study hard the methods by which other countries had beaten them in even Irish markets. They had to educate themselves as other countries had been educated, and they could only do that if they could bring to the aid of their movement the cordial co-operation of every class and every section of the community throughout the length and breadth of the country. (Applause.) What they had to do was to find a common platform upon which every man who wished well to Ireland, and was ready to help Ireland, could work and meet shoulder to shoulder, until they had elevated Ireland to the condition to which, if he knew their minds, they intended to elevate her. (Applause.) He might tell them that business took him for his holidays every year to America, and he knew that many of the Irish men he met had left their country in days of stress and storm, and he expected in the near future to see a large number of them coming back with new world enterprise, but with their old Irish spirit, coming back to a calm Ireland, just as the seagulls went back to the sea after a storm. (Applause.) When next he went to the States, and when he told his Irish/American friends what he had seen there that day and told them of the prospects that had been raised there of bringing a new national life to Ireland, and reviving the old Irish home, he was certain he would bring joy to many a homeless heart. (Applause.) The proceedings shortly afterwards completed.

The following article appeared in the *Ballymena Weekly Telegraph* in July 1931, under the heading 'Feis na nGleann in Ballymena attended by Lord Ashbourne':

The Feis of the Glens of Antrim was opened in the Ballymena Parochial Hall on Saturday by the veteran Gael, Lord Ashbourne. This festival, in which the keenest interest is taken, was formerly held in Cushendall. In order, however, that it might be more central for the Gaels of Antrim, Belfast and parts of Down it was decided that Ballymena should be the venue this year, and judging by the large entry and the splendid audience the change is evidently appreciated. The Feis, which occupies three days, includes language and literary competitions, native dancing, vocal and instrumental Irish music, Uilleann pipes, flute and fiddle competitions. The industrial section, larger than on previous occasions, was very attractive. The Feis also gives much encouragement to the development of Irish art, including sculpture, water colour and oil painting, wood carving and drawing. In the language, music, dancing and industrial section the entries totalled 66, with some

14 events in the sports meeting at Cushendall.

Very elaborate arrangements were made by the committee, of which the Rev. Thomas McGrattan, PP Glenariff, is chairman; Mr John Clarke, Glenarm, treasurer; Mrs Annie McAllister, Glenariff, secretary; and these officials are to be congratulated on the splendid results attending their efforts. The other members of the committee are: Rev. James McClenaghan, Carnlough; Rev. Liam Kirkwood, BA, CC, Ballymena; Messrs Arthur McAllister, RDC Cushendall; Francis McCarry, Ballycastle; Alister McMullan, Glenariff; Miss E. Kearney, PET, Cushendall; Mrs Mac Cormaic, PET, Glendun; Mrs G. Parry, Cushendun; Miss Ada McNeill, Cushendun; Miss Madge Logue, Ballymena; Miss M. O'Boyle, PET, Glenarm; Messrs G. Ramsden, PET, Ballycastle; Archibald McKinley, PET, Carnlough; Joseph P. Gregg, PET, Ballymena; E. Forde, PET, Glenravel; Archibald McSparran, RDC, Knocknacarry; E. O'Neill, PET, Glenariff; and Hugh Flatley, PET, Cushendall.

The judges
The judges, who carried out their difficult task with efficiency, were: Irish – Rev. Dean Gogarty, BA, Belfast; Mr Hugh Corvin, Belfast; Mr Andrew Dooey, Dunloy; Mr Jos. P. Gregg, PET, Ballymena. Irish History – Rev. P. McGouran, OMI, Dublin. Vocal and Instrumental Music – Mr C.J. Brennan, Mus.B., FRCO, LRAM, Belfast. Uileann Pipes – Mr R.L. O'Mealy, Belfast. Dancing – Mr Richard McGowan, Dublin. Art – M.J. Humbert Craig, RHA, Belfast. Industry – Miss A. O'Kane, Ballymena; Miss Dobbs, Cushendall; Miss R. Young, Miss Ada McNeill, Cushendun; Mrs Annie O'Mooney, Cushendall; Mrs Sydney Parry, Cushendall.

In all the classes a very high standard of excellence was attained, and from every point of view the Feis was a complete success. The patron of the Feis is the Most Rev. Daniel Mageean, DD, Lord Bishop of Down and Connor, and vice patrons Rev. D. Gogarty, BA, QUB; Miss M. Dobbs, Cushendall; and Mr Andrew Dooey, Dunloy.

Saturday's events
Saturday's programme was confined to the dancing and language competitions and the judging in the art and industry section. There was a record number of entries in the dancing section, and the judge – Mr Richard McGowan, Dublin – was busily occupied the entire evening, and his task was not an easy one in view of the general high standard. The dancers were all attired in Irish costume.
The language section was also very large, and the young competitors in Irish story-telling and general conversation showed a firm grip of their native tongue.

Art and Industry
Perhaps the most interesting feature of the Feis was the Arts and Industry section. Every encouragement is given to the development of drawing, painting, sculpture and wood carving, and the diversity and originality of the exhibits showed the interest in this class of work. Some of the drawings of the youthful competitors were highly commendable. A special attraction was an exhibition of water-colour and black and white sketches by Mr Joseph Dempsey, Belfast; and Mr John Clarke ('Benmore') and Mr John Holden. The sketches mostly depicted Irish scenery and were very much admired. A number of photographs of the sculpture work of John Hogan were also on view.

A specimen of Irish art, illustrated in an album and casket, containing a sermon in Irish on St Patrick, by Rev. Lambert McKenna, S.J. executed by Mr Joseph Dempsey, Belfast, was an object of much interest. The book is bound in morocco and Persian leather, and hand tooled. The text is inscribed on six vellum pages, profusely illuminated and preserving the Celtic unity and characteristics of Irish art illumination.

The industrial section, which had a record number of entries, was very attractive.

Opening ceremony

Rev. J.P. Clenaghan, PP, Carnlough presided at Saturday's opening ceremony, and among those on the platform were Rev. D. Gogarty, Dean of Residence, Queen's University; Rev. E.V. McGowan PP, Ahoghill; Rev. L. Kirkwood, CC, Ballymena; Senator T. McAllister, Miss M. Dobbs, Cushendall; Miss McNeill, Cushendun; Mrs McBride, Cushendun; Miss R. Young, Ballymena; Messrs J.P. Gregg, Ballymena; H. Flatley, Cushendall; John Clarke, Glenarm; and Miss A. McAllister (secretary of the Feis Committee.)

The Chairman

The Chairman, speaking in Irish, introduced Lord Ashbourne. They were, said Fr Clenaghan, very glad to have Lord Ashbourne with them and extended to him a thousand welcomes. He had done great work for the Irish language not only in Ireland but in foreign lands, and they thanked him for coming there.

Continuing, Fr Clenaghan said the Glens of Antrim Feis was primarily established to save the Irish language, dances and music, and to promote Irish industries. They were working not only for the town of Ballymena and the Glens of Antrim but for all Ulster.

A man without Irish could not call himself educated; every day he was using words the meaning of which he did not understand. The names of places around were Irish, but to a person who did not know the language they were barbarous and meaningless. In fact, the names of the people among whom he lived were as foreign and strange to him as the names of people in China.

As regards music, he said the native Irish music was almost forgotten and one heard nothing but the foreign music that came from America. The attitude to Irish dancing was much the same.

About three years ago, he continued, the chief inspector of schools appealed to the Board to give Irish a fair chance in the schools, but this was a voice crying in the wilderness, and the evil had gone on ever since in the Northern schools. 'We are met today' he concluded 'to do our best to remedy that evil'.

Lord Ashbourne

Lord Ashbourne (who was in Gael costume) spoke in Irish, and expressed the pleasure he felt in opening the Feis and being with the Gaels of Co. Antrim.
Proceeding in English, he emphasised the fact that they were not merely assembled to amuse themselves and compete for prizes, but to bring back the language of Ireland, first to the Glens of Antrim and then to all Ireland. That was the immediate object.

There were many, he proceeded, inside and outside the Gaelic movement who failed to understand their object. They were often accused by their enemies and praised by some of their friends on account of a thing for which they were not responsible. They were supposed to be trying to isolate Ireland and to hold the people back, to put an obstacle in the way of modern progress and to reach

Lord Ashbourne and Feis officials attending the 1931 Feis in Ballymena

back in their aspirations towards the past instead of moving forward towards the future with the intention of boldly taking their place in the world of today and preparing for the future. The truth was the direct opposite of this. It was precisely because they were convinced that the old order was rapidly passing away, and that a new world was upon them that they were determined to put back-bone and character into the people of Ireland, and to make it possible for them to hold their own in the intense struggle for existence that was coming. They believed strength of character and efficiency in every sense of the word depended on their being frankly what they really were, and ceasing to present to the world the ridiculous spectacle of a whole people vainly attempting to talk a language which was not their own, and deliberately putting artificiality in the place of reality. In doing this they realised that they stood for the nation as a whole, paying no attention to a boundary which was the result of the bungling of politicians of various colours. They were working for the whole of Ireland, the Ireland that God made, bounded by the sea, from Antrim to Cork. (Applause).

Literary competitions

Conversation and story-telling in Irish. Competitors under 18 years. Prize £5 scholarship (presented by Miss M. Dobbs (Cushendall) – 1 Donal O'Hara, Glendun PES; 2 Jas. McKillop, Glendun PES; 3 (tie) Margaret Hannon, St Louis High School, Ballymena and Evelyn O'Hara, St Louis High School, Ballymena.

Irish conversation and story-telling (junior) confined to children of the Nine Glens. Prize £2 10s scholarship – 1 Brigid McLaron, St Louis High School, Ballymena; 2 (tie) Jas. McKillop and Donal O'Hara, Glendun PES.

Conversation in Irish (junior). First prize, gold medal, presented by Mr A. McSparran, RDC, Cushendun; second and third prizes, books – 1 John Ervine, Christian Brothers' S.S., Belfast; 2 Martin Conway, Christian Brothers' S.S., Belfast; 3 Brigid McLarnon, St Louis High School, Ballymena; highly commended – Jas. McKillop, Glendun PES; Donal O'Hara, Glendun PES; Sally Heron, Ballycastle High School.

Conversation in Irish (senior). 1. Bella O'Donnell, Convent of Sacred Heart of Mary, Lisburn; 2 Fergal Breen, Christian Brothers' S.S., Belfast; 3 Monica Curran, Cross and Passion Convent, Ballycastle; 4 Bridie O'Connor, St Louis High School, Ballymena.

Story-telling (senior). First, second and third prizes, books – 1 Bella O'Donnell, Convent of Sacred Heart of Mary, Lisburn; 2 Mary McNeill, Glendun PES; 3 Eileen McDonagh, St Louis High School, Ballymena; 4 Teresa McGurk, Cross and Passion Convent, Ballycastle.

1954 saw the Golden Jubilee celebrations being held in Cushendun, as reported in the *Irish News*.

> The Golden Jubilee celebrations of Feis na nGleann were held in Cushendun. Large crowds representing people from almost every corner of Ireland and further afield flocked to the small seaside village.
>
> The oration was delivered by Mr S. O Mordha, Senior Lecturer in history at St Patrick's Training College, Drumcondra, Dublin, and editor of *An tUltach*. Mr O Mordha said during the past 50 years the Feis had existed to keep alive in the hearts of the people of the Glens loyalty to Ireland and the national culture. It was sometimes said that feiseanna had outlived their usefulness and that other means were now desirable for the restoration of the language. He went on to criticise the lack of use of the medium of radio to promote the Gaelic cause.
>
> Highlight of a crowded sports programme was a thrilling hurling match in which a star-studded Carey team came from behind to win the Feis Cup by 4–10 to 6–3 from a determined Loughguile team.
>
> In the dancing section dancers from all over the six counties earned the praise of the adjudicators for their polished displays of Irish dancing. The Feis championship for junior dancers was won by Alberta Woodside. She gave a delightful exhibition of dancing.
>
> A feature of the day was the arts and crafts exhibition, in which articles of social interest were on display.
>
> Amongst the spectators were a group of thirty students from Malaya and Ceylon. They were spending a week in Cushendun under the auspices of the British Council. Their national dress of long flowing and colourful saris was in sharp contrast to the short dancing customs worn by our own Irish dancers. The visitors, who came to learn about Irish culture and folklore, represented three

A section of the crowd at the Golden Jubliee celebrations in Cushendun continents – Europe, Asia and Africa. The men among them, some of them wearing very smart university blazers, were intensely interested in the hurling matches.

A young Malayan who said he was a student at Glasgow University when asked what he thought of our summer weather, surprisingly replied 'he expected it to be much worse'. From Africa came Fr Joseph Mawanda of the diocese of Masaka, Uganda, who is studying education at Bristol University. Fr Mawanda, between forays to the ice cream stall, said in his short stay he had already learned a few words of Irish.

Three dancers practising their steps

FEISEANNA REMEMBERED

Dancers competing at the Centenary Feis 2004
(Courtesy H Boyle)

High standard in dancing competitions

Adjudicators were loud in their praise of the standards attained by competitors in the dancing competitions on Sunday. A delightful exhibition of dancing was given by Alberta Woodside, who won the Junior Feis Championship and six first prizes.

The following were the results:

Feis championship, Junior (under 15 on 1 July 1954) – Alberta Woodside.

Single jig or reel (under 10) – 1. Marie C. Carey; 2. Sandra Woodside.

Four hand reel (under 10) – 1. Martin 'A' team, Randalstown; 2. Carey 'B' team.

Double jig or reel (under 12) – 1. C. Letters; 2. Ethna McCambridge.

Slip jig (under 12) – 1. Ethna McCambridge; 2. Sandra Woodside.

Three hand reel (under 12) – 1. Allen School, Portglenone; 2. Allen School, Corkey.

Double jig or reel (under 15) – 1. Alberta Woodside: 2. Patricia Graham.

Hornpipe (under 15) – 1. Alberta Woodside; 2. E. McCambridge.

FEIS NA nGLEANN

The Higgins sisters, Glenravel

Any set dance (under 15) – 1. Alberta Woodside; 2. Patricia Graham.

Four hand reel or Humours of Bandon – 1. Carey 'A' team; 2. Martin 'C' team.

Any figure dance (over 15) – 1. Martin School, Randalstown.

Single jig or reel (under 10) – 1. Sandra Woodside; 2. Marie C. Carey.

Four hand reel (over 10) – 1. Carey 'A' team; 2. Allen 'A' team, Portglenone.

Double jig or reel (under 12) – 1. (tie) Ethna McCambridge and C. Letters; 2. Sandra Woodside.

Slip jig (under 12) – 1. Ethna McCambridge; 2. Sally Scullion.

Three hand reel (under 12) – 1. Allen School, Corkey; 2. Martin School, Antrim.

Double jig or reel (under 15) – 1. Alberta Woodside; 2. Maura McCambridge.

Hornpipe (under 15) – 1. Alberta Woodside; 2. E. McCambridge.

Any solo dance (under 15) – 1. Alberta Woodside; 2. Gwen O'Doherty.

Four hand reel or Humours of Bandon (under 15) – 1. Carey 'A' team, Ballymena; 2. Martin 'A' team, Antrim.

Any figure dance (under 15) – Martin 'A' team, Antrim; 2. Allen School, Corkey.

Open

Double jig or reel (over 15) – 1. Bridie Barr; 2. Maura Mallon.

Hornpipe – 1. Bridie Barr; 2. Maura Mallon.

Any set dance – 1. Bridie Barr; 2. (tie) Maura Mallon and E. McCann.

Any six-hand reel or jig – 1. Judge 'A' team; 2. Naomh Joseph 'A' Bhealfeirste.

Any figure dance – 1. Craobh Gaedheal Uladh, Bhealfeirste; 2. Naomh Joseph 'A', Bhealfeirste.

Sports events

Boys (under 12) – 1. Joe Mitchell; 2. John Walsh; 3. Gerard Mullhall.

Girls (under 12) – 1. Mary Hamill; 2. Margaret Scally; 3. Jean Lynn.

Girls (under 15) – 1.Mary Hamill; 2. Mary Jamieson; 3. Patricia Allen.

Final (under 15) – 1. Pat Black; 2. Sean McAleese; 3. Dan McBeth.

Girls (under 18) – 1. Mary Hamill; 2. Anne Reid; 3. Mary Jamieson.

Youths (under 18) – 220 yds – 1. John Brogan; 2. Hugh Casey; 3. William McLaughlin.

100 yards (open) – 1. Robert Close; 2. Seamus McCrory; 3. J. Deery.

440 yards – 1. Eamon Kearney; 2. J. Deery; 3. G. Drain.

One mile relay – 1. Eamon Kearney; 2. John Brogan; 3. G. Drain; 4. J. Deery.

17
FIELD EVENTS AT THE FEIS

Introduction
Pádraic Ó Cléireacháin

Hurling in some form has been known in Ireland for as far back as records go. Earliest references are in old Irish manuscripts that are mostly unknown to the public, but after about 1600 records are often in English. It would appear that there were two traditions of hurling in Ireland. One of these survives to the present day in Scotland under the name camánacht or shinty. It was played in the northern part of the country, especially in Counties Antrim, Down, Derry and Donegal. In a ruined fifteenth-century church at Cloncha in Inishowen there is a grave-slab with a representation of a camán and a ball. The camán is almost identical with the present-day Scottish shinty stick.

Camánacht was played using a camán with a fairly narrow boss and a straight end. The ball used was made of wood and this fact, along with the narrow stick, meant it was played on the ground. It was a winter game often associated with Christmas and the New Year. In southern counties after 1600 several changes came in gradually. The boss of the camán became wider over the years and a softer leather-covered ball was used. The game came to be played mostly in summer, and at some stage handling of the ball was allowed. It is of interest that rules of hurling covering the game as played in Trinity College, Dublin, in 1870 restricted the width of the boss to two inches but allowed catching the ball in the hand.

When the GAA was founded in 1884, rules were introduced on an all-Ireland basis and were based mainly on the southern summer game, since it was much more widespread than the older camánacht version which in Ireland had survived only in the Glens of Antrim and in the Ards Peninsula in Co. Down. It should be noted that the early camáns were relatively narrow-bladed. The broad blade as we know it only became popular in the 1920s and 1930s.

In southern counties hurling enjoyed patronage from the Anglo-Irish gentry. Rival landlords would arrange matches between teams from their estates, and bets were often placed on the result. This patronage gradually ceased after the Act of Union in 1800 but hurling matches still took place between neighbouring parishes. Until the 1950s and 1960s most parishes relied on the goodwill of a farmer to allow matches to take place on a reasonably flat field. Official grounds under GAA control were few and far between, and some counties had only one or two. However, in the 30 years following the Second World War most clubs acquired their own grounds complete with changing rooms as the GAA went from strength to strength.

FIELD EVENTS AT THE FEIS

Warming up for a hurling match at Glenariff *(Courtesy Ulster Museum/MAGNI)*

Hurling was an important event at all Glens Feiseanna. F.J. Bigger commissioned a special trophy for the 1904 Feis – a magnificent piece of work fashioned in copper. It is still in possession of Carey Faughs GAC, who in the final beat Cushendun, who had earlier defeated Glenarm. A Glenariff team was playing in 1905, but at that time Carey were unbeatable. In 1906 the first of the North v. South Antrim matches appears to have taken place at the Feis. This contest continued as a feature of the Feis after its revival in 1928 until the late 1950s, when the North Antrim Board allowed the final of the North Antrim Championship to be played at the Feis. A cup was provided for this competition. The present Feis Cup is dedicated to the memory of Alastair McAllister, long-term treasurer of the Feis until his untimely death in 1984.

Athletics does not seem to have been given much prominence in early Feiseanna, although there were usually field events for children. With the development of level pitches in the post-war era, several attempts were made to bring some sort of order to athletics. In the late 1950s field events in Glenariff were held under National Athletics and Cycling Association (N.A.C.A.) rules. This was the only athletic association that operated on an All-Ireland basis. Strict rules had to be followed in measuring and marking the track, and entrants had to meet certain criteria. There were entries from as far away as Armagh and most of the prizes went to members of organised N.A.C.A. clubs. Since there were no such clubs in North Antrim, the local population was not too pleased.

Another attempt at organising athletics involved competitions for members of GAA clubs. Most North Antrim clubs participated, but a dispute arose when it was claimed that several winners of events were not registered GAA players. The County Registrar was later able to confirm that they were in fact registered. Since then athletics has been confined to children's sports, which continue each

Kings of the road, Craobh Rua Cluain Ard, road race prize winners, 1986

year on an informal basis and are very popular.

Over the past 30 years the finals of the North Antrim Junior and under-16 championships have been played at the Feis. The under-16 final for the McMullan Cup (in memory of Joe McMullan, long-term committee member) has proved to be very popular and rivals the senior final in public interest. Junior and senior camogie competitions have been taking place for a number of years, and in recent times under-12 ground hurling competitions and senior seven-a-side hurling as well as a football competition have been organised, with finals played at the Feis. This has meant that some matches must be played on Saturday. The Feis Committee are very appreciative of the help and support they receive from the North Antrim Board and the Camogie Board in running these competitions.

The committee of Feis na nGleann extends congratulations to the Camogie Association of Ireland and to the four North Antrim hurling clubs, Carey Faughs, Cushendun Emmets, Glenariff Oisins and Glenarm Shane O'Neill, who are also celebrating their centenaries at this time.

FIELD EVENTS AT THE FEIS

Carey Hurlers who won Shield in 1904

Carey Faughs GAC
Pat McVeigh

During the summer of 1903 following the successful establishment of the Gaelic League within the Glens of Antrim, it was decided to establish the GAA in North Antrim. Hurling was introduced to the Carey area by the two school teachers in the parish at the time. Denis Maguire coached the men in the skills of the game and Patrick Moore who provided the backbone of the team by playing in the full back position. Moore, who hailed from Co. Kerry, was related to the Gillan family of Lossett. He also held the position of North Antrim chairman between 1905 and 1908. The club won the first Feis trophy, commissioned by Francis J. Bigger, a magnificent copper shield, which is still held by the club to this day; they were also successful in the Feis cup of 1954. Carey Faughs has gone from strength to strength over the years and is today a thriving club with both a strong juvenile and senior membership.

Cushendun team, 1931, winners of county championship

Cushendun GAC
Malachy McSparran

The Cushendun club was formed 100 years ago, in 1904. Hurling games may have been played before that year, but there are no reports of any official league or championship competitions being organised before that date.

Feis na nGleann, also held for the first time in 1904, had a hurling competition. The prize for the winners was a copper shield, 'the Shield of the Heroes', which can still be seen in Carey Parochial Hall. The teams that took part in that competition were Carey Faughs, Cushendun Brian Borus, Glenarm Sean O'Neills and Glenariff Michael Dwyers. In the following year, 1905, a committee under the presidency of Fr Magill of Carey was elected to organise a competition for the Athy Cup. The teams that took part in this tournament, held in Glenarm, were Glenariff Ossians, Mullaghsandall Shamrocks, Feystown Owen Roes and Glenarm Sean O'Neills.

At the Antrim county convention in early 1906 a resolution was passed that a separate GAA committee should be formed in North Antrim. This was duly done at a meeting held a fortnight later. It was then decided that the winners of the North Antrim championship should play the winners of South Antrim to decide which team would be county champions.

Cushendun were one of the strong teams in these early days. The team won the North Antrim championship in 1907 and 1908, but lost on both occasions to the South Antrim winners. This success did not last long and it was to be 1931 before they contested the county final again. This time they were successful, and won their one and only senior championship.

The fact that Cushendun is a very small parish meant that there was always a great difficulty in having a sufficient pool of players. Emigration was also a factor, as there was very little employment locally and many young men found it necessary to travel to America, England or Scotland to find work.

For most of the last century, Cushendun were a junior or intermediate team. They won the county junior championship in 1963, the intermediate championship in 1973 and 1992, and had some success in league competitions. But it is difficult to win trophies when the neighbouring clubs are regular winners of the championships and leagues. There is naturally a temptation for good players to join a winning team. Great credit must be given to those players who remain loyal to their home team.

Cumann Oisin 1904–2004
Charlie McAllister

The oldest oral tradition of a shinney match in Glenariff is from the last Glens Gaelic speaker, who recalled 'it lasted all day till dark, everybody played and it

Glenariff Oisins County Champions 1935 Back Row: Alex McMullan (secretary), Charlie McDonnell, Dan McAllister, Willie Graham, Charlie McAllister (President), Robert McMullan, Charlie Black, Mick McKillop, Bob Graham, Fr Dan Magennis BA, CC (Vice President); front Row: Alex McDonnell (Captain), Mick Graham, Eneas Black, Jim Mullan, Archie Darragh, Charlie McAllister, Dan McKillop, George Harvey

went from townland to townland'. Play began in Innisdubh – a large meadow in the middle of the Glen in Clonreagh townland, and he heard his forebears relate the proceedings of the day. No score was kept and everyone had his own shinney, which was cut from a hedge or young tree.

There were many other fields that were referred to as 'hurling fields', but they were used by the youths of the local townland just for practice and pastime as there were few competitive matches then. The game was played with a caman and a nig. The caman or shinney, a curved stick with a narrow head, got its name from the Gaelic word *camanach*, meaning bent or bowed. It was akin to today's hockey stick. A nig, which was a hard wooden ball, got its name from the Gaelic word *cnag*, meaning a lump or ball. Shinney was a ground game and the nig was not to be handled.

Prior to the formation of the present Oisin club there were the Michael Dwyers and 'the Old Osheens', as older generations wrote. These two teams appear to correspond to the then existent schools, viz. The Bay, Kilmore and Tamlaght, where shinney was the lunch-break pastime for the pupils. It was played on the roads, as they were reasonably free of traffic in those days. The names associated with the Michael Dwyers were: Dan O'Neill (Grenaghan), Felix and Paddy McHenry (Crignagat), Charlie McCormick and John O'Boyle (Barrahooley), Randal McDonnell, Willie Delargy, Edmund and Robert Harvey, Johnnie Sharpe, Arthur and Neil McCarry (all Kilmore), Alex McIntosh (Foriffe), Charlie McCafferty (Clonreagh), Harry Hunter (Grenaghan), Jimmy

Glenariff Oisins, 2004 team
Back Row: Norris Murray, Alastair McAllister, Padraig McIlwaine, Paul Shepherd, Gerald Black, Mark Nulty, Seamus Reid, Johnnie McIntosh, Hugh O' Connor; front Row: Michael McKillop, Ryan McDonnell, Christopher Kelly, Alex McDonnell, Michael McAllister, Michael Gettens, Christopher Shepherd, Paul Darragh, Niall O'Hagan

McAuley and Malachy McCollum (Glassmullan), Frank and Neil John O'Boyle (Foriffe), James McAuley (Bellahuriman). This team was named by Arthur McCarry, who was killed in France during the 1914–18 war.

The Osheen or Oisin club was so named by James McAuley, Waterfoot, the village shopkeeper. Probably he chose the name on account of Oisin, the legendary Glens Fianna warrior, who held court in Lig na Bhfiann. From this hollow, on Lurgeadan, there is a panoramic view of the coast and Glen. James, or Jamey Harry Og, as he was more often called to distinguish him from the many of the same name in the Glen, was looked upon as an authority on local history, folklore and Glens Gaelic. It was he that taught Professor Hamilton Delargy his first words in Irish on Red Bay pier.

Names associated with the Old Oisin team were: Pat, Michael and Archie Kinney (Foriffe), Owen McAuley (Waterfoot), Arthur Harvey (Waterfoot), Robert and Paddy McDaide (Waterfoot), James McMullan (Foriffe), Frank and Dan Higgins (Waterfoot), Joe Harvey (The Bay), Ned O'Kane, James, Pat, Neil and Alex Connolly (Carrivemurphy), Johnnie and Willie McMullan (Waterfoot), James and Willie Murphy (Red Bay).

The names listed above were probably the more active participants, but it would be unfair to assume that their contemporaries were not strong supporters and just as enthusiastic in promoting our Gaelic culture.

A hurling enthusiast of early years told of a disagreement between Oisins and Michael Dwyers during a challenge match. It was refereed by Johnnie McKillen and he was accused, being a village resident, of favouring the Oisins, so the Michael Dwyers captain, Mick Kinney, led his team off the field. The teams were: (Michael Dwyers) Mick Kinney, Dan O'Neill, Felix McHenry, Paddy McHenry, John O'Boyle, Randal McDonnell, Willie Delargy, John Sharpe, Edmund Harvey and Robert Harvey; (Oisins) Pat Kinney, Owen McAuley, Arthur Harvey, Robert McDaide, Paddy McDaide, James McMullan (Foriffe), Archie Kinney, Willie McMullan, Johnnie McMullan, Willie Murphy (Red Bay).

The list supplied has only ten players on each side – perhaps a memory slip, or only that number of players may have been available on the day.

The first chairman was Charles McKenzie, who died in 1943.

From around 1895 Gaelic League branches were being formed in the Glens; this brought Francis Joseph Bigger, Bulmer Hobson and their troupes of dancers, musicians and Irish language enthusiasts to the Antrim coast. Their host at Glenarm was John Clarke (pen-name 'Benmore'), who was the proprietor of the Antrim Arms Hotel and author of 'Blossoms in the Shade', 'Blossoms in the Hedgerows' and many other poems.

In 1896 and 1897 members of the Belfast Gaelic League marched behind their pipers from Parkmore railway station through the Glen, via Tamlaght and Drumnacur side, to Waterfoot. Its secretary wrote of the people leaving their fields to converse with his members in Irish. Before leaving Waterfoot they also talked to a Scottish fisherman who carried on a conversation in his native

Highland Gaelic. The parade moved on to Cushendall, where a League member explained their aims and objects. Benmore and other Gaelic enthusiasts had begun, through the Gaelic League, Irish and music classes along the coast to Cushendall, thus sowing the seeds of a nationalist culture, the awakening of which had a perfect platform in the first Feis na nGleann, held in Glenariff in 1904.

This was a period of great endeavour to preserve and foster Irish culture and pastimes. Regular meetings of Belfast and Glens members were held in Garron Point School. The massive crowd that attended the Feis was treated to such entertainment by our national game that each parish aspired to the formation of its own team. Given the choice of musical instruments, to form a band, or a hurling 'rig-out', the youth of the day opted for the latter. This, which comprised gold jerseys, green linen shorts and orange, white and green socks, was donated by Francis Joseph Bigger. One of the first sponsors was Johnny Black, of Calisnagh. He made the first set of hurls with the promise that he would replace any broken ones provided the Oisins won the match. According to a contemporary, Glenariff must have won many matches for Johnny made many hurls.

There was little, if any, revenue from gate collections; in these early years, a club official went around the spectators with cap in hand seeking donations. Ash trees were well examined to select a branch or trunk shaped like a hurl. When cut it was taken to the Black family sawmills, Calisnagh, where whatever number possible was cut, to the required shape and size. Each player would then trim and fashion a stick to his own taste. Even though ready-made hurls were available from Belfast suppliers, this practice continued until clubs could afford to buy them. Broken sticks were not discarded; they were spliced for further use and in many cases this was the only supply of hurls for the juveniles. Players dressed and undressed behind a ditch for a match, and often a few team members played a match in their everyday attire.

The only means of transport, in early days, were bicycle and pony and trap. It seemed no great sacrifice for delegates attending meetings to cycle from Loughguile, Ballycastle, Glenarm, etc. to Cushendall. A contemporary wrote of the 1906 era: 'everyone went on bicycles except the less fit who availed of the transport supplied by Johnnie McDade, Waterfoot and Hugh O'Mullan, The Bay, who had what were termed "Posting Cars"'. This mode of transport was available to both team and supporters. As society became more affluent, the type of transport improved.

The hurl, as seen in photographs from the early 1900s, was said to have been introduced to the area by Masters Hugh Flatley, who taught in Cushendall, and Dan Delargy, who taught in Tamlaght School. While they were on a cycling tour of Ireland, in the late 1890s, they saw the hurls being used in Galway and bought two of them and a hurling ball.

In the *Irish Weekly* coverage of the 1904 Feis, 'Benmore' reports that

Cushendun Emmets beat Glenarm Shauns, thus reaching the final. Local tradition relates that Carey Faughs beat Glenariff Old Osheens on the same day, to reach the final also. The *Irish News* of 1904 (article also written by 'Benmore') states that Carey defeated Cushendun in the Feis cup final. However, 'Benmore' in an article written in the early 1930s, just before he died, said that Glenarm played Carey in the final – perhaps he had a memory lapse. Support for the different versions depends on what part of the Glens you come from!

All the matches were played on Feis day, on which, according to a press report, 'caman and athletics were played on the shore'. The final was refereed by Dan Dempsey and one of the umpires was Roger Casement.

In Glenariff that autumn (1904), the Old Osheens brigade gave way for a younger Oisins team to represent the Glen in outside competition, playing under the auspices of the recently formed GAA Pat Kinney (Foriffe) and Pat and Dan Higgins (Waterfoot) were students at St Malachy's College, Belfast, where hurling was gaining momentum, and they passed on their skills to the younger Oisins. This period saw the demise of the Michael Dwyers.

Many enthusiastic young hurlers had not gained their place on the newly formed Oisins team, so another team was formed. They originally played in Coille Vig (the small wood) – a field opposite Calisnagh Bridge – hence they were named 'The Coille Vigs'. They did not play in any outside organised competitions. They and the Oisins had many hard-fought struggles, as everyone was vying for his place on the official Glenariff team. After a short time the venue was moved to Innis Crig (the island of the rock), a small river field opposite Coille Vig. Probably the latter, a larger and flatter field, was needed for cultivation.

In a competition for the Athy Cup, held at a Glenarm Gaelic tournament in Feystown on 16 September 1905, Glenariff beat Feystown and Glenarm beat Mullaghsandall. In the final, Glenarm beat Glenariff by 3–1 to 3–0. The *Irish News* reported that it was a thrilling match and the best ever seen. Glenariff was very much improved and had won laurels in some hard-fought battles. This is the only documentary evidence that would lead us to believe that a Glenariff team played in 1904. The Athy Cup, presented by the Gaelic League, was a magnificent silver trophy modelled on the Ardagh Chalice.

At these sports Archie Kinney (Foriffe) won a gold medal in the mile race and his brother, Pat, won a silver medal for second place in the same race.

The first team in print was in the *Irish News* on 17 June 1906, after Glenariff played Carey in the Co. Antrim Championship at Cushendun. The result was Faughs 17 points, Oisins 2 points. The Glenariff team was as follows. Goals: James Connolly (Carrivemurphy). Backs: Arthur Harvey (capt.) (Waterfoot), Alex McIntosh (Foriffe), Joe Harvey (The Bay). Halves: Arthur McCarry (Kilmore), Alex Murray (Waterfoot). Centre Half Backs: Harry Hunter (Grenaghan), Paddy McDaide (Waterfoot), Johnnie McAllister (Kilmore), Neil Connolly (Carrivemurphy). Three quarters: Pat Connolly (Carrivemurphy), Pat

Darragh (The Bay), Paddy Maguire (Kilmore). Forwards: Hugh Mullan (The Bay), Willie Murphy (Red Bay), Ned Kane (The Bay), Jamie Delargy (Foriffe), Alex Connolly (Carrivemurphy).

Although the golden era for the Oisins was from 1930 until the mid-1940s when they won every trophy in Co. Antrim, there are recordings of outstanding matches and excellent players from the Glen. Willie Graham (Drumnacur), Danny McAllister (Kilmore) and Dan McKillop (Foriffe) were probably the first Glensmen ever to play in an All-Ireland Hurling final. This was in 1943 when the Antrim team, of which they were playing members, defeated Kilkenny and Galway on their march to Croke Park, where they were beaten by Cork. Notables of an earlier era were Arthur Harvey, Jamey Delargy, Ned O'Kane and Paddy McDaide, who played for North Antrim in the 1906 Feis at Cushendall. The Glenariff club was honoured again in 1971 when Niall Wheeler was selected as a replacement All-Star.

Like every other club, Glenariff had its lean years; having such a small area for choice and many of the youth at sea or working elsewhere, it was often difficult to field a team. One of these years was 1955, when Glenariff won the Junior County Championship against all odds. But through the latter half of the last century the team has been prominent in competing in league and championship competitions, narrowly missing county honours on many occasions. Most notable of these was the 1966 county final when Ossians were narrowly defeated by Loughguile in a replay.

In one of his notebooks, Professor Hamilton Delargy wrote: 'the young men at one time played hurling on the Tillicks, where older generations used to live'; in a later era the young men practised their hurling skills on the mountain top above Drumnacur, as the land in the valley was needed for cultivation.

The first official home venue was Neil John Black's field at The Bay. Next was Alex McMullan's field at Waterfoot. The latter, on which the school is built, remained the venue for hurling and Feiseanna until 1947, when the present park came into use. Two fields were bought by the committee under the chairmanship of Fr Hugh O'Neill, curate at the Bay, with a donation of £100 from the Feis committee, a GAA grant and generous donations from other supporters. The men of the Glen did all the necessary work. With voluntary labour, over the years, the present park was created. The vice-chairman of Feis na nGleann, Mr Pádraic Mac Cormaic, Cushendun, visited the park in the spring of 1947 and reported: 'I was glad to see the voluntary spirit which existed where men with picks and shovels, horses and carts were giving voluntary services each evening to get the grounds in order'.

The name, McAllister McVeigh Memorial Park, was selected by contemporaries of the two men, Charlie McAllister and Pat McVeigh, who were shot dead by Crown Forces in 1922 on Glenariff braes.

Cuireann sé bród orainn uilig go bhfuil an iománaíocht beo bríomhar go fóill ar fud na nGlinnti. Go maire sí slán go deo.

18
FEIS NA NGLEANN
GLENARM'S INVOLVEMENT
Felix McKillop

Following an initial meeting in the School House, Cushendall, in February, 1904 (chaired by Francis Joseph Bigger, M.R.I.A.) it was agreed that a grand Feis na nGleann should take place on 30 June 1904 in Glenariff. At that meeting Miss Barbara McDonnell, Cushendall was elected president while Miss McNeill, Cushendun, was chosen as secretary.

The three Glenarm representatives on the 1904 Feis na nGleann committee were as follows.

- John 'Benmore' Clarke, manager of the Seaview Hotel, Glenarm, was a major influence in the formation and organisation of Feis na nGleann, as well as the Glens of Antrim Gaelic Society, which he had helped form in December 1903. A life-long supporter of the Feis and all its aims, he died in 1934.
- Mrs Annie McGavock, daughter of Glenarm grocer Archie MacNeill, was a sister to Eoin MacNeill, co-founder of the Gaelic League in 1893 and later Minister of Education in the Irish Free State.
- James McRann, teacher in Seaview National School, Glenarm, was a native of Co. Sligo.

Along with members from every Glen, these three worked tirelessly to make the first Feis na nGleann the major success that it became.

Shane O'Neill Senior Hurlers (c1905)
Front L-R: Alex Petticrew (captain), Willie McGavock, James McGavock, Alex Robinson, Dan McNeill, J.J. Dodds, Pat McCollum, Paddy McLaughlin, Archie Heggarty, Frank McGavock, John O'Neill, James McAuley; front L-R: George Heggarty, James McNeill, [?], James O'Hara, James McNeill (the mason), Owen McNeill, Dan McAuley

Eoin (John) MacNeill, the eminent Gaelic scholar and brother of Annie McGavock, adjudicated in the Irish language section at the 1904 Feis. The Church of Ireland rector of Glenarm, Rev. Canon Dudley Janns, won first place for his historical notes on local duns and abbeys etc., while 'Benmore' wrote a play, *The Fate of Shane O'Neill*, specially for the occasion. Among those from Glenarm who also claimed first places at the 1904 Feis were Owen McNeill, in the 'whistling an Irish air' section, James McRann for flute playing, and James McNeill in the senior hornpipe, reel and jig, while Martha McKay excelled in the recitation section.

Shane O'Neill's GAC, which had been formed in the winter of 1903, was involved in the hurling tournament on the strand at Waterfoot. At the beginning of the day's proceedings a procession beginning at Cushendall was headed to the grounds at Glenariff by the O'Neill war pipers, Armagh. Behind them came the contingent of Glenarm hurlers, carrying the O'Neill banner, presented to the club by Francis Joseph Bigger. The Red Hand of the O'Neill's had premier place on the front of the procession of clans, flanked by the banners of the McQuillan and MacDonnell clans.

Though it has been suggested in recent years that Cushendun and not Glenarm played Carey Faughs in the 1904 hurling final, writing in November 1931 in the *Glensman* magazine 'Benmore' acknowledged that Shane O'Neill hurlers, Glenarm were beaten by Carey Faughs in the final, played on Waterfoot strand. The prize – a Celtic shield, 'The Shield of the Heroes' (donated by Francis Joseph Bigger and made by Mr Jack Morrow) – was won by the Carey men. One of the Shane O'Neill team, Frank McGavock, confirmed in a letter to *The Irish News* in September 1968 that Glenarm and Carey contested the first Feis final. The referee of this match was Dan Dempsey; Roger Casement, Rev. Patrick Magill and Daniel Magill acted as umpires.

David James Hogg, Belfast took photographs of participants in the first Feis, some of which appeared in the *Weekly Telegraph* some days later.

Shane O'Neill Senior Hurling Team (2004).
Back L-R: Martin Davey, John McAllister, Jim Petticrew, Barry McMullan, Johnny O'Boyle, Conor McNeill, Kevin Cottrell, Seamus McNeill, Hugh Feeney, Bryan O'Neill, John Magill, Seamus O'Kane, Sean O'Neill (manager); front L-R: Ciaran Campbell, Donal McAuley, John Milliken, Brendan McAllister, Ronan Matthews, Hugh Martin McKay, Brendan McDermott, Niall Hamill, Sean Waide, Dean Mitchell, Brian McDermott

19

SEAMUS CLARKE
LOCAL HISTORIAN AND CHAIR OF FEIS NA nGLEANN

Eamon Phoenix

Seamus Clarke was born in Ballycastle in 1914 into a family deeply influenced by the Gaelic Revival. His father, John, was a member of a family that had been evicted from the Carey district during the Land War of the 1880s. His mother, Annie Kenny, was a native of Co. Sligo and an Irish speaker. A constant visitor to the Clarke household in Seamus's youth was his father's cousin, John Clarke, ('Benmore'), one of the founders of the Feis and a prominent writer on Irish history and archaeology. The young Seamus also knew Louis J. Walsh, the playwright and Sinn Fein politician who was a solicitor in Ballycastle until 1922.

The Clarke family were engaged in the licensed trade and had a public house in Ann Street. Seamus was educated at St Patrick's Boys' School in the town and later at Ballycastle High School, where he was taught history by the prominent local historian, Hugh Alexander Boyd. He developed an early interest in the Irish language through the influence of his Aunt Mary, a keen Gaelgeoir, and went on to attend Gaelic League classes in the town. He was also involved in hurling and, while still in his twenties, became Secretary of Ballycastle Hurling Club.

Mr Clarke came from a highly politicised family – his grandfather was a Parnellite and his parents had been ardent Home Rulers – and by the late 1930s he had been elected as a Nationalist member of Ballycastle Town Council. By this time he had succeeded his father in the family business.

Over the years Seamus was fascinated by Irish history, building up an extensive library, which he recently donated to the University of Ulster at Coleraine. Following in 'Benmore's' footsteps, he became a leading figure in Feis na nGleann from the 1930s onwards. He researched extensively into the career of Roger Casement, who had been a friend of 'Benmore'. Seamus took a principled stand on the controversial 'Black Diaries', strongly refuting their authenticity in a series of letters to Irish newspapers. In the 1970s he published a book on *Casement and the Irish Language*, dealing with the patriot's efforts to revive Irish and his links with North Antrim.

For some 40 years he was chairman of the annual Casement commemoration at Murlough Bay and in this capacity he brought a host of major public figures to the event, including Eamon de Valera (in 1953) and the former Dáil Minister, Sean MacBride, whose grandfather hailed from Glenshesk.

Over a long lifetime Seamus has collated a series of scrapbooks on Irish historical subjects, the GAA in North Antrim and the life of Casement. He is the author of a history of Feis na nGleann, published in 1995, and edited a book of poetry associated with the Feis and its founders entitled, *The Poetry of Feis na nGleann*. He is a fund of information on the rich history and traditions of his native area and has been consulted by numerous scholars over the years. For many years he has served as chairman of the Feis.

In 2004 Mr Clarke celebrated his 90th birthday. His wish is to live to see 'a prosperous Ireland at peace with itself'. As for a united Ireland, he believes this will be achieved in time when a section of northern Protestants favour unity.

20
CENTENARY CELEBRATIONS
Nuala McSparran

The Centenary year got off to a flying start on 12 March 2004 with a celebratory dinner in the Marine Hotel, Ballycastle. Among the honoured guests was GAA President, Sean Kelly, who praised the Feis committee for their dedication and reminded those present of the link between Kerry and North Antrim. He said that culture was not confined to any particular people and it was right that everyone should share it.

Miriam O'Callaghan, President of the Camogie Association, said the Feis gave a sense of community and it was significant that women had so much to do with its foundation. Dr Eamon Phoenix, lecturer and historian, gave a history of the Feis against the political background of the time and the personalities involved. He spoke of North Antrim as a place apart where Gaelic Ireland and

Centenary trophies

Feis na nGleann Committee, 2004, at the centenary dinner with guests Sean Kelly, President of the GAA, Miriam O'Callaghan President of the Camogie Association and Dr Eamon Phoenix.

CENTENARY CELEBRATIONS

Barnish Primary School choir with their principal, Mrs Wisner-Clarke, and Choir Mistress, Mrs Maureen McCarry

Scotland met. The Feis, he said, had a dual significance and was an important landmark in a vision for a united Ireland.

The year continued at a hectic pace with language competitions in May, with a large entry and keen competition for the Gaeltacht scholarships.

There has always been a strong musical tradition in the Glens of Antrim and this was evident again in our Centenary year, with competitors taking part from as far afield as Dungannon.

In an Ordnance Survey memoir written in 1835, James Boyle referring to the native inhabitants, wrote:

> many beautiful Irish airs are sung in both the English and the Irish language, particularly in Glenariff.
> The fairs in Cushendall are resorted to as much for music as for business and until very lately each public house regularly employed two fiddlers or pipers on fair days and two rooms in each of these houses were set aside for dancing but dancing in this parish has, by the Priest's orders, been discontinued.
> There are many beautiful Irish airs in Glendun but it is to be feared many have been lost.

Irish traditional music was very much a social music, with instrumental music, song and dance flourishing together. It was an oral tradition as few could read

FEIS NA nGLEANN

Musicians showing off their talents

music. Tunes and songs were learnt by ear. Seán Ó Riada described it as 'an untouched, unwesternized orally-transmitted music'.

At the 1904 Feis there were competitions for fiddle, war pipes and uilleann pipes, flute and harp. Traditional music received a great boost with the foundation of *Comhaltas Ceoltóirí Éireann* in 1951. There are at present eight branches in Co. Antrim – six of them in North Antrim, including the Ballycastle and Glens of Antrim branches. Classes in instrumental music and sessions are organised by these branches and by the closely associated Glens Traditions Group.

Singing is to a great extent taught in schools. The Feis Committee appreciates that in the busy world of today's classroom there are compelling academic demands so that it is difficult for teachers to find time to develop the cultural side of the children's education. With this in mind the Music Committee try to produce an attractive *Clár* to suit both teacher and pupil. In instrumental music there are solo competitions in tin whistle, flute, fiddle, accordion and miscellaneous instruments as well as duos and trios. There are solo singing competitions in both Irish and English. All of these competitions cater for six different age groups. A new section for traditional groups has proved very popular with teenagers, and a competition for novices has been introduced in most sections to encourage those who on Feis Day failed to win a prize. Similar competitions are now held at the annual Co. Antrim *Fleadh Cheoil* and the two programmes complement each other.

CENTENARY CELEBRATIONS

There are choir competitions for primary and post-primary schools in both Irish and English and an open competition for singing in Irish. The Music Committee's main aim is to ensure that the Feis plays its part in keeping alive traditional music and song, especially those tunes and songs with a Glens of Antrim connection, and in reviving songs that may be to a great extent forgotten. In this they hope to maintain the aims of the founders in the modern era.

Dancing has been a favourite pastime in the Glens for many generations. In 1835 James Boyle wrote:

> Dancing, until very lately, was their favourite amusement and they frequently indulged in it both in their own homes and at the fairs at Cushendall, to which many came for no other purpose.

Comtemporary dancing costumes, 2004

This year was no exception, with dancers competing for special Centenary prizes.

The Feis weekend, 18–20 June, drew large crowds, and they were entertained by fine displays of hurling, camogie and football. Visitors to the field included the Armagh Pipers, Glens Comhaltas Group, the Armagh Rhymers and Francis O'Boyle, storyteller, musician and artist from Shropshire (his father was born in Glenariff). Two marquees held extensive displays of arts and craft including demonstrations of traditional bread-making, lace-making and crochet.

Centenary mass was held in St Patrick's and St Brigid's Church, Glenariff on 25 June.

The celebrant was Bishop Donal McKeown. Mass hymns were sung by the Glens Choir.

Éigse na Feise – 'Feis na nGleann – Céad Bliain ag Fás' – was held in Kilmore House, Glenariff, on 29 and 30 October.

The year concluded with a visit from the famous group *Siamsa Tíre* from the National Folk Theatre of Ireland, Tralee, performing 'The Children of Lir' through mime, music and dance in St MacNissi's College, Garron Tower.

THE POETRY OF FEIS NA nGLEANN

Traditional dance, music and storytelling were prevalent pastimes in the Glens of Antrim through the centuries. Irish was the spoken language until the mid-nineteenth century. The Ordnance Survey memoirs of 1830 record that traditional airs were popular in every Glen, especially Glendun and Glenariff. Poems from the early twentieth century by such poets as Dan McGonnell and Stoddard Moore are still recited locally. An anthology of poems about the Glens Feis or by poets associated with Feis na nGleann was compiled by Seamus Clarke in 1995. The poems that follow are taken from this publication, except 'The Antrim Glens' by Joseph Duffy (Séamus Ó Dubhaigh).

Joseph Duffy was a local schoolmaster and member of the first Feis committee in 1904. He was not only a language enthusiast but was deeply interested in all aspects of Irish culture.

The Blue Hills of Antrim

The blue hills of Antrim I see in my dreams,
The blue hills of Antrim, the glens and the streams,
In sunlight and shadow, in weal and in woe,
The sweet vision haunts me wherever I go.

The wind's in the heather of sunny Cnoc-leithid,
And soft thro' the vale of Gleann-seasg hath it played,
O'er young Margie's wemplings and deep Mael's roar,
It croons in my heart, and will croon evermore.

Sliabh Treastain's in shadow, and Gleannan in tears,
Looks sorrowing up at her love through the years,
That sad look at Treastain I cannot forget,
My heart pines in darkness, my lashes are wet.

The sun's on Gleann-duinne and old Sliabh-an-air
Thinks only of peace now and never of war,
My heart's in the sun now, it sings like a bird,
Of question or quarrel it never had heard.

O'er lone Luirg-eadain the dim shadows creep
And Cois-abhann-dalla is silent in sleep,
As night's on the mountain, as sleep's on the stream,
My heart is in darkness, my soul is a-dream.

Red dawn is at breaking and Sliabh-Mis is glad,
In smiles to the green fields and fallows of Braghad,
Carraig-bile is waking from night's dewy sleep,
And Cealla's young stream with my new pulses leap.

Down wild Sliabh-na-ngaoth the Lammas winds roar,
Their pealings re-echoed from rocky Pairc-Mor,
Gleann-airbh is troubled – my brain is afire,
For love unrequited and hindered desire.

Meek eve calms the rough brow of mighty Beann-uamhain,
And Dubh-ais for sorrow looks out at the moon,
As day sets on Sean-cill and Dun-mor macAirt,
The sweet light of memory is quencht in my heart.

As fleet as the changes on the mountain and vale,
So fleet are my moods and so many their tale.
I sigh with the shadow, I laugh with the shine,
And with joy in the hill's heart there's gladness in mine.

The blue hills of Antrim I see in my dreams,
The blue hills of Antrim, the glens and the streams,
In sunlight and shadow, in weal or in woe,
The sweet vision haunts me wherever I go.

Seosamh MacCathmhaoil (Joseph Campbell)

THE POETRY OF FEIS NA nGLEANN

The Feis in the Glen

When I was young I took a day from Time
And keep it still – no glint of all the sun
That shone that day, but shines in the fixed clime
In which I keep the hours he can't outrun.
Oh, I went down that morning to the Feis
With everyone to watch the way I'd go
I wore a linen frock with cuffs of lace
I wore a yellow hat with a cherry bow.

The day the sun shone as it never shone, ever,
On sea and on glen and on bright waterfall,
The day I was wise, and the day I was clever,
The day I knew all things, and nothing at all.

Through the green, golden glen the birds were singing
And all the little brooks were tuned to me,
The pipers in their saffron kilts were swinging
Down to the glen's foot, where it meets the sea.
And, oh, the prizes! Fat books for my winning,
For I knew everything that was to know –
We are so sure of things in the beginning –
I wore a yellow hat with a cherry bow.

The day the sun shone over smooth, over hilly,
The day when my heart could go thro' a stone wall,
The day I was wise, and the day I was silly,
The day I knew all things, and nothing at all.

I took a day from Time when I was young
And kept it still, sun, trees and streams and sea,
So small a song was mine, but it was sung
And still is singing. He I loved loved me
First love that keeps a ribbon for a token,
The small sweet vanities that with it go
The day I sealed from Time with seals unbroken
I wore a yellow hat with a cherry bow.

The day when the sun on the sea was a river
Of gold for my sailing beyond the world's wall,
The day I was wise, and the day I was clever,
That day I know all things, and nothing at all.

Siobhan Ní Luain

The Antrim Glens

The Antrim Glens stretch to the Moyle
That silver streak of sea
Where Lir's long daughter wandered long
Awaiting to be free

This lady fair oft visited
In turn, each Glen of Nine
And asked Dame Nature's care for all
That mortals might not pine

That Antrim Glens might fruitful be
And plenty might abound
That pestilence should be unknown
And invalids made sound

That through all time, the gas, ozone
From mountains top to shore
Should youth preserve, destroy disease
And heal the sick and sore

In Antrim Glens the virgin Spring
Disputes stern Winter's reign
And ere he half his course has run
She claims the Glens' domain

In these sweet spots, the sun's strong rays
Of Summer make a home
Reluctantly she moves away
More southern climes to roam

When Autumn comes upon the Glens
He asks a lengthened stay
And wrestles long with Winter fierce
Before he moves away

The spell of Winter here is short
And this he knows full well
So off he scampers to the North
A whining tale to tell

J. Duffy, 1900

THE POETRY OF FEIS NA nGLEANN

Autumn Day in Glenariff

The calm sea sleeps upon the shore –
Each wavelet like a dreamer's breath
Soft swells and falls, it could no more
Of stillness offer save in death.

And Lurig's hushed brow of calm
Looks down in peace upon the bay –
Or northward reared, like battled ram
Disputes each white-sailed cloudlet's way.

And sunshine hoarded through the length
Of Summer days, 'gainst Summer's will –
Now burning August's gathered strength
Hurls in fierce splendour o'er the hill.

Roger Casement

Glenariff, Co. Antrim

If Only I Were in Articoan

If only I were in Articoan,
Near that mountain that is far away,
O King! my visit would be light-hearted
To the Cuckoos' Glen on Sunday.

Chorus

Agus och, och éirí 'lig is ó
Éiri lionndubh is ó
My heart is heavy and wounded.

Many's a Christmas I would be,
In Cushendun when [young and] foolish,
Hurling on the white strand,
My white hurl in my hand.

Chorus

Am I not miserable here by myself,
Not hearing the voice of cock, blackbird or
Sparrow, thrush, or even the snipe,
And I do not even recognise Sundays.

Chorus

Many's the sight that I saw
From Garron Point to the Moyle,
A great fleet driven by the wind;
And King Charlie's armada.

Chorus

If I were in Cushendun,
Where all my friends are,
I would find music there, drink and games,
And I would not die alone.

Chorus

My seven curses on the world,
It is more treacherous than death;
It lured me from my own people,
As the lamb would be lured from the sheep.

Chorus

If only I had a skiff and oar,
I would row upon the flood-tide,
Hoping to God to arrive safely,
So that I will be in Ireland when I die.

Chorus

      John McCambridge

Áird a' Chuain

Á mbeinn phéin in Ard a'Chuain
In aice an isléibhe úd atá í bhfad bhum,
A Rí! gurbh aighearach mo chuairt
Go Gleann na gCuach Dé Domhnaigh.

Loinneog

Agus och, och éiri 'lig is ó
Éiri lionndubh is ó
'Sé mo chroí atá trom is é leonta.

Is ioma' Nollaig a bhí agam péin
I mBun Abhann Doinne is mé gan chéill,
Ag iomáin ar an tráigh bhán,
Mo chamán bán in mo dhorn liom.

Loinneog

Nach tuirseach mise anseo liom péin,
Nach n-airím guth coiligh, londuibh nó traon',
Gealbhan, smólach, naoscach phéin,
Is chan aithnim péin an Domhnach.

Loinneog

Is ioma' amharc a bhí agam péin
Ó Shrón Ghearráin do dtí an Mhaoil
Ar loingeas mór ag cáith ar ghaoith,
Agus cabhlach an Rí Seorlai.

Loinneog

'Á mbeinn phéin i mBun Abhann Doinne,
Far a bhfuil mo chairdean uile,
Gheobhainn ceol ann, ól is imirt,
Is chan fhaighinn bás in uaigneas.

Loinneog

Mo sheacht mallacht ar an tsaol,
Is caraí é go mór ná an t-éag;
Mheall sé mé ó mo mhuintir phéin,
Mar mheallfaí an t-uan bhón chaora.

Loinneog

'Á mbeadh agam péin ach coit' is rámh,
Ná go n-iomairinn ar dhroim an tsnáimh,
Ag dúil as Dia go ruiginn slán
Is go bhfaighinn bás in Éirinn.

Loinneog

INDEX

Note: references with the letter 'n' refer to notes, references with the letter 'p' refer to photographs.

Abbey Theatre, 36, 38
Act of Union, 35, 36, 158
Adair Arms Hotel, Ballymena, 53, 54
Africa, 47, 50, 55, 154
    Congo, 48, 55, 56, 63, 100
    South Africa, 57, 112
    West Africa, 100
Ahoghill, 25, 28, 37, 102, 151
Aifreann Feirste, 120
All Ireland Hurling final, 168
Allen School, Corkey, 155, 157
Allen School, Portglenone, 155
Allen, Patricia, 157
Altan, 143
America (USA), 32, 61, 100, 136, 149, 151, 163
    Philadelphia, 135
Amhrán na bhFiann, 7
An Claidheamh Soluis (The Sword of Light), 91
An Clár, 133
An Tuirne Beag (The Little Spinning Wheel), 99, 133
An tUltach, 24, 127, 153
Andrews, John, 84
Anglo-Irish Treaty, 75
'Annals of Tigearnach', 23
Annals of Ulster, The, 39
Antrim Arms Hotel, 165
'Ard Righ', 65, 69, 70, 74, 75, 77, 79, 81, 82, 98, 99, 112
Ardery, Mary Jane (mother of F.J. Bigger), 66
Armagh Rhymers, 177
Armagh, Co., 170
    Lurgan, 82
    South Armagh, 4, 23
    Flurry Bridge, 81
Armour, Rev. J.B., 59, 60, 61
Armoy, 55
'Art and Industrial Exhibition', 131
Asgard, 74
Ashbourne, Lord, 42, 69, 149, 151–2
Ashbrooke, Co. Fermanagh, 22
Asia, 154
Asquith, [Herbert], 90
Astley, Nanette (mother of Ada McNeill), 45
Athy Cup, 162
Aud, 62
Australia, 100

'B' Specials, 28
Ball, Anne (maternal grandmother of Sir Roger Casement), 53
Ballinderry, 53
Ballintoy, 119, 120

Ballycastle, 3, 4, 5, 6, 7, 10, 11, 12, 25, 33, 43, 46, 47, 53, 55, 56, 57, 59, 72, 83, 95, 96, 97, 99, 103, 112, 114, 118, 119, 120, 129, 133, 141, 143, 146, 150, 166, 171, 176
Ann Street, 171
    Churchfield House, 46, 47, 53
Ballycastle High School, Ballycastle, 171
Ballycastle Hurling Club, 171
Ballycastle Pipe Band, 114
Ballycastle Rural District Council, 100, 102
Ballycastle Toy Factory, 33
Ballygullion, 84
Ballymena, 8, 21, 23, 25, 33, 34p, 41, 42, 54, 59, 78, 101, 113, 116, 117, 134, 145, 149, 150, 151, 157
    Harryville, 8, 53, 117
    Henryville, 8, 53
Ballymena Academy, 54, 99–100
Ballymena Cricket Club, 55
Ballymena Diocesan School, 54
Ballymena Feis, 42
Ballymena Observer, 115
Ballymena Parochial Hall, 149
Ballymena Weekly Telegraph, 145, 148, 149, 170
Ballymoney, 60, 61
Ballymoney Free Press, 61
Ballymoney Town Hall, 60
Ballyvoy, 99
Bann, River, 18
Bannister, Eilis (sister of Mrs Sydney Parry), 15, 32
Bannister, Gertrude *see* Mrs Sydney Parry
Bannister, Una (sister of Mrs Sydney Parry), 15, 32
Bannside, 40
Barr, Bridie, 157
Barrahooley, 164
Bartley, Fr Tom, 7
Bay, The, 165, 166, 167, 168
Beathaisnéis a Dó, 29n
Beathaisnéis a hAon, 29n
Beatty, Dr, 113
Beauclerc estate, Ardglass, 68
Beckett, J.C., 77n
Belfast, 3, 15, 16, 17, 19, 21, 27, 60, 65, 66, 67, 68, 69, 71, 73, 74, 75, 78, 81, 82, 84, 95, 96, 98, 107, 112, 120, 131, 141, 149, 150, 151
    Antrim Road, 74
    Beersbridge Road, 107
    Bigger's Entry, 65
    Castlereagh Road, 78
    Cave Hill, 69, 81
    Church Street, 69
    Crown Entry, Belfast, 65
    Deramore Park, 33
    Donegall Street, 95
    Falls Road, 23

    Hercules Street, 66
    Loretto Cottage, 78, 79, 82
    Malone Road, Belfast, 21, 33
    MacArt's Fort, 81
    North Street, 95
    Queen Street, 95
    Ravensdale Street, 78
    Rea's Building, Donegall Street, 66
    Shaw's Bridge, 81
    West Belfast, 73
Belfast Central Library, 66
Belfast Coiste Ceantair, 3, 98
Belfast Council, Gaelic League, 67
Belfast Evening Telegraph, 61, 84
Belfast Harp Festival 1792, 3, 16
Belfast Literary Theatre, 38
Belfast Lough, 69
Belfast Naturalists' Field Club, 66, 67, 98
Belfast Philharmonic Society, 84
Belfast Public Library, 17
Belfast Revivalists, 19
Belfast sectarian violence, 1920–2, 75
Belfast Telegraph, 71, 77
Belfast: Origin and Growth of an Industrial City, 77n
'Benmore' *see* John Clarke
Biggar, Joseph Gillis, 66
Bigger, Colonel F.C. (brother of F.J. Bigger), 71, 75
Bigger, David (grandfather of F.J. Bigger), 66
Bigger, Francis Joseph, 2, 3, 4, 25, 41, 56, 57, 64p, 65–77, 76p, 79, 81, 82, 83, 84, 96, 98, 99, 112, 114, 115p, 116, 121–2, 129, 131, 132, 133, 141, 146, 147, 148, 159, 161, 165, 166, 169, 170
Bigger, Joseph (father of F.J. Bigger), 65
Bigger, William (great-grandfather of F.J. Bigger), 66
Biggerstown, Mallusk, 65, 66
Birds of Ard Righ, The, 75
Birmingham, George A. *see* Canon James Hannay
Bishop Mageean Cup for the Irish Language, 5
'Black Diaries', 63, 171
Black, Charlie, 163p
Black, Denis, 3, 100
Black, Eneas, 163p
Black, Gerald, 164p
Black, Johnny, 166
Black, Kevin, 143
Black, Martin, 143
Black, Neil John, 168
Black, Pat, 157
Blacker, Eliza, 28
Blaney, Hugh, 145
Blaney, Mary, 136
Blayney, Alexander, 87
'Blossoms in the Hedgerows', 165

'Blossoms in the Shade', 165
Blythe, Ernest (Ernie), 38, 73, 74
Bodleian Library, 23
Bolg an tSólair, 16
Book of Leinster, The, 39
Book of Revelations, The, 35
Book of Rights, The, 39
Boundary Commission, 93–4
Boyd, Dr Bill, 119
Boyd, Hugh Alexander, 171
Boyle, James, 175, 176
Boyne, 35
Brady, Fr Brian, 7
Brady, Rosemary O'Rawe, 129, 134
Braid, 117
Braid River, 53
Breathnach, Micheál, 22, 23
Breen, Fergal, 1 52
Brennan, C.J., 150
Breslin, Michael, 117
Bristol University, 154
British Council, 153
Brixton Prison, 45, 51, 74, 98
Brogan, Eddie, 7
Brogan, John, 157
Brogan, Mr, 28
Brooke, Charlotte, 16, 24
Brookeborough, Rosemary, Lady, 20p, 21, 22, 25
Broughshane, 60
Broxley Park, 21
Bunting, Edward, 119
Burns, Kathleen, 11
Burns, Paddy, 9, 11, 144
Byrne PP, Fr, 43

Caird, Dr Donald, 119
Camogie Association of Ireland, 11, 160, 173
Campbell, Chris, 9, 11
Campbell, Ciaran, 170p
Campbell, Isobel (wife of John 'Benmore' Clarke), 96
Campbell, James, 2
Campbell, John, 2, 78–86, 130, 133
Campbell, Joseph, 41, 65, 69–70, 73, 75, 78–86, 146
Campbell, William (father of John and Joseph Campbell), 78
Canada, North-West, 31
Canmer, Catherine (mother of John and Joseph Campbell), 78
Canmer, Josephine (sister of John and Joseph Campbell), 78
Capuchin Annual, 77n
Carbery, Ethna *see also* Anna Johnston, 2, 33, 95
Carey, 3, 9, 11, 19, 58, 97, 99, 117, 118, 153, 155, 156, 157, 159, 167, 170, 171
Carey Faughs GAC, 3, 159, 160, 161, 162, 167, 170
Carey Parochial Hall, 162
Carey, Marie C., 155, 156
Carlisle, Alex, 73
Carnegie, Peggy, 1
Carnlough, 3, 5, 8, 42, 56, 98, 116, 147, 150, 151
    College Farm, 101
    High Street, 102
    Waterfall Road, 102
Carnmoney, 65, 66, 70

Carrickfergus, 21, 32, 35, 87
Carrivemurphy, 165, 167, 168
Carson, Robert, 60
Carson, Sir Edward, 45, 59, 60, 90, 91
Casement and the Irish Language, 171
Casement, Admiral, 47, 59
Casement, Agnes Jane (Nina) (sister of Sir Roger Casement), 53, 58
Casement, Charles Adam William Ball (brother of Sir Roger Casement), 53
Casement, Hugh (great-great-grandfather of Sir Roger Casement), 53
Casement, Hugh (paternal grandfather of Sir Roger Casement), 53
Casement, John (uncle of Sir Roger Casement), 53, 54, 55, 100
Casement, Roger (great-grandfather of Sir Roger Casement), 53
Casement, Roger (father of Sir Roger Casement), 53
Casement, Sir Roger (David), 2, 3, 8, 15, 21, 26, 32, 33, 37, 38, 39, 41, 45, 46, 47, 48, 49, 50, 51, 52p, 53–63, 73, 74, 75, 79, 84, 92, 96, 98, 99, 109, 111, 112, 114, 115p, 116, 141, 167, 170, 171
Casement, Thomas Hugh Jephson (brother of Sir Roger Casement), 53, 58
Casey, Hugh, 157
'Castle Sean' *see* Jordan's Castle
Cattle Raid of Cooley, The, 37
Caulfield, Miss, 147
Cavan, Co., 66
Ceannt, [Eamonn], 92
Celtic Society, The, 16
Celtic Twilight, The, 79
Ceylon, 153
Chambers, James, 73
Chapel School, Ballycastle, 95
Charlemont, Lord, 35
China, 151
Christian Brothers' Secondary School, 152
Churchill, Lord Randolph, 91
Clarke, James (uncle of John 'Benmore' Clarke), 95
Clarke, John (father of Seamus Clarke), 171
Clarke, John 'Benmore', 2, 3, 4, 5, 11p, 56, 67, 75, 81, 95–7, 103, 112, 115p, 150, 151, 165–6, 167, 169, 170, 171
Clarke, Seamus, 5, 8, 11, 77n, 85n, 171–2, 179
Clarke, Stephen, 2, 33, 49, 72–3, 115
Clarke, Tom, 91
Clenaghan, Rev. George, 11p, 114, 151
Clerkin, Patrick J., 7, 11
Clifton Street Cemetery, Belfast, 69
Cloch Cheannflaolaidh, 21
Clonegagh/Clonreagh 107, 164
Close, Robert, 157
Cloughs, 144
Coast Guard station, Cushendun, 50
Coláiste Chomhghaill, Belfast, 23
Colaiste Uladh, Co. Donegal, 25, 26
Collected Poems (Moira O'Neill), 32
Colum, Pádraic, 79, 84, 85
Columbia University, 7
Comhaltas Ceoltóirí Éireann, 12, 118, 176
Comhaltas Uladh, 7, 117
Comhchoiste na Gaeilge Aontroim Thuaidh, 118, 119
Comhdháil le Rincí Gaelacha, 8
Community Relations Council for Northern Ireland, 119

Con Magee's GAC, 101
Conal Cearnach, 39
Concannon, Helena *née* Walsh (wife of Thomas Concannon), 83
Concannon, Thomas, 83
Congested Districts Board, 41
Connolly, Alex, 165, 168
Connolly, James, 74, 79, 165, 167
Connolly, John, 11
Connolly, Joseph, 74
Connolly, Neil, 165, 167
Connolly, Pat, 165, 167
Connolly, Senator Joseph, 103
Conradh na Gaeilge, 118
'Consul Casement' *see* Sir Roger Casement
Convent of Sacred Heart of Mary, Lisburn, 153
Convery PP, Fr, 108
Conway House, Dunmurry, 23
Conway, Martin, 152
Cora Cainnte Thír Chonaill, 126
Cork, Co., 7, 152, 168
    Carraig an Ime, West Cork, 18
    Carraig na bhFear, 24
    Macroom, 18
    Mallow Castle, 53
    Queenstown, 62
Corr Éan, 126
Corvin, Hugh, 150
Cottrell, Kevin, 170p
Coyle PP, Fr Eddie, 119
Craig, [James], 45
Craig, J. Humbert, 5, 37, 150
Cranfield, Randalstown, 68
Craobh Gaedheal Uladh, Bhealfeirste, 157
Craobh Rua Cluain Ard, 160
Crignagat, 164
Croke Park, Dublin, 168
Crommelin, Constance, 36
Crommelin, Nicholas de Lacherois, 38
Crommelin, Samuel de Lacherois (husband of Maria Dobbs), 38
Crone, Dr John S., 66, 68, 69, 77n
Cross and Passion Convent, Ballycastle, 152, 153
Crossing the Bar, 76
'Crown and Shamrock', Carnmoney, 71
Cruitne, The, 39
Cú na gCleas, 15, 27
'Cú Uladh' *see* P.T. McGinley
'Cuchullain', 81
Cuideachta Ghaeilge Uladh *see* Ulster Gaelic Society
Culfeightrin, 119
Cumann Gaelach Reachtainn, 143
Cunnradh na Gaedhilge, 89
Curran, Monica, 152
Cushendall, 2, 3, 4, 5, 7, 9, 10, 11, 15, 17, 35, 39, 41, 42, 43, 49, 56, 58, 98, 99, 101, 102, 103, 108, 112, 117, 118, 119, 120, 129, 132, 133, 134, 136, 145, 146, 147, 148, 149, 150, 151, 152, 166, 168, 169, 170, 175, 177
    High Street, 135
    Kilnadore House, 99, 147
    Laney, 3, 102
    Legge Green, 4, 42
    Monavart, 2, 31, 71, 98, 134
    Shore Street, 135
    Tully, 140
'Cushendall Toy Making Industry', 136

INDEX

Cushendun, 3, 5, 7, 8, 10, 24, 25, 36, 41, 43, 45, 50, 51, 56, 67, 98, 109, 150, 151, 152, 153, 159, 162, 163, 167, 168, 169, 170
    Ballyloughan Torr, 140
    Calisnagh Bridge, 167
    Calisnagh, 140, 166
    Castlegreen, 140
    Rockport, 31
Cushendun Brian Borus, 162
Cushendun Emmets, 3, 160, 167
Cushendun, Lord *see also* Ronald McNeill, 25, 98
Cushleake, 147

Dáil Éireann, 93
Dáil Uladh, 112
'Dalriada', 39
Daniel (Biblical reference), 35–6
Darragh, Archie, 163p
Darragh, Dan[iel], 95, 96
Darragh, Pat, 167–8
Darragh, Paul, 164p
Davey, Martin, 170p
Davey, Patrick, 120
de Blacam, Aodh, 24
de Búrca, Seán, 117
de Valera, Éamonn, 93, 119, 171
Deery, J., 157
'Deirdre and the Sons of Uisneach', 9
Delargy, Dan, 101, 166
Delargy, Jamie, 168
Delargy, Mr, 147
Delargy, Ollamh, 125
Delargy, Prof. James Hamilton, 116, 119, 165, 168
Delargy, Rugadh, 125
Delargy, Willie, 164, 165
Dempsey, Dan, 167, 170
Dempsey, Joseph, 150, 151
Dennis, Patricia, 11
Department of Agriculture and Technical Instruction, 148, 133
Derry Sentinel, 89
Derry, Co., 101, 158
    Ballinascreen, 16
    Coleraine, 25, 99
    Derry City, 93
    Maghera, 118
    South Derry, 19, 68
Dervile, Sr, 7
Devlin, Joseph (Joe), 73, 91
Devlin, Rev. E., 43
Diamond, Rev. Edward, 11p
Dickson, Rev. William Steele, 69
Dixon, Roger, 74, 77
Dixon, Sir Daniel, 126
Dobbs, Conway Edward sen. (grandfather of Margaret Dobbs), 35
Dobbs, Conway Edward (father of Margaret Dobbs), 21, 32, 35, 36
Dobbs, Chaplain Rev. Conway Ed., 40
Dobbs, Lieutenant Conway Ed., 40
Dobbs, Francis (father of Maria Sophia Dobbs), 35–6
Dobbs, Henry Hugh (brother of Margaret Dobbs), 40
Dobbs, James (brother of Margaret Dobbs), 21

Dobbs, Margaret (Emmeline), 2, 3, 4, 7, 15, 20, 21, 25, 27, 28, 29, 32, 34p, 35, 36–40, 45, 59, 67, 96, 102, 109, 115p, 116, 117, 141, 150, 151, 152
Dobbs, Maria (wife of Samuel de Lacherois Crommelin), 38
Dobbs, Maria Sophia (wife of Conway Edward Dobbs sen.), 35
Dobbs, Nithsdale (brother of Margaret Dobbs), 40
Dobbs, Rev. Richard Stewart, 36
Dobbs, Richard, 36
Doctor and Mrs McAuley, The, 38
Dodds, J.J., 169p
Domville Dolls' House, 134p, 136
'Donal agus Morag', 143
Donegal, Co., 4, 19, 25, 27, 51, 73, 74, 82, 107, 119, 149, 158
    Árainn Mhór (Aranmore island), 26, 43
    Cairdeas Chloich Cheann Fhaola, 120
    Caiseal na gCorr, 25
    Cloncha, Inishowen, 158
    Cloughaneely, 25, 37, 45, 50
    Donegal town, 10
    Glenswilly, 107
    Gort an Choirce, 25
    Tory, 26
Donegore churchyard, 67
'Donn Byrne' *see* Brian O'Byrne
Dooey, Andy, 4, 41, 42, 67, 115, 120, 150
Dooey, Pearse, 7
Doomsland, 69
Down, Co., 19, 35, 149, 158
    Ardglass, 68
    Ardglass Golf Links, 69
    Ards Peninsula, 158
    Ballyvalley, Banbridge, 66
    Bangor, 3
    Bannville, 18
    Clandaboy/Clandeboye, 18, 87
    Donaghadee, 65
    Downpatrick, 68
    Downpatrick Cathedral, 68
    Loughinisland, 16
Doyle, Lynn, 38, 84
Drain, G., 157
Dramatic Legend, 78
Drone, The, 78
Drumnasole, 8
Drury, Miss, 23
Duanaire Gaedhilge, 21, 23, 24, 28
Dublin, 12, 15, 16, 20, 23, 28, 32, 33, 36, 37, 49, 56, 62, 66, 73, 75, 77, 88, 89, 90, 111, 119, 120, 143, 145, 149, 150
    Doyle's Cottage, Lawson Terrace, Sandycove, 53, 99
    Four Courts, 87, 89
    O'Connell Street, 89, 91
    Rotunda, 92
Dublin Castle, 73, 75
Dudgeon, Jeffrey, 53, 54, 57, 63n, 77n
Duffy, Joseph, 2, 3, 99, 108, 109, 115, 147, 148, 179
Dún na dTuar, 136
Dundalgan Press, 38
Dundarave *see* Upper Clogher Court
Dungannon Convention of 1782, 35
Dunkin, Lady, 28
'Dunleath Arms', Ballywalter, 71
Dunleath, Lord, 35

Dunloy, 7, 9, 10, 67, 117, 118, 119, 120, 150
Dunsford Catholic Church, 69

Easter Rising, 4, 33, 62, 73, 74, 75, 77, 90, 92, 93, 97
    'Dublin Plan', 92
Eccles, Miss, 135, 136, 147
Éigse na Feise, 177
Éigse na nGlinntí, 17, 119, 120
Eire Ogs, Glenarm, 114
Elder Dempster Shipping Company, 55
Elliott, Seamus, 9
Ellis, Albert, 62
Emerson, Mr & Mrs, 85n
Emerson, Rose, 129
Emmet, Robert, 69
Emmet, Thomas Addis, 69
England, 35, 45, 62, 91, 92, 98, 100, 136, 144, 163
    Liverpool, 55, 66
    London, 15, 23, 63, 135,
        House of Commons, 66, 90
        House of Lords, 90
        Stanley Gardens, 23
        Tower of London, 62, 100
    Newcastle-on-Tyne, 135
    Oxford, 23, 26
    Shropshire, 177
    Sussex, 53
Eoin MacNeill: Scholar and Man of Action, 63n
Eriu, 39
Ervine, John, 152
Europe, 92, 154
    Belgium, 102
    France, 40, 165
        Boulogne, 53
        Paris, 19, 53
    Germany, 62, 100
        Berlin, 61
    Low Countries, 76
    Russia, 131, 133
        Moscow, 131, 133

Fáinne, 12, 120
Fairhead, 147
Farrelly, Una, 26
Fate of Shane O'Neill, The, 170
Feeney, Hugh, 170p
Feis Cheoil, 110
Feis Na nGleann, A History of the Festival of the Glens, 85n
Felix Devlin GAA, Belfast, 114
Ferguson, Sir Samuel, 67, 68
Ferns, Co. Wexford, 31
Feystown, 167
Feystown Owen Roes, 162
Fianna Éireann, 73
Field events, 158–68
Fife, Mr, 147
Finlay, P.T. (Cú Uladh), 41
'Fionn Mac Cumhaill' *see* Maghnus Mac Cumhaill
First World War (Great War), 4, 42, 61, 74, 114
Fitzgerald, Desmond, 73
Fitzgerald, Mabel, 73
Flatley, Hugh, 2, 3, 4, 11p, 36, 41, 59, 101, 150, 151, 166
Fleadh Cheoil, 119, 176

187

Fogarty, Fr, 42
'Foggy Dew, The', 143
Forde, E., 150
Foriffe, 164, 165, 167, 168
From Corrib to Cultra: Folklife Essays in Honour of Alan Gailey, 77n
'From Moscow to the Moyle', 129, 131
Fullerton, Fr Robert, 73

Gaelic Athletic Association, 1, 2, 3, 5, 10, 11, 63, 83, 95, 117, 118, 119, 120, 122, 145, 158, 159, 161, 162, 168, 172, 173
Gaelic Journal, The, 89
Gaelic League, 1, 2, 3, 5, 15, 16, 19, 20, 25, 28, 33, 36, 45, 49, 50, 56, 58, 61, 65, 67, 69, 81, 83, 89, 90, 91, 94, 95, 98, 102, 103, 107, 112, 114, 116, 117, 122, 145, 161,169, 171
    Coiste Gnótha, 67, 98, 112
Gaelic of Isla: A Comparative Study, The, 124
Gaelic Revival, 1, 15, 45, 85, 97, 98, 112, 131, 171
Gaelic Society of Dublin, 16
Gaelscoileanna, 12, 120
Galgorm, 3, 21, 23, 25, 55
Galgorm Castle, 57, 67, 109
Galgorm House, 15, 21, 32, 102
'Galloping Horse, The', 135
Galway, Co., 166, 168
    Aran Islands, 49
    Inis Meán, Aran Islands, 16, 36, 88
    Maam Cross, 21
Garrett, P.H., 17
Garron Tower, 3, 7, 23, 117
Garron Point, 11, 166
Gaughan, J.A., 77n
General Assembly of the Presbyterian Church, 108, 109–110
German Mausers, 39
Gettens, Michael, 164p
Gill, Mr, 41
Glasnevin Cemetery, 62, 100
Glass, Katie, 143
Glasscock, R.E., 77n
Glassmullan, 165
Gleann Airbh go Glas Naíon, 126
Glenann, 3, 101
Glenariff, 1, 3, 4, 6, 7, 8, 9, 10, 11, 15, 19, 23, 32, 36, 41, 43, 57, 71, 79, 81, 96, 101, 107, 112, 115, 116, 119, 131, 141, 144, 145, 147, 148, 150, 159, 163, 166, 167, 168, 169, 170, 175, 177, 179
    Bay Lodge, 36
    Drumnacur, 101, 165, 168
    Glenariff Lodge, 32, 36, 103
    Kilmore House, 11, 119, 177
Glenariff Michael Dwyers, 162, 165
Glenariff Oisins, 160, 163p, 164p, 165, 166, 167, 168
Glenarm, 1, 3, 5, 19, 36, 42, 56, 58, 67, 81, 83, 87, 96, 103, 112, 114, 150, 159, 166, 167, 169, 170
Glenarm Catholic Church, 87
Glenarm Gaelic League, 103
Glenarm Shane O'Neill's, 3, 160, 162, 167
Glenballyeamon, 101
Glencloy, 3, 102, 147
Glencorp, 57, 102
Glendun, 3, 7, 11, 24, 32, 37, 41, 100, 101, 109, 147, 150, 152, 175, 179

    Ballure, 100
    Dunurgan, 100
    Shannish, 100, 101
Glendun PES, 152, 153
Glendun Viaduct, 108, 109, 110, 111
Glendun Lodge, 45
Glenravel, 4, 42, 101, 147, 150
Glens Comhaltas Group, 177
Glens of Antrim Gaelic Society, 169
Glens of Antrim Hotel, Cushendall, 38
Glens Traditions Group, 176
Glenshesk, 99, 171
    Teoghs, 100
Glensman, The, 38, 85n, 95, 170
Glentaisie, 99, 147
Glenville, 136
Glór na Maoile, 118, 119
Glór na nGael, 118
Glynns, The, 39, 40, 129, 140
Gogarty, Rev. Dean, 150, 151
Golovin, Aleksandr, 133
Gorta Mór (Great Hunger), 141
Gough, Miss, 25
Gracehill, 55
Graham, Bob, 163p
Graham, Mick, 163p
Graham, Patricia, 155, 156
Graham, Willie, 163p, 168
Grange, Nora, 114
Grannd, Seumas, 124
Grattan's Parliament, 66
Graves, Alfred Perceval, 68
Great International Exhibition, Crystal Palace 1851, 136
Green, Alice Stopford, 60, 61, 69, 72p, 73, 76
Greene, Sean, 106p
Gregg, Joseph P., 42, 150, 151
Grenaghan, 164, 167
Griffith, Arthur, 71, 82
Gwynn, Stephen, 58, 83, 146

'hag of Béarra', 18
Hamill, Mary, 157
Hamill, Niall, 170p
Hamill, P[atrick], 3, 102
Hamilton, Mrs, 24
Hannay, Canon James, 69
Hannon, Margaret, 152
Hanover House, Clifton Street, Belfast, 84
Harbinson, Janet, 119
Harbour Road, Carnlough, 102
Hardbeck, Carl, 2, 41
Harvest Storm, 143
Harvey, Annie, 9
Harvey, Arthur, 165, 167, 168
Harvey, Edmund, 165
Harvey, George, 163p
Harvey, Joe, 165, 167
Harvey, Robert, 164, 165
Harvey, Vincent, 11
Heggarty, Archie, 169p
Heggarty, George, 169p
Henry and William Seeds Solicitors, 66
Henry Joy McCracken Literary Society, Belfast, 95
Heron, Mr (School Inspector), 113
Heron, Sally, 152
Hewitt, John, 37
Hicks, Miss F.A., 134, 135
Higgins, Dan, 165, 167

Higgins, Frank, 165
Higgins, John, 3, 101
Higgins, Pat, 167
Higginson, Nesta, 31– 2, 36, 146
'High King and Queen of Ireland', 3
Hill, Rev. George, 67
History of the Linen Hall Library, A, 77n
Hobson, Bulmer, 2, 73, 74, 77n, 83, 91, 165
Hogan, John, 150
Hogg, David James, 170
Holden, John, 150
Holden's Hall, 2p, 3, 4, 137, 146
Holmer, Professor (Ollamh Nils), 19, 124
'Homage of the Nine Glens to the Ard-Rí', 42
Home Rule, 1, 39, 59, 60, 61, 66, 73, 74, 90–1, 92, 95, 97, 171
Hope, Jemmy, 69, 74
Howth gun-running, 74
Howth Gun-running, The, 77n
Hughes, Fred[erick], 41, 79, 82, 84
Hughes, Frederick (father of Hubert and Fred Hughes), 84
Hughes, Herbert, 69, 79, 82, 84, 85
Hughes, Lena (sister of Hubert and Fred Hughes), 84
Hunter, Harry, 164, 167
Hurst, Mabel, 136
Hutton, Margaret, 15, 20, 21, 23, 27, 33, 37
Hyde, Dr Douglas, 1, 23, 24, 25, 28, 37, 38, 56, 67, 81, 89, 141

Iberno Celtic Society, 16
Immediate Education Act 1877, 87
In Remembrance. Articles and Sketches by Francis Joseph Bigger, 77n
Independent Liberal Unionist, 73
Inglis, Brian, 63n
Innis Crig, 167
Invest NI, 134
Ireland Yesterday and Tomorrow, 77n
Irish Archaeological Society, 16
Irish Brigade, 62
Irish Civil War, 4, 42, 75
Irish College, Belfast, 23, 67, 114
Irish College, Cloch Chrannflaolaidh, 21
Irish College, Paris, 19
Irish College, Rathlin Island, 4, 25, 114
Irish Dancing Commission, 8
Irish Decorative Arts Association, 131
Irish Dialects and Irish-Speaking Districts, 29n
Irish Free State, 93
Irish Independence Party, 8, 90, 97
Irish Manuscripts Commission, 94
Irish National Literary Society, 1
Irish Volunteers, 35, 61, 92, 94, 103
Irish News, 3, 61, 77n, 96, 107, 114, 116, 117, 153, 167, 170
Irish Peasant Home Industries, 99, 133
Irish Popular Songs, 28
Irish Primer Compiled and Published under the Patronage of the Ladies Gaelic Society, An, 17
Irish Republican Brotherhood (IRB), 7, 62, 73, 74, 75, 83, 91, 92
Irish Transport and General Workers' Union, 74
Irish Weekly, 166
Irish White Cross, 114
Irvine, Archie, 103
Isle of Man, 53

INDEX

Jail Journal, 71
Jamieson, Mary, 157
Janns, Rev. Canon Dudley, 147, 170
Jephson, Annie (mother of Sir Roger Casement), 53
Jephson, James (maternal grandfather of Sir Roger Casement), 53
John Turnly Memorial Trophy, 9, 131
Johnston, Anna (wife of Seamus MacManus) *see also* Ethna Carbery, 33, 95
Johnston, Netta Jane Nicholl (Miss), 3, 102
Jones, Alfred, 55
Jordan's Castle, Ardglass, 68
Joseph Campbell, Poet & Nationalist 1879–1944. A Critical Biography, 86n
Journal of Irish Literature, The, 86n
Journal of the East Belfast Historical Society, 86n
Joyce, Dr, 28

Kane, Mary, 11
Kane, Ned, 168
Kearney, Eamon, 157
Kearney, Eileen, 42, 150
Keats, [John], 54
Kelly, A.A., 86n
Kelly, Christopher, 164p
Kelly, Sean, 11, 173, 174p
Kerry, Co., 161, 173
    Banna Strand, 62, 92, 100
    Coill Bheag, Killarney, 116
    Tralee, 11
    Tralee Bay, 62
Kilkenny, 168
Killen, John, 77n, 85n
Killough, Brendan, 102
Kilmore, 4, 164, 167, 168
King James (I and VI), 19
King, Mrs (wife of Rev. Dr King), 54
King, Rev. Dr, 54
King, Travers (son of Rev. Dr King), 54
Kings, Lords and Commons, 29n
Kinney, Archie, 165, 167
Kinney, Michael, 165
Kinney, Pat, 165, 167
Kintullagh Convent schools, 43
Kirkwood, Rev. Liam, 11p, 150, 151
Knocknacarry, 150
Knocknacarry Primary (National) School, 99, 108
Korovin, Kostantin, 133

Lady of the House, The, 136
Lagan, River, Belfast, 81
'Lancers, The', 140
Land League, 1, 95
Land Purchase Act, 68, 74
Land War, 171
Lanyon, John, 55
Larne, 32, 39, 134
Larne Board of Guardians, 102
Larne Rural District Council, 102
Layd, 4
Leitch, Mick, 32
Lenaghan, Fr, 42
Letters of P.H. Pearse, The, 77n
Liberal Party, 60
'Life of Colmcille by O Donnell, the', 23
Lig na Bhfiann, 165
Linen Hall Library, Belfast, 71

Little Cowherd of Slainge, The, 78
Lives of Roger Casement, The, 63n
Lloyd, Owen, 85, 147
Logan, Annie, 11
Logue, Cardinal, 76p
Logue, Madge, 11p, 43, 150
Londonderry, 113
Longfield, Lady, 137
Lord Mayor of Cork, 7
Lossett, 161
Loughgiel (Loughguile), 7, 9, 10, 11, 119, 153, 166, 168
Louth, Co., 32, 35
    Omeath, 7
Lurgeadan, 165
Lynch, Patrick, 16, 19
Lynn, Jean, 157
Lynn, Robert, 79

Mac Amhlaigh, Bharney, 125
Mac Amhlaigh, Briain, 116
Mac Amhlaigh, Seamus Bhriain, 116, 125
Mac Cathmhaoil, Seosamh, 80
Mac Cormaic, Pádraic, 4, 7, 9, 38, 41, 42, 43, 115, 168
Mac Cormaic, Sibéal (wife of Pádraic Mac Cormaic), 4, 7, 42
Mac Cumhaigh, Art, 23
Mac Cumhaill, Maghnus, 27
Mac Curtain, Tómas, 7
Mac Dónaill, Dr Séamus *see* Dr James McDonnell
Mac Giolla Domhnaigh, Gearóid, 126
Mac Gréagóir, Aoidhmín, 125
Mac Gréagóir, Luaidheann, 126
Mac Maoláin, Chuir, 127
Mac Maoláin, Seán, 119, 126
Mac Piarais, Pádraig *see* Pádraig Pearse
Mac Póilín, Séamus, 19
MacAdam, Robert, 16, 17, 27
MacAulay, Hugh, 147
MacAuley, Henry, 107
MacAuley, James, 108
MacAuley, Rev. Dr Charles, 87
MacAuley, Rosetta (mother of Eoin MacNeill), 1, 87
MacBride, Sean, 171
MacDermott, John (Sean), 74, 75, 91
MacDonald, William, 83
MacDonnell, Annie, 147
MacEldowney, Hugh, 57–8
MacErlean, John, 87
MacGonigle, Margaret, 100
Mackey, H.O., 54, 63n
Mackle, Fiona, 11
MacManus, Anna *see* Anna Johnston
MacManus, Seamus (husband of Anna Johnston), 33
MacNabb, Fr Vincent, 87
MacNabb, Joseph, 87
MacNeill, Archibald (father of Eoin MacNeill), 1, 87, 103, 169
MacNeill, Eoin, 1, 3, 25, 26, 36, 56, 58, 67, 76p, 81, 87–94, 95, 112, 126, 141, 169, 170
MacNeill, James (brother of Eoin MacNeill), 103
MacNeill, Máire, 16
Madden Cup, 4
Madden, Dr, 43

Madden, Peter, 4
Madonna and Child, 69
Magee, Jack, 86n
Mageean, Most Rev. Daniel, 150
Magennis, Fr Dan, 163p
Magherintemple *see also* Churchfield House, 53, 54, 55, 56, 62, 100
'Magic Mouse Trap, The', 135
Magill, Daniel, 170
Magill, Fr Patrick, 162, 170
Magill, John, 170p
Maginnis, Denis, 115p
Maguigan, Michael, 114
Maguire, Denis *also known as* Dominic, 3, 41, 99, 161
Maguire, Paddy, 168
Malaya, 153
Mallon, Maura, 157
Mallusk, 65, 76, 99
Man and a Brother, A, 38
Marine Hotel, Ballycastle, 173
Markievicz, Countess, 73
Marley, Peter, 42
Marshall, Dr J.D., 141
Martin School, Antrim, 157
Martin, F.X., 77n
Martin, Mr, 108
Martinstown, 4
Masaka, Uganda, 154
Masefield, John, 35, 36, 38, 39
Masque of the Nine Glens, The, 3
Matthews, Brigid, 70, 74
Matthews, Ronan, 170p
Maunsel & Co., 85
Mawanda, Fr Joseph, 154
Mayne, Rutherford *see* Sam Waddell
Maynooth, 87, 119
Mayo, Co., 36, 99, 108
    Westport, 69
McAleese, John, 7
McAleese, Sean, 157
McAllister McVeigh Memorial Park, 168
McAllister, Áine, 42, 43
McAllister, Alastair, 10, 164p
McAllister, Anna, 4, 31
McAllister, Annie, 11p, 150, 151
McAllister, Arthur, 42, 150
McAllister, Brendan, 170p
McAllister, Charlie, 163p, 168
McAllister, Daniel, 3, 98, 101, 148, 163p, 168
McAllister, Johnnie, 167, 170p
McAllister, Marie, 11
McAllister, Michael, 164p, 165
McAllister, Senator T., 151
McAteer, Matt, 7
McAuley, 'Big Jim' *see* Seamus Bhriain Amhlaigh
McAuley, Catherine, 100
McAuley, Charles, 5, 37
McAuley, Dan, 169p
McAuley, Donal, 170p
McAuley, Eileen, 11
McAuley, Frank, 4, 7
McAuley, James, 8, 165, 169
McAuley, Jimmy, 164–5
McAuley, John H., 4
McAuley, Neale, 100
McAuley, Neil, 3
McAuley, Owen, 165
McBeth, Dan, 157
McBride, Mrs, 151

189

McBrinn, Joseph, 129, 131
McCafferty, Charlie, 164
McCambridge, Ethna, 155, 156, 157
McCambridge, John, 3, 17, 102, 103, 126
McCambridge, Maura, 156
McCambridge, Phrodustanach, 126
McCamphill, Hugh, 7
McCann, E., 157
McCann, Jack, 116
McCarry, Aileen, 8, 11
McCarry, Arthur, 164, 165, 167
McCarry, Francis, 150
McCarry, James, 11
McCarry, Maureen, 175p
McCarry, Neil, 164
McCartan, Hugh, 77n
McCartan, Pat, 91
McClenaghan, Rev. James, 150
McCloskey, Anne-Marie, 11
McCluskey, Eibhlin (mother of John 'Benmore' Clarke), 95
McCollum, Malachy, 165
McCollum, Pat, 169p
McCormick, Alexander (great-great-grandfather of Moira McNeill), 139
McCormick, Anne (great-great-grandmother of Moira McNeill), 138, 139
McCormick, Charlie, 164
McCormick, Mrs, 28, 43, 150
McCracken, Fr, 42
McCracken, Henry Joy, 69, 74, 95
McCracken, Mary Ann, 69
McCrory, Seamus, 157
McCullough, Denis, 41, 73, 74, 75, 83, 91
McCurdy, Augustine, 141
McCurdy, Joseph, 141
McCurdy, Neil, 58, 141, 142, 143, 147
McDade, Johnnie, 166
McDaide, Paddy, 165, 167, 168
McDaide, Robert, 165
McDermott, Brendan, 170p
McDermott, Brian, 170p
McDonagh, Eileen, 153
McDonnell, Alex, 163p, 164p
McDonnell, Barbara, 2, 15, 31, 41, 57, 71, 77n, 98, 133, 134, 136, 146, 148, 169
McDonnell, Charlie, 163p
McDonnell, Dr James (forebear of Barbara McNeill), 2, 15, 16, 27, 119
McDonnell, Miss, 136, 147
McDonnell, Randal, 164, 165
McDonnell, Ryan, 164p
McElderry, John, 60
McElroy, Rev. Albert, 7
McGarry, Rev. Canon Patrick 'Paddy', 145
McGavock, Annie (sister of Eoin MacNeill), 3, 41, 56, 103, 111, 112, 115, 169, 170
McGavock, Frank, 169p, 170
McGavock, James, 169p
McGavock, William (husband of Annie McGavock), 103
McGavock, Willie, 169p
McGeown, Stephen, 100
McGinley, P.T., 95, 107
McGonigle, Miss, 3
McGonnell, Dan, 179
McGouran, Rev. P., 150
McGowan, Rev. E.V., 41, 151
McGowan, Richard, 150
McGrattan PP, Rev. Thomas, 115p, 150
McGrogan, Rose, 23

McGuire, Dominic, 147
McHenry, Felix, 164, 165
McHenry, Margaret, 85n
McHenry, Paddy, 164, 165
McIlhatton, Bobby, 11
McIlroy, Mary, 147
McIlwaine, Padraig, 164p
McIntosh, Alex, 164, 167
McIntosh, Johnnie, 164p
McKay, Alexander, 147
McKay, Hugh Martin, 170p
McKay, John, 10
McKay, Martha, 170
McKay, Rosie, 147
McKechnie, Rev. John, 6, 43, 115, 116
McKeever, Fr Willie, 10
McKendry, Mary, 147
McKenna, Rev. Lambert, 151
McKenzie, Charles, 165
McKeown, Dr Donal, 121, 177
McKeown, Stephen, 3
McKillen, John, 3, 102
McKillen, Johnnie, 165
McKillop, Dan, 163p, 168
McKillop, Jas., 152
McKillop, Michael, 164p
McKillop, Mick, 163p
McKinley PP, Rev. A., 114
McKinley, Archie, 11p, 150
McKissock, Mr, 107, 108
McLarnon, Brigid, 152
McLaughlin, Paddy, 169p
McLaughlin, William, 3, 101, 157
McLoughlin, Charles, 95
McMaster, John, 60
McMullan Cup, 160
McMullan, Agnes, 147
McMullan, Alex, 116, 163p, 168
McMullan, Alister, 150
McMullan, Barry, 170p
McMullan, Dan, 38
McMullan, James, 165
McMullan, Joe, 8, 160
McMullan, Johnnie, 165
McMullan, Mairéad, 10, 11
McMullan, Robert, 163p
McMullan, Willie, 165
McMullen, Archibald, 43
McNally, Rev., 76p
McNamee, John, 3, 101
McNaughton, Cathal, 11, 129p
McNeachtin, James 'Seanachie', 108
McNeill, Ada, 2, 3, 4, 15, 20, 23, 25, 27, 28, 32, 37, 38, 41, 42, 45–51, 57, 59, 61, 67, 98, 109, 111, 112, 115p, 116, 141, 148, 150, 151, 169
McNeill, Conor, 170p
McNeill, Daniel (father of Ada McNeill), 45, 169p
McNeill, James, 169p, 170
McNeill, James (the mason), 169p
McNeill, John, 147
McNeill, Mary, 153
McNeill, Moira, 131, 138
McNeill, Owen, 147, 169, 170
McNeill, Ronald (cousin of Ada McNeill) see also Lord Cushendun, 45, 98, 109
McNeill, Seamus, 170p
McPeake, Francis, 68
McRann, James, 3, 103, 147, 169
McShane, W., 23

McSparran, Archibald, 150, 152
McSparran, Ellen (wife of Daniel McAllister), 98
McSparran, Nuala, 11
McVeigh, Biddy, 23
McVeigh, Pat, 11, 168
'Mechanical Ostrich', 135
Meenaboy, Co. Donegal, 25
Memoirs of Senator Joseph Connolly, 77n
'Mermaid, The', Kircubbin, 71
Messrs Henry and William Seeds, 66
Miles, Catriona, 119
Mill Street, Cushendall, 98, 101
Miller, Charlotte (wife of Sir Roger Casement), 46
Milligan, Alice, 2, 3, 33, 41, 69, 70, 79, 95
Milliken, John, 170p
Mitchel, John, 71
Mitchell, Dean, 170p
Mitchell, Joe, 157
'Mo Choill', 143
Moley, Fr John, 117
Molyneux, William, 36
Montgomery, Leslie Alexander, 84
Mooney, Mrs, 43
Moore, Brian, 87
Moore, Master, 99
Moore, Patrick, 161
Moorhead, Thomas, 3, 101
Morris, William, 131
Morrison, Alex, 124, 127
Morrow, Jack, 83, 84, 147, 170
Moyle, 131, 133
Mulholland, Annie (wife Nicholas Crommelin), 38
Mulholland, Sarah (daughter of St Clair Kelburn Mulholland), 35, 36
Mulholland, St Clair Kelburn (father of St Clair Kelburn Mulholland), 35
Mullaghsandall, 167
Mullaghsandall Shamrocks, 162
Mullan, Hugh, 168
Mullan, Jim, 163p
Mullhall, Gerard, 157
Munster, 10, 23, 108
Murlough Bay, 63, 100, 171,
Murphy PP, Very Rev. E., 114
Murphy, James, 165
Murphy, Willie, 165, 168
Murray, Alex, 167
Murray, Norris, 164p
Mussolini [Benito], 47

National Athletics and Cycling Association (NACA), 159
National Folk Theatre of Ireland *see Siamsa Tíre*
National Library of Ireland, 54
National Museum of Ireland, 98, 136
National Romanticism, 131
National University of Ireland, 93
Neagh, Lough, 39, 68
Neeson, Kevin, 145p
New Ireland Literary Society, Dublin, 89
New Songs, 82
New Zealand, 135
Newe, G.B., 102
Ní Bhriain, Cait, 114
Ní Chonaill, Eibhlín Dhubh, 18
Ní Dhochartaigh, Roisín, 114
Ní Fhaircheallaigh, Una, 42

INDEX

Ní Ógáin, Róis *see also* Rose Young, 15, 21, 24, 32, 102, 109
Ní Ógáin, Úna, 23
North Antrim Championship, 159
Northern Patriot, The, 33, 95
Northern Star, The, 16
Nulty, Mark, 164p

Ó Broin, Donncha, 119
Ó Buachalla, S., 77n
Ó Catháin, Seán, 23, 27
Ó Cléirigh, Pádraig, 7, 107
Ó Clérigh, Séan, 42
Ó Coileáin, Pádraig, 119
Ó Cuív, Prof. Éamonn, 19, 119
Ó Dionnshléibhe, Aindrias, 19
Ó Doibhlin, Brendan, 119
Ó Doibhlin, Deaglan, 119
Ó Dubhaigh, Aindreas *see also* Andy Dooey, 119, 120
Ó Dubhaigh, Séamus *see* Joseph Duffy
Ó Duibhín, Dochtúir Ciarán, 125
Ó Duinnín, Urramach, 125
Ó Faogáin, Éamonn, 120
Ó Fiannachtaigh, Tomás, 16
Ó Grianna, Séamus, 27
Ó hUiginn, Pól, 27
Ó Laoghaire, Art, 18
Ó Luain, Sibéal, 41
Ó Mongáin, Dominic, 28
O Mordha, Mr S., 153
Ó Muireadhaigh, An tAthair Lorcán, 23–4
Ó Murigheasa, Enrí (Henry Morris), 7
Ó Neill, Eoghan, 18, 19
Ó Riada, Seán, 175
Ó Ruairc, Peadar, 145
Ó Searcaigh, Seamus, 4, 26, 41
Ó Suilleabhain, Tomas, 114
Ó Tuathail, Eamonn, 26
Ó Tuathall, Fr Domhnall, 41
O'Boyle, Frank, 165, 177
O'Boyle, John, 164, 165
O'Boyle, Johnny, 170p
O'Boyle, Maggie, 11p, 150
O'Boyle, Neil John, 165
O'Byrne, Brian, 4
O'Byrne, Cathal, 2, 69, 73
O'Callaghan, Miriam, 11, 173, 174p
O'Connor, Bridie, 152
O'Connor, Hugh, 164p
O'Connor, John, 8
O'Doherty, Gwen, 157
O'Donnell, Bella, 152, 153
O'Donnell, Bernard, 3, 102
O'Donovan, Cornelius, 147
O'Donovan, John, 67
O'Grady, Standish, 132
Ógrianna, Seamus, 15
O'Growney, Fr Eoghan, 1, 88
O'Hagan, Niall, 164p
O'Hara, Donal, 152
O'Hara, Evelyn, 152
O'Hara, James, 169p
O'Kane, Miss A., 150
O'Kane, Ned, 165, 168
O'Kane, Seamus, 170p
O'Laverty, Monsignor James, 67
O'Loan, Mr, 147
O'Lochlainn, Colm, 77
Olympic Games, 144

O'Mealy, Richard Lewis, 84, 147, 150
O'Mooney, Annie, 150
O'Mullan, Hugh, 166
O'Neill Crowley Gaelic Club, Belfast, 95
O'Neill, Bryan, 170p
O'Neill, Captain, 23
O'Neill, Dan, 164, 165
O'Neill, Ellen, 139, 150
O'Neill, Fr Hugh, 43, 168
O'Neill, John, 17
O'Neill, John, 169p
O'Neill, Lady, 23
O'Neill, Moira *see* Nesta Higginson
O'Neill, Nellie, 24
O'Neill, Rosina, 147
O'Neill, Sean, 170p
O'Neill, Shane, 51
Or Fifty Years Ago, 85n
O'Rahilly, The, 91
Orangemen, 28, 91
Orr, William, 69, 74, 87
O'Shea, P.J., 67
O'Toole, Fr, 43
Owen, J.K., 68
'Owl and the Pussycat Rowboat', 135

Paris Exposition 1900, 129, 148
Parkhill, David, 83
Parkmore, 107, 108, 165
Parliament Act 1911, 90
Parnell, Charles Stewart, 66, 74, 95, 96
Parry, Mrs Sydney *née* Gertrude Bannister, 4, 15, 20, 32, 42, 59, 61, 62, 150, 150
Patriot King and the Irish Chief, The, 35
Patton, Caoimhin, 117
Pearse Club, Cushendall, 114
Pearse, Pádraig (Patrick), 7, 15, 21, 25, 27, 33, 71, 73, 91, 92
Pentonville Prison, 51, 62, 100
Petrie, George, 67
Petticrew, Alex, 169p
Petticrew, Jim, 170p
Phoenix, Eamon, 11, 173, 174p
Picts of Dalriada, 39
Pius XI, 94
Plunkett, Joseph Mary, 26, 92
Plunkett, Sir Horace, 3, 132, 146, 147, 148
Pobal an Chaistil, 119
Poetry of Feis na nGleann, 172
Poets and Poetry of Munster, 28
Pogosskaia, Anna, 131
Portglenone, 11, 55, 156
Portnagolan, Cushendall, 7, 15, 32, 37, 40, 67, 109, 116
Portrush, 131
Protestant Home Rule, 60, 61
Protestant IRB, 73
Protestant Nationalist Society, 83
Protestant Nationalists, Gaelic Leaguer, 65
Purcell, Lewis *see* David Parkhill

Queen's College Belfast, 66
Queen's University Belfast, 151

R.I.C., 74
  mutiny, 69
'Rakes of Mallow, The', 140
Ramsden, Mr G., 150

Randalstown, 155
Ranelagh, 136
Rathlin Co-Op, 143
Rathlin Island, 3, 4, 8, 19, 25, 57, 61, 72, 106p, 107, 112, 113, 114, 118, 120, 141, 143, 147
  Ballygill South, 141
  Cleggan, 141
  Kenramer, 141
  Raghery, 37, 58, 146, 147
Rebellion of 1798, 68, 74, 95
  1798 Centennial, 131
  Battle of Antrim, 66, 95
Red Arch, 3
Red Bay, 37, 58, 83, 141, 165, 168
'Red Hand of the O'Neills', 68, 160
Redmond, John, 91, 92
Reeves, Bishop William, 23, 32, 54, 102
Reid, Anne, 157
Reid, B.L., 55, 60, 63n
Reid, Forest, 79
Reid, Seamus, 164p
Republic, The, 73
Republican 'Dungannon Clubs', 73, 83
Revue Celtique, 39
Reynolds, William, 84
Rhys, Professor, 23, 26
Riddell, Frances, 3, 99, 129, 133, 146
Robinson, Alex, 169p
'Roddy MacCorley', 33
Roger Casement: The Black Diaries, 63n, 77n
Roger Casement: The Truth about the Forged Diaries, 63n
Roger Casement's Diaries, 63n
Roise na hAmhran (Rosie of the Songs), 143
Rooney, Mr, 23
Roscommon, Co., 25, 67
Rowan, Colonel, 23
Royal Belfast Academical Institute, 66, 98–9
Royal College of Music, London, 82
Royal Irish Academy, 67, 94
Royal Society of Antiquaries in Ireland, 67
Royal University of Ireland, 1, 87
Russell, George Æ, 79, 82
Russian Peasant Industries, 148
Rutherford Mayne, Selected Plays, 85n

'Santa Claus', 136
Saunders, Norah, 86n
Saunders, Sr Assumpta, 86n
Savage, Grace Charlotte (wife of John Young), 21
Sawyer, Roger, 53, 63n
Scally, Harry, 7, 115
Scally, Margaret, 157
Scholarly Revolutionary, The, 126
School House, Cushendall, 169
Scoil Eanna, 21, 33, 73
Scotland, 7, 100, 114, 115, 142, 158, 163, 175
  Glasgow, 6
    Glasgow University, 154
    School of Scottish Studies, 115
  Glenluce Bay, 65
  Nithsdale, 65
  West Highland, 47
  Western Isles, 114
Scottish Mod (festival), 6
Scullion, Sally, 156
'Sean the Proud', 68

Seaview Hotel, Glenarm, 103, 169
Seaview National School, Glenarm, 103, 169
Sebastian Erard concert harp, 85
Second World War, 5, 103, 115, 140, 158
'Seveen Canmer' *see* Josephine Canmer, 78
Shan Van Vocht, 33
Shane O'Neill Carn, 51
Shane O'Neill Gaelic Athletic Club, 83, 96, 103, 170
Sharkey, Hugh, 100
Sharpe, Canon, 102
Sharpe, Johnnie, 164, 165
She Moved through the Fair, 84
Shelley, [Percy Bysshe], 54
Shepherd, Christopher, 164p
Shepherd, Paul, 164p
'Shield of the Heroes', 147, 162, 170
Shiels, George, 38
Siamsa Tíre, 11, 177
Sinn Fein, 71, 82, 171
Sligo, Co., 103, 169, 171
Smith, Jean Kennedy, 119
Songs of the Glens of Antrim, 32, 36
Songs of Uladh, 79, 83, 84
South America
    Amazon Basin, 63
    Putamayo, 39, 50, 100
Spence, Arthur, 134, 135, 136
SS Bonny, 55
SS Clydevalley, 39
St Anne's, Belfast, 53
'St Anthony's Tray', 70
St Brigid's Church, Glenariff, 177
St Joseph's Training College, Belfast, 7
St Louis Convent Grammar School, Ballymena, 6, 7, 152, 153
St Louis World's Fair 1904, 133
St MacNissi's College, Garron Tower, 177
St Malachy's College, Belfast, 1, 72, 87, 114, 167
St Mary's Chapel, Belfast, 120
St Mary's Hall, Belfast, 23
St Mary's Larne, 114
St Patrick's Boys' School, Ballycastle, 171
St Patrick's Church, Glenariff, 177
St Patrick's Training College, Drumcondra, 153
St Peter's Church, Belfast, 71
St Peter's Churchyard, Dublin, 69
Statistical accounts of parishes of Ardclinis and Layd, 36
Stockman, Ollamh Gearóid, 126
Strahan, George, 66
Sturge, Miss, 134
Summer School of Gaelic in Ulster, 50
Sunday Independent, 24

Táin Bó Cualinge (the *Táin*), 15, 33, 39
Tamlaght, 165
Tamlaght School, 166
Tate's Lane, Newtowncrommelin, 101
Teach Comber, Claudy, 117
Tenisheva, Princess, 131
Tennyson, [Lord Alfred], 54
'The Ballymoney Farce', 61
'The Laney Man' *see* John McCambridge
'The Ould Lammas Fair', 4
'The Trench', 66
Tierney, Mark, 63n
Tillicks, the, 168
Times, The (London), 61
Tír na nÓg Irish Summer School, 117
Toal, Rev. Tom, 115p, 116
Tone, Wolfe, 95
Toomebridge, 100
Torr Road, 47
Tracey, Nancy, 24
Transactions of the Royal Academy, 141
Treaty of 1921, 93
Trinity College Dublin, 54, 55, 91, 158
Trinity Manse, Ballymoney, 60
Truce of 1921, 114
Turnball, Agnes (paternal grandmother of Sir Roger Casement), 53
Turnley, Francis, 58
Turnly, John, 8
Tyrone, Co., 18, 28
    Binn an Phréacháin, 24
    Carrickmacross, 148
    Dungannon, 35, 175
    Muinter Luinigh, 19

Ui Dercu Cein, 39
Úirchill an Chreagáin, 23
Ulad (Ulster), 79
Ulster, 19, 53, 56, 60, 61, 65, 66, 67, 68, 73, 79, 82, 85, 91, 97, 102, 117, 132, 141, 151
Ulster College of Irish, Cloghaneely, Donegal, 45
Ulster College *see* Colaiste Uladh
Ulster Folklife, 77n
Ulster Gaelic Society, 16, 17
Ulster Journal of Archaeology, 39, 67
Ulster Ladies Gaelic Society, 17, 18
Ulster Land War, The, 74
Ulster Liberal Party, 7
Ulster Literary Theatre, 69, 78–9, 83, 84
Ulster Reformed Public House Association, 70
Ulster Theatre Group, 41
Ulster Theatre in Ireland, The, 85n

Ulster Volunteer Force (UVF), 40, 91
Ultach Trust, 119
Unionist party, 60
United Irishmen, 69, 74, 87, 122
United Irishmen, The, 82
University College Dublin, 90
University of Ulster, Coleraine, 171
Upper Clogher Court, Bushmills, 28
Uppsala University, 19

Waddell, Helen, 78
Waddell, Sam[uel], 2, 41, 78, 79
Waide, Sean, 170p
Walsh, Dr Micheline Kearney, 119
Walsh, John, 157
Walsh, Louis (Lughaidh), 41, 42, 83, 171
Waterfoot, 3, 41, 85, 101, 107, 108, 120, 146, 165, 166, 167, 168, 170
    Main Street, 102
Waterfoot National School, 108
Watson, Ollamh Seosamh, 125
'Waves of Tory, The', 140
Weekly Telegraph see Ballymena Weekly Telegraph
Welch, Robert J., 83
Wheeler, Niall, 168
White, Sir George, 60
White, Capt. Jack (son of Sir George White), 60
Whiteford, James, 135
William, Prince of Orange, 35
Wilson, John, 119
Wisner-Clarke, Mrs, 175p
Wood/Art exhibits, 84
Woodside, Alberta, 153, 155–7
Woodside, Sandra, 155–6

Yeats, [William Butler], 70, 79
Young, Ethel (sister of Rose Young), 23
Young, George (brother of Rose Young), 28
Young, John (father of Rose Young), 21
Young, Mary (sister of Rose Young), 23
Young, Robert M., 67
Young, Rose (Maud), 2, 3, 15, 20, 21, 22, 24, 25, 27, 28, 32, 34p, 37, 41, 45, 57, 67, 98, 102, 109, 115p, 116, 150, 151
Young, Willie (brother of Rose Young), 23

Zeitschrift fur Celtische Philologie, 125